Get Better at Flatter

Markus Reitzig

Get Better at Flatter

A Guide to Shaping and Leading Organizations with Less Hierarchy

Markus Reitzig
University of Vienna
Vienna, Austria

ISBN 978-3-030-89253-1   ISBN 978-3-030-89254-8   (eBook)
https://doi.org/10.1007/978-3-030-89254-8

© The Editor(s) (if applicable) and The Author(s), under exclusive licence to Springer Nature Switzerland AG 2022

This work is subject to copyright. All rights are solely and exclusively licensed by the Publisher, whether the whole or part of the material is concerned, specifically the rights of translation, reprinting, reuse of illustrations, recitation, broadcasting, reproduction on microfilms or in any other physical way, and transmission or information storage and retrieval, electronic adaptation, computer software, or by similar or dissimilar methodology now known or hereafter developed.

The use of general descriptive names, registered names, trademarks, service marks, etc. in this publication does not imply, even in the absence of a specific statement, that such names are exempt from the relevant protective laws and regulations and therefore free for general use.

The publisher, the authors and the editors are safe to assume that the advice and information in this book are believed to be true and accurate at the date of publication. Neither the publisher nor the authors or the editors give a warranty, expressed or implied, with respect to the material contained herein or for any errors or omissions that may have been made. The publisher remains neutral with regard to jurisdictional claims in published maps and institutional affiliations.

This Palgrave Macmillan imprint is published by the registered company Springer Nature Switzerland AG.
The registered company address is: Gewerbestrasse 11, 6330 Cham, Switzerland

Preface and Acknowledgments

For a scientist, writing a book for managers in today's world has become an affair of the heart, for many reasons. Let me name just two. First, we have—in modern academe—come to weigh scholarly achievements in citations and journal publications, so being the author of a book for practitioners no longer tilts the career balance. Second, even books dedicated to practitioners—in our modern daily life—often lose against vlogs and online snippets in competing for executives' attention.

So why this book? My motivation was to write about a topic I feel passionate about to this day. Having studied novel organizational forms for the better part of my professional career, having taught numerous students about how to manage without hierarchy, and having witnessed just as many executives struggle with the challenges of doing so, I hoped simply to provide them a science-based yet actionable guide to designing flat structures. A guide that would be easier to understand, and better to follow, than other contemporaneous approaches.

Whether I've succeeded or not, others will have to tell.

What I can say is that I thoroughly enjoyed the process. It gave me a chance to read up on the works of my colleagues, friends, and co-authors of many years, and to reflect on the insights that my students and I have created over almost two decades. I am indebted to so many of them for years of joint work, and I would at least like to thank my most frequent collaborators—Professors Oliver Alexy, Helge Klapper, Boris Maciejovsky, Phanish Puranam, and Olav Sorenson—for their having contributed to my understanding of how organizations work, and without whom this book would not exist.

Several of them, as well as others, have also supported me during the actual process of writing this piece. Helge Klapper, Boris Maciejovsky, Costas

Markides, Mariana Sailer, and Stefan Thau provided feedback on early versions of selected chapters.

So did a range of executives to whom I am profoundly grateful for assessing the book's viability from a practitioner perspective—notably Robin Colgan (Jaguary Landrover), Christoph Fischer (BayernLB), Steve Morgan (Pegasystems), and Carsten Strube (Mercer Management Consultants). This book is intended to make your lives easier, and I'm glad that you helped me work toward this goal.

Parts of the book could not have been completed without the generous support of senior executives who went on record and, originally for this book, shared with me their experiences of delayering hierarchical organizations or growing startups in a flat manner. Special thanks go to Richard Borek (Borek), Georg Rätker (T-Systems), and Andreas Schuster (wirDesign). I owe Florian Bernschneider (AGV Braunschweig) for establishing contacts with the aforementioned companies.

While I am deeply grateful to all of the above, three friends stand out in terms of providing substantial information and help in the context of this book project. Not only did they meticulously read every chapter in its original version; they also shared their contacts and helped promote the ideas portrayed herein wherever there was an opportunity. They are Michael Lander (Siemens), Sridhar Raghavachari (formerly ITC), and my co-author of longstanding, Professor Phanish Puranam.

Irrespective of the support I received from the aforementioned persons, I couldn't have finished this volume without the tremendous help I received from all my internal and external team members in this production process over the past two years.

Lorena Schivo and Sandra Perger provided excellent assistance in compiling references and publicly available documentation. Kristen Ebert-Wagner did an outstanding job in getting the manuscript ready for publication. My heartfelt thanks to all of you! I would equally like to thank my editor, Liz Barlow (Palgrave Macmillan), for her serious interest in and commitment to this book from the very beginning, and for excellent cooperation along the entire way.

Two of my graduate students provided particularly comprehensive and important support over the course of the last two years. My special thanks go to Tomas Lego and Robert Janjic for endless hours of sparring on the fundamental ideas behind the chapters in this book, for digging up case material, challenging my thinking, discussing both the scientific literature and my related inference, and correcting my initial chapter drafts. More than once they spotted glitches in my original writings. I owe both of them.

Finally, I thank my student assistant, Lenz Söder. He has been my closest companion along the way in writing this book, served as my (almost) daily discussion partner for over a year, was the first to review each chapter draft, and became my key aide in compiling materials and drafting illustrations for this book. Without his support, this book would not have come together in its current form in time.

Writing a classic is reserved to the fewest of us, and I do not hold such ambitions. In fact, it may not even be desirable. For, as Mark Twain allegedly once put it:

"Classic"—a book which people praise and don't read.

Rather, I have to admit that—inasmuch as I enjoyed the process of writing—I would be lying if I said that I wouldn't want to see this book diffuse among colleagues and practitioners and make their lives a little easier. And to witness that social science can have an impact on corporate practice.

Those whom I hold dear saw less of me while I was working on this book. It is to them that I devote this book in gratitude for their patience and understanding—first and foremost among them my daughter, Lola, who writes funnier stories than her dad.

Vienna, Austria   Markus Reitzig

Praise for *Get Better at Flatter*

"Professor Reitzig has produced a rarity of a book: a managerial book full of practical insights that is based on rigorous academic theory and evidence-based research. This makes Get Better at Flatter the go-to book for any senior executive interested in learning when to reduce the hierarchy of their firm and how to do so successfully. This superb book is full of fresh ideas and practical advice, written in a clear style and enriched with real company examples. You should not just buy this book, you should read it!"
—Costas Markides, *Robert P. Bauman Chair of Strategic Leadership, Professor of Strategy and Entrepreneurship, London Business School*

"When it comes to organization design today, "flat" (and each of its near synonyms) is a cool idea. It may also be a stupid idea for your organization. This is the first book I have read on this topic that analyses rather than proselytizes. It shows how to think through the "why's" and "how's" of getting flatter in a systematic manner. A must read for anyone who would rather be a thoughtful manager than be among the herd of the "thought led"."
—Phanish Puranam, *Roland Berger Chaired Professor of Strategy and Organisation Design, Professor of Strategy, INSEAD*

"Organization charts have fewer and fewer levels. But surprisingly little academic attention has been given to this important trend. Reitzig provides a much-needed theoretical framework for understanding when and why firms can benefit from flattening their structures. He also offers detailed practical advice on how to do it. Importantly, both his theoretical framework and his practical guidance account for the fact that firms vary in how flat they have historically been and in what they hope to achieve through a decentralized design. Anyone contemplating a reorganization should read it."
—Olav Sorenson, *Joseph Jacobs Chair in Entrepreneurial Studies, Professor of Strategy, UCLA Anderson*

"This book strikes an unusually well-done balance between hands-on ideas and a carefully researched evidence base and will be equally useful for executives and academics interested in organizational design and hierarchy."
—Stefan Thau, *The Cora Chaired Professor of Leadership and Learning, Professor of Organisational Behaviour, INSEAD*

"Prof. Reitzig's book is a welcome and timely contribution to the discussion about flat organizations. To date, the discussion has often been comparing two polar extremes—the boss-less organization versus a traditional hierarchy. Reitzig convincingly makes the case that the more useful discussion is the continuum between those

polar extremes. The book provides actionable insights to managers who struggle with how much, what kind, and when to grant freedom to their employees."
—Linus Dahlander, *Lufthansa Group Chair in Innovation, Professor of Strategy, ESMT Berlin*

"Flat, decentralized organizations have come a long way since the turn of the millennium, and are now on the brink of becoming a part of mainstream managerial practice. Reitzig's timely and insightful book explains why this is the case, and provides managers with crucial, evidence-based insights as to what they can achieve by "going flatter," when and with what approach, and how to make it happen. If you want your company to be faster and more innovative, and unleash the potential of employees, you should read this book."
—Oliver Alexy, *Professor of Strategic Entrepreneurship, TUM School of Management*

"On a topic where fads and fictions have prevailed, this 'user manual' for leading flat organizations—grounded in Reitzig's deep expertise and decades of research—makes the complex simple, the hyped-up real, and the unforeseen predictable. A must read for anyone frustrated by hierarchy and red tape."
—Ethan Bernstein, Edward W. Conard *Associate Professor of Business Administration, Harvard Business School*

"With this book, Prof. Markus Reitzig manages to free the flowery debate about New Work and New Leadership from its word cloud and makes it clear what one should really focus on when it comes to the practical application in a company. This practicality is not based on anecdotes or a subjective gut instinct, but builds on a solid empirical foundation. This makes it not only a book on management which is worth a read, but provides real added value for every executive."
—Florian Bernschneider, *Chief Executive of the Employers' Association (AGV) Braunschweig*

"An eminently readable book that addresses one of the big issues faced by managers; making organisations 'match-fit' for a new generation of talent in a post-covid world. Professor Reitzig blends theory, primary research and his own industry experience to inform and provide clear, actionable insight."
—Robin Colgan, *Managing Director, Asia Pacific Importers at Jaguar Land Rover*

"As much as I enjoy chatting about my current favorite topic with like-minded or curious people after the transformation of wirDesign, the wonderfully scientific perspective of Prof. Markus Reitzig's well-founded book surprised me and enriched my point of view. Anyone who wants to have a say in future discussions, instead of idly chatting, should invest their time well and read this book."
—Andreas Schuster, *Co-founder and Board Member of wirDesign*

"Get Better at Flatter by Prof Reitzig is an expertly-written book providing practical, yet deeply-researched guidance regarding the do's and don'ts of flat organizations, beyond the usual buzzword bingo of agile, scrum and kanban."
—Dr. Christoph Fischer, *Division Head, BayernLB*

"Prof. Markus Reitzig does a great job of providing orientation on a highly topical issue.

Flat hierarchies and flexible organizational models are of great interest as part of a "new way of working". Established companies in the industry deal with this topic while trying to optimize organizational structures that have evolved over time.

Prof. Reitzig manages to describe both advantages and limits of fewer levels of hierarchy in a clear and succinct fashion. His approaches combined with practical examples provide orientation in this complex and emotional environment. Making use of a straightforward chapter structure, he offers an efficient reference tool, thanks to the clear summary at the end of each chapter.

As I can confirm from my own daily practice, the book has real added value for managers and helps to recognize mistakes or, ideally, to already avoid them at the outset."

—Michael Lander, *Co-Chapter Lead of Global Business Consulting & Digitalization, Siemens AG*

Contents

Introduction   xix

Part I   Why Flat Structures Work at All   1

1   What Does It Mean to Move Toward a "Flatter" Structure?   3

2   What Managers Can Effectively and Efficiently Delegate   19

3   Why Would Employees Ever Assume Extra Work in a
    Decentralized Organization?   43

**Part II   What Managers Can Do to Make Flat Structures
           Work Well**   61

4   What Type of Persons Should You Take on the Journey?   63

5   How to Enforce and Foster Effective Self-organization?   79

6   How to Design the Playing Field for Efficient Quasi-
    decentralization?   93

Part III	When, Why, and How Flat Structures Can Beat Traditional Hierarchies	103
7	When Can Flat Structures Beat More Centralized Structures?	105
8	Where Does a Flat Structure Reach its Limits?	121
9	The Guide(s) to Successful Decentralizing	135
Part IV	Test Your Understanding	153
10	Delayering the Hierarchical Firm: The Case of Borek	155
11	Flat Growth: The Case of wirDesign	163
12	Flat Fads or More? From *a* as in "agile" to *z* as in "zi zhu jing ying ti" …	173
Glossary		195
Index		201

List of Figures

Fig. 1.1	Line of command, consisting of one CEO, one mid-level manager, and one shop-floor worker. (© Markus Reitzig 2021)	11
Fig. 1.2	Two-layered command hierarchy with span of control of two at all layers. (© Markus Reitzig 2021)	12
Fig. 1.3	Authority structure with triple leadership and four jointly supervised subordinates. (© Markus Reitzig 2021)	13
Fig. 1.4	Authority structure with single leadership and span of control of six. (© Markus Reitzig 2021)	13
Fig. 1.5	Authority structure with single leadership and span of control of four. (© Markus Reitzig 2021)	14
Fig. 2.1	The fundamental problems of organizing. (© Markus Reitzig 2021)	23
Fig. 8.1	Information exchange among nine members of an organization. Left: Decentralized setup. Right: Hierarchical setup. (© Markus Reitzig 2021)	122
Fig. 8.2	Three sources of unidirectional influence in a traditional command hierarchy: Decision rights (straight line); status (long dashes); control over information (dotted line). (© Markus Reitzig 2021)	129
Fig. 8.3	Unidirectional normative influence and bidirectional information flow in a learning hierarchy. (© Markus Reitzig 2021)	130
Fig. 8.4	Decentralized decision rights, unidirectional normative influence from status, and bidirectional information flow in a learning hierarchy. (© Markus Reitzig 2021)	131
Fig. 9.1	Delayering of a traditional hierarchy to a teams-based structure. (© Markus Reitzig 2021)	136
Fig. 9.2	Horizontal growth of a teams-based structure. (© Markus Reitzig 2021)	136

Fig. 9.3	Guide to delayering a hierarchy in order to make the company more creative. (© Markus Reitzig 2021)	138
Fig. 9.4	Guide to delayering a hierarchy in order to make the company faster. (© Markus Reitzig 2021)	140
Fig. 9.5	Guide to delayering a hierarchy in order to attract and retain talent. (© Markus Reitzig 2021)	144
Fig. 9.6	Guide to growing a company in a flat manner. (© Markus Reitzig 2021)	148
Fig. 12.1	On the relationship between design solutions, design principles, and Logics of Organizing (LoO): The example of agility. (© Markus Reitzig 2021)	178

List of Tables

Table 2.1	Dimensions of structural decentralization for our sample corporations. Unless a narrow scope is mentioned explicitly, de-facto decentralization refers to the corporate-wide structure. (© Markus Reitzig 2021)	33
Table 3.1	A conceptual map linking motivational mechanisms to dimensions of informal decentralization. (© Markus Reitzig 2021)	52
Table 3.2	Dimensions of informal quasi-decentralization and reported motivations among employees of our sample corporations. (© Markus Reitzig 2021)	54
Table 4.1	Personality traits associated with extra motivation gained from autonomous work.	66
Table 4.2	Personality traits associated with cooperation in relevant games in behavioral economics.	69
Table 5.1	High delegation and decentral information requirements. (© Markus Reitzig 2021)	85
Table 12.1	Design solutions emerging from contemporary approaches to nontraditional ways of organizing. (© Markus Reitzig 2021)	185
Table 12.2	Categorizing and mapping approaches to nontraditional ways of organizing to the 4+1 framework. (© Markus Reitzig 2021)	187

Introduction

The idea of working in "flat structures"—organizational hierarchies with few or potentially no middle layers of management—exudes an air of freshness and energy. It has diffused among millennials as much as among seasoned employees who have spent the better part of their professional lives in traditionally run companies. And there's something to be said for such flat structures: they have the potential to do better than established hierarchical organizations in certain instances. This potential has left many managers wondering whether and how to level their corporate structures in order to both make their employees happy and increase performance. At the same time, this potential is easily overestimated, and moving to a flatter structure is erroneously perceived to guarantee a revitalized business. Many contemporary writings in management contribute to this situation.

To give flat structures the platform they deserve, but to help leaders approach the situation realistically, this book complements extant writings by taking a slightly different approach to the topic. Unlike many writings on the subject, this book does not begin from the premise that organizations with little or no hierarchy will always work and outcompete their traditional counterparts. Rather, I argue that flat structures ***can*** be very powerful and potentially superior to hierarchical firms under certain conditions. And just because they can, most managers will begin to experiment with flat structures at some point in their career, or feel pressured to do so. When you reach this point, it will be important for you to know how to ***make flatter*** the **better** structure for your purpose.

This book will teach you how to successfully move from a hierarchical organization to a flat, teams-based form of organizing—or to maintain the latter in your new venture while scaling, if this is where you're coming from.

Whether your goal is for your corporation to become—or remain—creative, fast, or attractive to current and future talent by removing—or not even implementing—layers of management, the framework developed in this book will help you avoid some of the most frequent pitfalls in the process. And pitfalls there are plenty. Most fall into just three categories, however.

- *Mismatch between corporate goal and flat structure.* Delayering a large corporation can take very different forms; so can keeping a startup flat. Only if your goal—say, to be fast to market—can be attained by the specific structure you put in place will the move to a flatter structure succeed.
- *Mismatch between the flat structure and how you treat your staff within it.* Flat structures shift responsibility and more accountability from managers to team members. In turn, this means that you must not treat your staff the way you do in traditional hierarchical companies; you must appreciate them in their specific roles.
- *Mismatch between the flat structure and the staff you took or take on board.* There's only so much you can do as an organizational designer to make employees behave in a way that suits the company. Much of the success will hinge on their inner disposition—so picking the right folks for the job in the beginning is key.

Why Read *this* Book?

Rarely if ever did organizational bureaucracies have a reputation as bad as today's.

Over the past two decades, the use of formal command hierarchies within companies has been blamed for hampering their ability to react faster to unforeseen developments, to foster the creativity of their staff, to crank out innovative products speedily, and, in turn, attract young talent to the workforce and keep it.

With traditional management models being up against the ropes, "novel" forms of organizing appeared to have an easy opponent—at least, in the popular management literature. Flattening the decision-making structure by removing (sometimes all middle) layers of authority from a hierarchy has been increasingly hailed as a silver bullet for founding successful startups, transforming giant corporations into agile players, and enabling the current and future workforce to be happy and productive at the same time.

Related management concepts or tools abound—such as agility, holacracy, and scrum.

So why another book?

The short answer: because, as is so often the case, upon closer inspection the truth is more complex than the latest management fashion may suggest. First, hierarchies have been around for a reason, and they will remain important in certain domains. Second, doing without them where possible requires more than a one-size-fits-all template for managers to execute.

To appreciate my first point, let's begin from the following two observations.

One: in 2017, in the United States, around 128 million people were in the labor force, over 67 percent of them working for a company having 100 or more employees on its payroll, and more than half (~53 percent) working for one having 500 or more. Those 100-plus-employee companies account for over 75 percent of total revenues in the US economy, the 500-plus-employee ones for about 64 percent. So big companies matter.[1]

Two: on average, a CEO in the US does not supervise more than six managers, and a mid-level manager in Europe just under three, according to scientific studies. The lowest-level managers within companies, on average, supervise teams of around 15 in the median. For an 800-person company, this easily means four or more layers of management. And that number can rise drastically when company size increases. In other words, large firms use hierarchies of significant depth.[2]

If we put these two observations together, we have to conclude that most economic value is generated in deeply hierarchical organizations.

But why does the most significant part of the economy seem to rely on hierarchies if they are as bad as we are being told?

I can think of three explanations, all of which may have some validity.

First, maybe traditional forms of organizing, despite their alleged and real downsides, are not always that bad. Maybe they are superior at delivering performance under certain conditions. As I will argue in Chap. 8, such conditions exist, partly explaining the continued existence of bureaucracies.

Second, maybe where flat structures could do well, managers simply have yet to try them out and will do so only in the future. There are good reasons to believe that we'll increasingly see more decentralized organizations form and persist in the future (see also Chap. 8 for further thoughts on this). It's unlikely this will hold for all organizations, though.

Third, maybe managers of (currently large) companies have already tried to move to flatter structures but simply did a less-than-perfect job and returned to their traditional management models in frustration—perhaps because they underestimated the challenges of establishing a flat startup culture, or because they struggled with transforming their traditional companies. The list of examples is long (see Chap. 1).

This book seeks to help executives prepare for the second challenge and to deal with the third—and to avoid mistakes when moving to flatter structures. Having managers appreciate where traditional structures should remain because they are superior will save decision-makers predictable disappointment.

What the Book Does for You Exactly

This volume encourages you to view organizations as systems that can be engineered to make different individuals collaborate toward a common goal.

I will demonstrate that just as cars can be designed to run on electricity rather than fossil fuels, organizations can be designed to require fewer (if any) layers of management when dividing labor and reintegrating work.

Just as electric vehicles cannot resolve every transportation problem—being CO_2 neutral while providing sufficient cruising range—in every situation—urban traffic versus countryside—flat organizations will have different options and limits in meeting different goals. To give an example: a flat organization may be better both at providing fast solutions to its clients and showing a high degree of corporate-wide quality standardization when operating in a local as opposed to a global context.

For managers to eventually create the flat organization that suits their purposes, they must therefore determine what exactly it is they want to achieve when delegating more decision-making to their subordinates.

To be able to define meaningful and realistic goals at all, however, they must first do away with unrealistic expectations, nurtured and fueled by ideological rather than scientific accounts of what organizational design can and should do. To the contrary, managers should first understand the operations of their engine: why flat(ter) organizations work at all, and under which conditions they do (well) in which regard. By understanding what is possible, they'll be able to design what meets their desires best—rather than beginning from wishful thinking just to hit the hard wall of reality eventually.

Such an understanding, so I propose, requires executives to develop a more nuanced understanding than has been provided in the popular management literature of what moving to "flat" structures really means.

First, creating flatter structures can range from removing interim layers of authority within a hierarchy to quasi-decentralizing decision rights. There's a huge difference between eliminating a few mid-level managerial positions in an inflated hierarchy and giving responsibility to staff on the shop floor to structure their workday, however. The former problem seems simple in comparison to the latter.

Second, high delegation to achieve quasi-decentralization is not a monodimensional problem. It can occur, to different degrees, along a series of organizational design dimensions. For example, while some companies let employees choose which tasks to work on, others would rather allow them to choose who to form teams with; yet other firms will have their staff determine their own salaries, decide how to communicate with one another, or resolve disputes among peers. All in all, this leaves managers with the need to pick the right design option from a plethora of potential structures. Only when the potential structure fulfills what management hopes to achieve, and when it is suited to their corporate staff, will the high-delegation initiative eventually succeed.

The challenge for executives to think about creating functional flat structures is thus not trivial. Despite abundant practical advice, extant management tools in the field often either lack scientific grounding or focus on isolated difficulties of quasi-decentralization.

With this book I seek to fill this void. While providing actionable advice for managers eventually, the writings presented here draw on the scientific knowledge gained in the fields of organizational design and organizational behavior of the past 60 years. A fair share among these are studies conducted by my co-authors, graduate students, and myself over the past decade. Structuring what we have come to know from about a hundred studies through a scientific and practice-proven lens on nonhierarchical forms organizing developed jointly with Oliver Alexy and Phanish Puranam and enriching these insights with illustrative case material from more than a dozen selected companies, I provide readers the understanding and skills to become truly "better at flatter" management—from hiring to execution. Here, they will benefit from the feedback I received on the book's core ideas over the course of many executive seminars, master classes, and public presentations—including two TEDx talks in 2016 and 2020—on the subject.

How to Read This Book

There are two ways to read this book, depending on how much time you have to spare.

Ideally, you'll peruse the different chapters in order. Chapters 1, 2, 3, 4, 5, 6, 7, and 8 will take you through the different steps of understanding the functionality of flat designs, while Chap. 9 will synthesize them in a managerial framework that allows you to tackle the practical cases in Chaps. 10 and

11 to test your own understanding. I recommend this way of going through the book if you want to ensure that you end up having a profound understanding of the challenges that designing flat organizational structures brings about.

Should you have less time on your hands, you may want to read Chaps. 1 and 2 and then jump to Chap. 9. In this case, you may find yourself needing to selectively revisit earlier parts of the book that I refer back to, depending on where questions arise when applying the framework.

Irrespective of how you read the book, it's my hope that you'll walk away not only confident but also inspired to (re)structure your company.

Notes

1. See U.S. Census Bureau, "2017 SUSB Annual Data Tables by Establishment Industry," and OECD, "SDBS Structural Business Statistics (ISIC Rev. 4)." For OECD countries, the distribution is skewed slightly less toward large companies, but shows a similar picture overall.
2. For more details, see Rajan and Wulf, "The Flattening Firm," and Smeets and Warzynski, "Too Many Theories, Too Few Facts?" Admittedly, these studies from the late 2000s suggest that companies had become flatter during the preceding decades. If that trend had prevailed thereafter, depths of hierarchies might have decreased even further since 2008. However, barring radical changes, the overall inference presented here would remain the same.

Bibliography

OECD. "SDBS Structural Business Statistics (ISIC Rev. 4)." https://stats.oecd.org/Index.aspx?DataSetCode=SSIS_BSC_ISIC4# (accessed December 2020).

Rajan, R. G., and J. Wulf. "The Flattening Firm: Evidence from Panel Data on the Changing Nature of Corporate Hierarchies." *The Review of Economics and Statistics* 88, no. 4 (2006): 759–73.

Smeets, V., and F. Warzynski. "Too Many Theories, Too Few Facts? What the Data Tell Us about the Link between Span of Control, Compensation and Career Dynamics." *Labour Economics* 15, no. 4 (2008): 687–703.

U.S. Census Bureau. "2017 SUSB Annual Data Tables by Establishment Industry." https://www.census.gov/data/tables/2017/econ/susb/2017-susb-annual.html (accessed December 2020).

Part I

Why Flat Structures Work at All

1

What Does It Mean to Move Toward a "Flatter" Structure?

As mentioned in the introduction, high hopes have been attached to the flattening of corporate structures over the past: to make companies be more creative, react faster to market developments, make their employees happier, and so forth. And there are instances when such aspirations have materialized. They provide the obvious inspiration for us to engage with the topic of this book, so let's hear from some of them—and begin with the German company T-Systems, which recently moved to a flatter structure than it had operated before.

> **T-Systems International GmbH**
>
> **Background**
> T-Systems emerged from Deutsche Telekom's acquisition of the majority of stakes of Debis Systemhaus in 2000[1] and is, as of this writing, one of the leading providers of digital services around the world. The company offers services ranging from cloud & infrastructure to IT security and 5G technology, and is aiming to become "Your Digitization Partner with Industry Expertise."[2] Employing over 28,000 people around the world, the Telekom subsidiary is generating annual revenues of 4.2 billion €.[3] As one of the most advanced digital service providers, the company is involved in high-tech projects around the world, such as setting up electro stations in Austria[4] or implementing a flight operation system at Beijing Airport.[5]
> T-Systems's Global Delivery Unit Auto-MI has a workforce of around 1000 people in Germany. They offer services such as IT consulting, software development, and implementation, with a focus on the automobile and manufacturing industry. Most people working in the unit have an engineering and IT background.
>
> *(continued)*

(continued)

Moving to a Flat Structure

In 2014 the T-Systems GDU Auto-MI embarked on a delayering process spearheaded by their new Vice President, Georg Rätker. Prior to the transition, four layers of senior, mid-level, and lower-level management had separated the VP from the workforce. When the transition was complete, the number of layers was reduced to just two. The intention behind the transformation was twofold: first, senior management wanted to accelerate the flow of information within the unit. As Rätker put it, "You have to imagine it like this: when something has come from the top, and has cascaded through the four respective hierarchical layers, one question is, of course, 'How long does it really take, until it has reached the bottom?' and even more so 'How will this actually be understood at the bottom?'"[6] Further, the delayering process was supposed to help with fostering creativity and innovation in employees by involving them more closely in the company's decision-making process.

The people working at T-Systems had mixed feelings about moving to a flatter structure. Some were on board right away and "took the chance. They found it exciting, and did indeed get involved more themselves."[7] Others were skeptical about the transformation, and yet again others totally neglected the new work organization. At this point, the company began educating employees on the new practices such as Design Thinking or HR Leadership.

Although "I believe I, myself, was already quite agile in many basic characteristics, even before restructuring,"[8] naturally, the transformation to a flatter structure brought with it more delegation. For starters, Rätker's direct reports were granted a bigger say in the strategic planning of the unit's activities and have since enjoyed more freedom in shaping their area of responsibility. This move was helped by the modular project structure typical of the IT service sector. In the process, Rätker reduced his role with his subordinates: he became more of a feedback partner than a supervisor. Also, employees gained the right to suggest which projects they wished to work on. Rätker explains that, because of the transparent project architecture, each employee could preselect projects of interest by "talking with people in advance. And if they thought that would work out, then it was never a problem to say 'Listen, I see an opportunity there. That interests me more, content-wise, and I'd like to do that.'"[9] Further, T-Systems began introducing several initiatives such as co-creating or idea management, which increased the opportunities for employees to participate in the company. The restructuring brought about changes in compensation practices, too. While overall compensation budgets were still determined by senior management, middle management now faced less bureaucracy and needed less approval when deciding on the remuneration of individual employees on their teams. Finally, events that were meant to keep all staff updated on the state of current projects across the unit became a habit, and this helped spread critical information across the entire organization more broadly.

What Happened

Seven years into the process, the company feels that the delayering initiative has met two of the initial goals—accelerating decision-making and fostering creativity—at least in part. As Rätker sums up, "We've certainly achieved more speed in some aspects. But on the other hand, the thing is, if you're no longer

(continued)

(continued)
that straightforward organization-wise, then sometimes you'll have some who get lost. They go this way, they go that way, and that way. So surely there'll be some examples, where you didn't get faster. [...] As regards creativity, I would connect this a little bit with empowerment, I'd say. I do think that some of those who didn't have the courage to speak up before, but had good ideas, can get involved more. That helps, definitely. For that I'd say I'd put an obvious checkmark next to it."[10]

Some more inspiration comes from the Finnish company Reaktor, which began as a flat organization and retained large parts of its structure over the course of its growth.

Reaktor Group Oy
Background
  Reaktor was founded in 2000 in Helsinki. As of this writing, the company employs 550 people spread across seven offices around the world. Reaktor considers itself a "strategy, design, and technology partner for forward-thinking companies and societies"[11] and boasts of clients such as Adidas, HBO, and Airbus. Its services are varied and highly customized, such as optimizing code for recycling robots and setting up a digital clinic. In 2018 Reaktor received wide attention when teaming up with the University of Helsinki to launch the free online course "Elements of AI," which has enrolled over 600,000 students as of this writing. More recently, it became public that Reaktor is heavily involved in the development of Finland's official COVID-19 tracking app.
  Sticking to a Flat Structure
  Back in 2012, however, the company's future was unclear. At that time, it employed around 150 people, and management was expecting some serious issues unless it changed parts of its operations. More specifically, top management feared that its organizational structure would slow the company's growth. This was because at that time company policy still foresaw to run all the essential decision by a centralized executive group. And, "since all the necessary information was rarely available [to that top management team], the executive group became a bottleneck."[12] Although operational success and employee satisfaction remained high, the executive group thought that an ounce of prevention was worth a pound of cure, so they sat down and discussed options for solving the issues at hand.
  Installing a layer of middle management was dismissed after brief deliberations because it did not seem appealing given the corporate background. Instead, management decided to "increase openness and transparency. [They] chose to give all Reaktorians more power and responsibility, to encourage them to increase self-organization, and to decrease the role of [their] executive group."[13]

(continued)

(continued)

By now, these changes have become part of the company's organizational design. It all begins when new projects are acquired: the company advertises them to their employees in an opening and "anybody could make known their interest to join the project,"[14] which gives them a say in their projects. Once involved in a project team, "they operate autonomously and make all necessary decisions concerning their projects."[15] Also, there is no approval process for vacation planning; people figure this out on their own in consensus with the project team they are currently enrolled in. In order to enable their employees to make solid decisions, Reaktor began increasing transparency with sensible information. Now, every employee is educated about the corporate financials monthly. Furthermore, an open data project was initiated that helps with sharing all the information about skills, interests, and utilizations across the company.

What Happened

According to former Reaktor CTO Hannu Terävä, "This all has resulted in a sharp decrease of issues brought to our executive group […] and has reduced the time for things to actually get done."[16] This did not come as a surprise, since "often, the greatest innovations that fuel our evolution have come from Reaktorians working with clients."[17] Additionally, the company witnessed employees' personal growth as they were constantly exposed to the challenge of taking on responsibility and making decisions on their own.

Naturally, Reaktor also faced issues in this organizational transition, notably when scaling up their operations while maintaining a decentralized structure. As CTO Mikael Kopteff noted, "We take our global business very seriously. So naturally, we need to have functions for all the operations that in a traditional company are run by managers. We are attempting to scale them and to distribute the responsibilities throughout the company."[18] When an increased number of recruiting interviews were needed, the company's top management, instead of relying on hierarchies to coordinate these issues, once again allocated responsibility to the entire workforce. The "20 percenter model" was introduced, which requires Reaktor employees to dedicate 20% of their worktime to tackling management problems that affect the entire company. Not only does it seem to work; it also helped bring people even closer together and spread information throughout the company. Also, Reaktor states that rather than HR hiring managers, having specialists such as coders and developers heavily involved in the recruitment process enhances the quality of new talent hired by the company, since "the best recognize the best."[19]

As of 2018, employees within Reaktor are organized in temporary project-depended teams that constantly change as a project evolves. Reaktor CTO Mikael Kopteff argues, "This "loose" structure gives us resilience and the ability to adapt to the changes in the market extremely rapidly."[20] In the process, former Reaktor CTO Hannu Terävä considers the role of the executive group as "facilitat[ing] the work of our teams by means of financial management, sales, recruitment, and administrative support."[21] Other than the project teams, there are several interest groups about work-related and non-work-related topics, such as programming and cycling, that are supported and embraced by the company.

However, when talking to practitioners and researching the media more carefully, doubts emerge about whether the above stories are representative of the experiences of many companies. Upon closer look, it seems that the realities of implementing or maintaining flat(ter) structures and the constraints on what they can achieve caught up faster with many companies than expected. Both Treehouse and Wistia illustrate the issues that many corporations appear to face when embarking on the venture of eliminating—parts of—their command hierarchies.

Treehouse Island, Inc.

Background

In 2010 Ryan Carson, along with Alan Johnson, founded Treehouse with the mission "to diversify the tech industry through accessible education, unlocking the door to opportunity, and empowering people to achieve their dreams."[22] The Portland-based company offers online coding courses to private and business clients and helps companies spot suitable tech talent. What began as a series of physical meet-ups and workshops teaching people how to code evolved into a 177-person online business serving customers such as Disney, Virgin, and Estée Lauder, among others.

Moving to a Flat Structure

By 2013 the company had grown to more than 60 employees and undergone a fundamental redesign of its organizational structure when it noticed workers' declining job satisfaction. As CEO Carson put it, "The notion of remaking Treehouse's management structure emerged […] when word filtered up that some front-line employees didn't feel their voices were being heard—and that one planned to boycott an all-hands meeting as a result."[23] To resolve the issue, Carson and Johnson went into a deep think and eventually came up with the idea of removing the seven middle management positions they did currently employ.[24]

When Carson and Johnson discussed the idea with the Treehouse workforce, "there were very strong feelings both ways."[25] Concerns about the loss of direction were raised; however, most people supported the vision and, ultimately, they decided to push it. As Carson and Johnson informed their investors of their plans towards more decentralization, the latter responded with excitement rather than skepticism. Kate Eberle Walker, the representative of Kaplan Ventures, a major investor of Treehouse, said: "When you give them the opportunity they will create work for themselves, effectively, and put more effort into it,"[26] so the company could count on full support from its investors and thus began the transformation process.

From now on, people were encouraged to propose their own projects and to choose what they would like to work on. At the time, the rule was that a "Treehouse employee can propose a project by submitting it on an internal company website. If enough of their colleagues sign on to help the project goes forward. If it doesn't attract others' interest, it's abandoned."[27] Only in a very last step would the Treehouse founders endorse a project or not, to ensure align-

(continued)

(continued)

ment with the strategic orientation of Treehouse overall. Interestingly, this step was explicitly requested by the employees. Along with autonomy, Treehouse began increasing transparency. As Carson states: "Treehouse is committed to sharing lots of information about the business with its employees, so they can make educated decisions about how to proceed."[28]

The more decentralized setup found its way into the workforce's compensation design, too. At the time, "workers evaluate one another each quarter, rating everyone they've worked on a project with (typically five to 10 people) on a scale of 1 to 5. Employees are asked to evaluate colleagues' judgment, communication, working style and skill level. Good reviews are they key factor in deciding who gets raises. Consistently bad reviews start a process that can lead to firing."[29]

Initially, converting to the flat structure seemed to pay off for the company: "Treehouse says it's increased productivity and employee enthusiasm by freeing workers from managerial oversight and giving them the information and latitude to do their jobs the way they see fit."[30] Yet, about two years and forty employees later, constraints on the no-bosses approach became transparent. Situations in which "employees felt adrift, lonely islands with no support"[31] accumulated. Also, the lack of accountability became a major problem because "projects went unfinished," Carson said, "and there was no one to hold accountable."[32] As one interviewer summed up Carson's thoughts: "You need to have a team of smart, motivated people or else this isn't going to work. They had to let some people go when they made this change. Some people weren't able to switch to this style. Some employees want to be managed."[33]

Reintroducing Hierarchy

Finally, the company ditched its heavily decentralized design. Already when introducing the flat structure two years earlier, Carson was troubled by the thought that workers could spend too much working time at evaluating their peers and was concerned that "as you scale, how do you get people to honestly evaluate each other?"[34] After re-installing management this fear proved true, as "[s]ome people weren't pulling their weight and it became clear really, really fast."[35] As he concluded: "The no-boss approach was fine when Treehouse was a small company—it employed 61 in 2013—but it became an obstacle for the business as Treehouse grew north of 100 workers."[36]

Treehouse did not resort to a traditional way of organizing without second thoughts, however, since by then "the no-boss approach was a core part of Treehouse's identity and something some employees deeply appreciated."[37] Not surprisingly, as a result of returning to traditional management, "some employees were disappointed and quit fairly quickly, and others suddenly felt dispensable."[38]

What Happened

Overall, the re-transition turned out to be rough. To mitigate some of the issues, Carson staffed management positions with employees who held "strong people skills, figuring they would be best positioned to manage the change."[39] So, in a way, Treehouse retains the "flat spirit" in some form. They have maintained a four-day work week, for instance, which they say "benefits recruitment, morale and—consequently—productivity."[40]

Wistia, Inc.

Background

Wistia is a Boston-based company run by its co-founders Chris Savage (CEO) and Brendan Schwartz (CTO). From its launch in 2006 until this writing, Wistia has grown to 107 staff. The company makes "marketing software, video series, and educational content based on the belief that anyone can use video to grow their business and their brand."[41] As of 2017, they raised 17.1 million dollars to buy out the company from its investors in order to fully focus on developing high-quality products rather than growing to merely meet external shareholders' expectations.

After Savage and Schwartz graduated from Brown University, the two friends strived to "build a company that let people run wild and free with their ideas—a place where you could come up with a marketing campaign at nine and set it in place by five."[42] They feared that bureaucracy and managers telling employees what to do might come in the way of their vision. That's why they started out using a rather flat organizational structure as a tool to avoid those issues. Savage described the early years of Wistia thus: "We didn't have a defined framework for making decisions. Instead, we focused on giving people autonomy."[43]

More specifically, Wistia's structure at the time granted its employees ownership over the available projects. Having ownership at Wistia then meant that people "are responsible for thinking about and organizing the progress on that part of the business."[44] In the early years, this structure worked well for the company. As Savage stated, "With individual ownership, our team members were more motivated to move their projects forward faster. [...] By entrusting people to own parts of the business from the get-go, people got up to speed very quickly and the business moved much faster."[45] Wistia became a company full of "huge opportunities for individuals to jump in and make a real difference"[46] and established itself as a place that "make[s] sure that [its] team is inspired to do meaningful, quality-driven work."[47]

Abandoning the Flat Structure

As Wistia grew beyond 30 permanent employees, however, problems started to emerge. Because everyone wanted to be enrolled in the most important corporate projects, other, more mundane tasks were delayed or remained unfinished. In the process of scaling up, "responsibilities were chopped into smaller pieces and it was hard to keep track who is responsible for what which clouds the decision-making process."[48]

The breakdown of the self-organization also manifested itself in the emergence of a shadow hierarchy—essentially, people began running every decision by Savage or Schwartz. As a result, the number of decisions the two founders had to make exploded, and their decision-making quality decreased. Savage concluded that "for us, it became hard to take risks—no one was clear on who was responsible for what. We moved more slowly, and it felt harder to learn and be creative."[49] In 2011 the company ditched its flat system and introduced an organizational structure that was more reminiscent of a traditional hierarchy.

(continued)

(continued)
What Happened
When Savage and Schwartz announced this change, some employees were thankful while others felt pushed back and feared a loss of autonomy and creativity. Still, Wistia saw no other option but to implement a senior management team responsible for running the business, and it drew up an organizational chart with hierarchy layers, defined roles and goals. Today, the company enjoys a number of perks from its more centralized structure. They experienced the speed of execution accelerating since there are clearly defined communication paths now. Contrary to expectation, creativity flourished working in a hierarchical system as people can focus on defined goals and are aware about the resources at their disposal. As CEO Savage summed up Wistia's journey: "A small flat company can have lots of autonomy and creativity if there is enough trust, but those values don't scale through flatness; they scale through an organizational structure."[50]

If the examples of T-Systems, Reaktor, Wistia, and Treehouse serve one key purpose, it's to show that moving to flatter structures brings both opportunities and threats that educated managers must carefully balance.

What the cases also illustrate, however, is that the abandoning of campaigns towards more decentralized decision-making is again no rarity. Beyond the success stories of vanguard corporations excelling in performance when reducing their hierarchical depth, many less glamorous accounts of perceived failures surface once one investigates more thoroughly. Finally, as the examples demonstrate, the explanation for why moving to a flatter structure eventually works in one instance but not in another is visibly not just a simple story of industry affiliation or corporate size; in fact, Wistia and Treehouse operate in markets similar to Reaktor's and T-Systems's, and the first three companies are roughly comparable in terms of their number of employees.

So what does it take to make a flat structure work for one's company? With regard to the four specific case corporations above, we jointly revisit this question in Chap. 9 after we've developed a more nuanced understanding of what it takes to be better at designing flatter structures in Chaps. 2, 3, 4, 5, 6, 7, and 8. At this point, let's build a general toolkit to help answer the fundamental question of what separates the wheat from the chaff.

To make fast progress in answering this question, we must not simply describe what some successful companies do and suggest how to imitate their approaches. Their situation may be very different from your company's. Instead, we must begin by getting a sense of what is possible at all when moving to flatter structures, why, and when.

This journey begins with defining what making a structure flatter actually means. To that end, we need to recall what command hierarchies actually are and what it means to reduce their steepness.

1 What Does It Mean to Move Toward a "Flatter" Structure?

The simplest form of such a hierarchy is a line of command (Fig. 1.1).

Here the CEO supervises a mid-level manager, who supervises one shop-floor worker, where supervising means exercising formal authority—demanding actions and behaviors commensurate with the employee's contract and the governing labor law. The CEO can also give direct instructions to the shop-floor worker if she wants to, because her authority extends to all members of the small organization.

More likely, the command hierarchy in the organization will have a pyramid shape (Fig. 1.2).

Here, the CEO presides over several, in the simplest case two, mid-level managers, and they both supervise several, in the simplest case two, shop-floor workers.

To have a common vocabulary, let's call the number of layers of authority in the hierarchy the depth of the hierarchy. In our examples, the depth is two (CEO and mid-level manager). Let's refer to the number of people each manager supervises as her span of control. In our second example, the CEO and the mid-level managers each have a span of control of two.

What does flattening now mean?

It refers to the process of reducing the depth of the hierarchy, broadly speaking. More narrowly, it refers to the same process while keeping the size of the overall organization largely unchanged, though.

In our example, flattening the hierarchy from depth 2 to depth 1 can take different shapes.

Fig. 1.1 Line of command, consisting of one CEO, one mid-level manager, and one shop-floor worker. (© Markus Reitzig 2021)

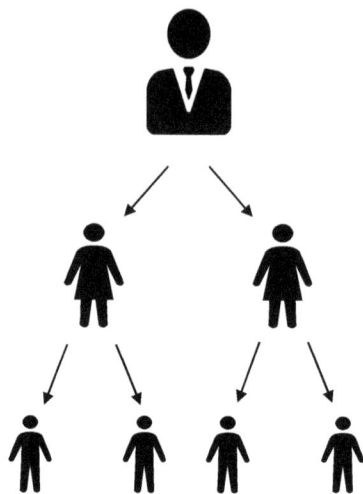

Fig. 1.2 Two-layered command hierarchy with span of control of two at all layers. (© Markus Reitzig 2021)

One possibility is that the former mid-level managers remain within the firm, in which case there are two scenarios. Either they join the CEO at her level for joint leadership, or they join the shop-floor workers.

Another possibility is, of course, that the mid-level managers leave the company.

Importantly, what all structures depicted in Figs. 1.3, 1.4, and 1.5 achieve is reducing the depth of hierarchy from 2 to 1. Strictly speaking, they are therefore no longer hierarchical structures, because there's only one layer of authority left above the shop-floor workers. In fact, these structures are better referred to as authoritative structures, not hierarchical structures.

Clearly, however, these three authoritative structures—while all "flatter" than the original hierarchy—will have very different implications for the functioning of the organization.

In the scenario depicted in Fig. 1.3, the average span of control is 1.33 as compared with 2 before. But three bosses now need to coordinate on who to supervise and how to make decisions for the company as a whole.

In the case depicted in Fig. 1.4, the span of control for the sole CEO increases to 6 from 2 before.

Finally, in Fig. 1.5 the span of control increases to 4 from 2 before.

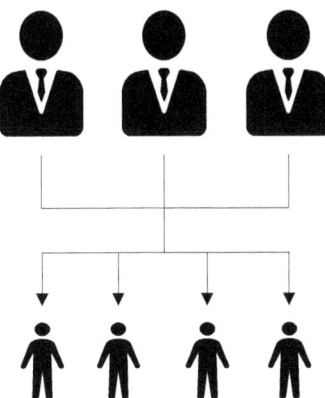

Fig. 1.3 Authority structure with triple leadership and four jointly supervised subordinates. (© Markus Reitzig 2021)

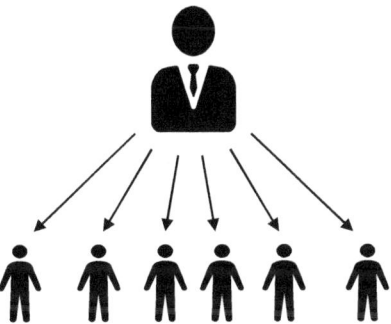

Fig. 1.4 Authority structure with single leadership and span of control of six. (© Markus Reitzig 2021)

With the exception of the shared leadership (Fig. 1.3), an admittedly rare scenario in most corporations, the workload for managers would go up quite dramatically compared to the original structure (Fig. 1.2), all else being equal, particularly their roles not changing. Their work in terms of monitoring and overseeing reports would double or even triple, their work in managing only bilateral conflicts by team members would go up from 2 to 6 and 15,[51] respectively.

It should be clear that with the exception of initially inflated hierarchies—in which the CEO had abundant time left over—moving to any of the new structures will impose an enormous burden on her, unless other things change. These other things, to be more precise, concern the work of the shop-floor employees. In essence, they must take over some of the managerial functions formerly executed by the manager; otherwise, the organization will become unstable.

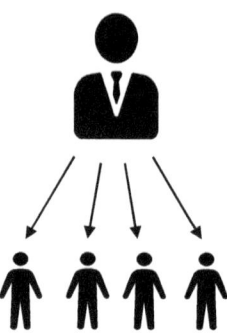

Fig. 1.5 Authority structure with single leadership and span of control of four. (© Markus Reitzig 2021)

"Flattening" an organization's structure, unless in rather trivial cases of deflating formerly blown-up structures, therefore always ***includes the challenge of decentralizing!*** In the context of command hierarchies, that means ***delegating decision rights within certain domains*** to employees and ***making them take over functions*** traditionally reserved for managers with authority.[52]

- But which functions could employees take over to save a manager's time (Chap. 2)? Unless we know where we can gain managerial time by delegating some of their former responsibilities, decentralizing will not work. This raises the next question, however.
- Why would employees ever want to assume new responsibilities if they could (Chap. 3)? Unless we understand why they would walk the extra mile in a more decentralized organization, we have no reason to believe that a flat structure can ever cope with the workload. Which raises the next question.
- Which type of staff should you ideally take on the journey (Chap. 4)? Are all employees equally enticed to working in a flat environment, or are some more prone to push the initiative? And how far down should you push the decision-making in your organization?
- And how can you enforce and foster collaboration among those employees and others who are less convinced that they want to work autonomously (Chap. 5)? Clearly, picking the right staff from the outset is important, but how to bring on the rest?
- How do you design the playing field for your people so that they don't get lost in the process of self-organization? How can you help them avoid duplication of effort, ensure compatibility of team efforts, manage information costs, and resolve conflicts (Chap. 6)?

- And once you've done all of the above, when should you ever put an efficient flat structure to use because it can beat a more centralized structure (Chap. 7)? What are the conditions?
- And just to be sure: when would moving towards more decentralization make no sense? Where does the flat structure reach its limits (Chap. 8)?

These are the key questions we need to address before we can draw an interim summary, which eventually provides us with

- The guide(s) to successful decentralizing (Chap. 9)

Finally, the last chapters of this volume are devoted to checking on our newly gained understanding and putting it to a practical and conceptual test.

- Tackling a practical case of removing hierarchical layers in a larger corporation—the transformation story of Borek (Chap. 10)
- Founding and growing a flat startup—the case of wirDesign (Chap. 11)
- Concluding thoughts—what to make of all the trends from *a* as in "agile" to *z* as in "zi zhu jing ying ti" (Chap. 12)

Notes

1. Boston, "Deutsche Telekom Confirms Purchase of DaimlerChrysler's Debis Division."
2. https://www.t-systems.com/de/en/about-t-systems/company (accessed June 14, 2021).
3. Ibid.
4. "Elektro-Tankstelle aus einem Guss," *T-Systems*, https://www.t-systems.com/at/de/referenzen/digital/comfort-charge (accessed June 15, 2021).
5. "Digital Air Traffic Control for Smooth Processes," *T-Systems*, https://www.t--systems.com/us/en/success-stories/digital/beijing-airport (accessed June 15, 2021).
6. Interview with Georg Rätker, 29 April 2021, via videocall.
7. Ibid.
8. Ibid.
9. Ibid.
10. Ibid.
11. https://www.reaktor.com (accessed February 5, 2021).
12. Terävä, "How Reaktor Grew without Hierarchy."

13. Ibid.
14. Ibid.
15. Kopteff, "Scaling Our Business beyond 500 with Distributed Responsibility, Free of Static Structures or Superiors."
16. Terävä, "How Reaktor Grew without Hierarchy."
17. Ibid.
18. Kopteff, "Scaling Our Business beyond 500 with Distributed Responsibility, Free of Static Structures or Superiors."
19. Ibid.
20. Ibid.
21. Terävä, "How Reaktor Grew without Hierarchy."
22. "About Treehouse," https://teamtreehouse.com/about (accessed 5 February 5, 2021).
23. Rogoway, "Portland Startup Treehouse Eliminates the Boss, Tells Workers to Manage Themselves."
24. Some former managers were happy to return to a frontline job; others feared that the company would lose direction.
25. Rogoway, "Portland Startup Treehouse Eliminates the Boss, Tells Workers to Manage Themselves."
26. Ibid.
27. Ibid.
28. Ibid.
29. Ibid.
30. Ibid.
31. Rogoway, "No-Boss Office Brings Back the Boss: 'We Were Naïve.'"
32. Ibid.
33. Siu, "Ep09: How Treehouse, an $8 Million Revenue Company Operates on a 4-Day Work Week and No Managers—Interview with Ryan Carson."
34. Rogoway, "Portland Startup Treehouse Eliminates the Boss, Tells Workers to Manage Themselves."
35. Rogoway, "No-Boss Office Brings Back the Boss: 'We Were Naïve.'"
36. Ibid.
37. Ibid.
38. Ibid.
39. Ibid.
40. Ibid.
41. "We're Wistia," *Wistia*, https://wistia.com/about (accessed February 3, 2021).
42. Savage, "Flat Is not a Value: How a Clear Org Structure Unlocked Growth at Wistia."
43. Savage, "Ditching Flat: How Structure Helped Us Move Faster."
44. Ibid.
45. Ibid.
46. Ibid.

47. "We're Wistia," *Wistia*, https://wistia.com/about (accessed February 3, 2021).
48. Savage, "Ditching Flat: How Structure Helped Us Move Faster."
49. Ibid.
50. Savage, "Flat Is not a Value: How a Clear Org Structure Unlocked Growth at Wistia."
51. The number of bilateral conflicts can be calculated as $n(n-1)/2$, where n is the number of subordinates. So in Fig. 1.5, with four subordinates, the CEO must manage $4(4-1)/2 = 6$ conflicts. In Fig. 1.4, the number is $6(6-1)/2 = 15$ conflicts.
52. Interested readers may note already that I am using the term "command hierarchy" and not just hierarchy in general. As we will discover later, notably in Chap. 8, the term hierarchy can extend to forms of influence other than just official command associated with formal decision-making rights. In fact, influence hierarchies of humans within organizations, more generally speaking, simply denote systems (1) in which two members in adjacent layers of the hierarchy have asymmetric influence over one another—whatever the nature of that influence may be—power, formal authority, or just status; and (2) in which these relations between such people are transitive so that if A has, say, more power than B, and B has more power than C, then A also has more power than C. As such, command and status hierarchies can exist in parallel within one company, and they must not necessarily be identical. How this affects the logic of decentralizing decision-making rights is an aspect we visit again in Chaps. 8, 9, and 10 of this book.

Bibliography

Boston, William. "Deutsche Telekom Confirms Purchase of DaimlerChrysler's Debis Division." *Wall Street Journal,* March 28, 2000. https://www.wsj.com/articles/SB954344023145547909 (accessed June 14, 2021).

Kopteff, Mikael. "Scaling Our Business beyond 500 with Distributed Responsibility, Free of Static Structures or Superiors." *Reaktor,* November 16, 2018. https://www.reaktor.com/blog/scaling-our-business-beyond-500-with-distributed-responsibility-free-of-static-structures-or-superiors/ (accessed February 4, 2021).

Rogoway, Mike. "No-Boss Office Brings Back the Boss: 'We Were Naïve.'" *Oregon Live*, June 18, 2016, updated January 9, 2019a. https://www.oregonlive.com/silicon-forest/2016/06/portland_startup_that_eliminat.html (accessed February 5, 2021).

———. "Portland Startup Treehouse Eliminates the Boss, Tells Workers to Manage Themselves." *Oregon Live*, December 19, 2013, updated January 10, 2019b. https://www.oregonlive.com/silicon-forest/2013/12/portland_startup_treehouse_eli.html (accessed February 4, 2021).

Savage, Chris. "Flat Is not a Value: How a Clear Org Structure Unlocked Growth at Wistia." *ChartHop,* September 24, 2020. https://www.charthop.com/blog/org-chart/flat-is-not-a-value-org-structure-growth-wistia/ (accessed February 6, 2021).

———. "Ditching Flat: How Structure Helped Us Move Faster." *Wistia,* October 15, 2015. https://wistia.com/learn/culture/ditching-flat (accessed February 5, 2021).

Siu, Eric. "Ep09: How Treehouse, an $8 Million Revenue Company Operates on a 4-Day Work Week and No Managers—Interview with Ryan Carson." *LevelingUp,* n.d. https://www.levelingup.com/management/ryan-carson/ (accessed May 27, 2021).

Terävä, Hannu. "How Reaktor Grew without Hierarchy." *Reaktor,* September 3, 2015. https://www.reaktor.com/blog/how-reaktor-grew-without-hierarchy/ (accessed February 4, 2021).

2

What Managers Can Effectively and Efficiently Delegate

Asking which functions decision-makers can delegate to their employees and save on managerial time requires recalling ***what it is that managers traditionally do.*** In essence, their job is to ensure that collaboration among employees arises so that the organizational goals are being met—not more, not less.

But what does that entail? While it would be easy to draw up a laundry list of all managerial tasks that come to mind, doing so would probably not be too helpful in structuring our thinking to arrive at a finite set of insights.

Several years ago, together with my colleagues Phanish Puranam and Oliver Alexy, I therefore tried to describe which fundamental problems managers need to address when setting up an organization. Here, our goal was to come up with the ***shortest possible but yet sufficiently comprehensive list.***[1] From this exercise emerged a framework which has, by now, been used to guide hundreds of executives to think about flat forms of organizing in depth. We refer to it as the 4+1 framework.

The terms "delegating" and "decentralizing" both feature prominently in this book. It seems important to recall the theoretical difference. Delegation involves the transfer of decision rights from a manager to her employees, but final control of and responsibility for the outcome remain with the manager. In a perfectly decentralized setup, the employees experience no final control and assume responsibility, but they are no longer accountable to a superior. In corporate life, if only for legal reasons, we will—strictly speaking—therefore never witness "formal decentralization" but rather a high degree of delegation—which differs from the usual low degree delegation observed in any type of company. For all practical purposes, however, it seems fair to refer to such high-delegation regimes as regimes of "informal," "quasi," or "de-facto decentralization."

© The Author(s), under exclusive license to Springer Nature Switzerland AG 2022
M. Reitzig, *Get Better at Flatter*, https://doi.org/10.1007/978-3-030-89254-8_2

The Fundamental Problems of Organizing—The 4+1 Framework

Organizations, in order to achieve more than what an equally large group of independently working individuals could, need to **divide labor and integrate effort** among their members.[2] Managers in charge of designing and running such organizations need to create the appropriate template for doing so; and they must supervise and enforce the process of collaboration, which includes the stimulation of the employees they're responsible for as well as the coordination and conflict resolution among them.

Division of labor is key to reaping the benefits of specialization—an insight dating back to the writings of Adam Smith. You may remember his example of the pin factory—which he uses to illustrate that individuals can become more efficient in performing their work if they repeatedly concentrate on just a subset of recurring tasks. With different employees each making specialized contributions to the overall product, however, the need for coordination arises. A company providing doors and windows, for example, may employ carpenters, glaziers, and locksmiths—all working on different parts of the final product. They all need to be motivated to work, and to work together to deliver the product to the client. And when they have a conflict, the manager is asked to resolve it—at least in a traditional company.

To these classic insights, Phanish Puranam, Oliver Alexy, and I added the understanding that division of labor always entails two challenges—but only two: task division and task allocation. And that integration of effort equally entails two challenges—but only two: the distribution of rewards and the provision of information. Jointly, these four challenges pose the first 4 fundamental problems of the 4+1 framework, and I elaborate on them below.

Task Division

Task division answers the question of **what needs to be done**. It's best conceived of as an exercise that involves decomposition and mapping. Decomposition here means that an overarching goal of an organization—say, to be a more attractive employer to sought-after top coders—is broken down into tasks. In the current example, such tasks could entail revisiting working hours for future employees, rethinking their remuneration, and so forth. Importantly, these tasks have to map onto the overarching goal the organization pursues. In traditional companies, the default is that a manager determines the goal and decomposes it into tasks and subtasks. Often, she will rely on standard tools such as workflow diagrams or business process maps to structure her own thinking and communicate with others.

Task Allocation

Task allocation answers the question of ***who does what***. Like task division, task allocation is a mapping—or matching—exercise. Finding the person who best fits the requirements that come with the different work packages is the challenge for the manager, at least in a traditional company. Key considerations in creating a good fit are usually the experience and the task-related skills that a person brings to the table, so that she can be efficient in what she does. In addition, and depending on how the tasks and subtasks have been divided above, managers often also consider whether assigning different sets of tasks to the same person reduces the need for her to coordinate with others and speeds up the production process; or whether synergies between different tasks suggest that one person should perform both. How the task allocation motivates an employee tends to be a secondary consideration in most traditional companies, as the assumption is that the employee should mainly care about the remuneration she receives.

Rewards Distribution

Reward distribution answers the question of ***who gets what***. In virtually all for-profit companies in the world, this remuneration will have a monetary dimension. In fact, in traditional corporations this part of the remuneration—whether fixed, variable, or based on shares—is considered the key motivator for employees to engage. This understanding goes back to the classic writings of Herbert Simon, who suggested that the reason why individuals sign a labor contract and put up with being administered by a manager is that they reduce uncertainty about their income.[3] Few people would probably disagree that such reasoning still holds to some extent for most employees, and it is conceivable that it is the primary motivation for many. Even traditional companies, however, have come to appreciate that other types of rewards also matter and motivate the individual. Status, and relatedly recognition by peers, the possibility to learn, the chance to advance one's own career—all these are so-called extrinsic rewards that employees may aim for when working for a given organization. So are the opportunities to do something 'meaningful,' take extended vacations, reduce workhours, or take a longer maternity or paternity leave than is guaranteed by law. Today, managers in most companies will seek to create compensation packages that entail parts of these rewards.

Information Exchange

Information exchange answers the question of ***who needs to know what***. Admittedly, in answering this question, corporations may be more lenient than secret services running undercover operations—abiding by the strict rule of providing their agents the minimal information needed for them to carry out their missions and thus reduce the risk of undesired information leakage. The general principle of parsimonious information exchange, however, has also governed much of corporate life. Traditionally, the goal of information exchange is achieved when the required coordination between employees becomes possible. So to the extent that two individuals know enough about what the other person does for them to adjust their own activities, information exchange is considered complete. In our earlier example of a company producing doors and windows, the locksmith may be happy enough to know when he receives the carpenter's door frame, and what the measurements are. The more standardized these operations, the less the two "need" to talk to one another, or maybe not at all. Traditionally, managers would determine the required level of exchange among their employees, its contents, frequency, and medium.

While addressing the questions of task division, task allocation, rewards distribution, and information exchange should facilitate the functioning of an organization overall, there may always be hiccups. After all, managers and employees are humans; they make mistakes in planning and execution; they may not show constant performance across all workdays; their life situations may change; and they may be substituted by new hires. In any of these situations, the workings of the organization experience a friction, which, unless it is intended to change the course of the company, would count as a temporary exception. ***Resolving these exceptions***, again, falls into the lap of the manager in a traditional company. Probably the most frequent conflicts she needs to address are mismatches between task division and goal attainment, which require adjusting the structure. And conflicts among employees, either because of their different interests (a.k.a. incentive conflicts) or because of their different views on how to get the work done (a.k.a. coordination conflicts).

Jointly, therefore, managers designing corporate structures and overseeing their operations in traditional companies need to address 4+1 fundamental

2 What Managers Can Effectively and Efficiently Delegate

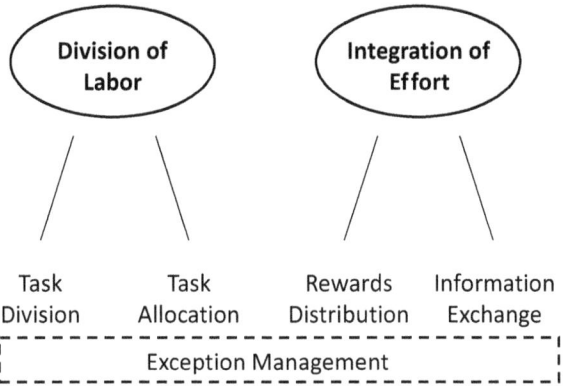

Fig. 2.1 The fundamental problems of organizing. (© Markus Reitzig 2021)

problems—task division, task allocation, rewards distribution, information exchange, and exception management (Fig. 2.1).

So, returning to our initial question in this chapter, which of these duties could they possibly give up and delegate efficiently to their subordinates?

Let's cut the question into its two parts and review them one by one in the next two sections.

First: what evidence is there that self-organization without managers can work at all? And along which of the 4+1 dimensions?

Second: what evidence is there that it frees up managerial time so that managers can address the wider span of control (see Chap. 1) they will face when working without middle layers in their corporate structures?

(Where) Does Self-organization Work Effectively?

What evidence is there that self-organization without managers can work at all? And along which of the 4+1 dimensions? The past 20 years, and certainly the last decade, have witnessed the emergence, some would say a renaissance,[4] of a plethora of organizations—both in the not-for-profit sector and in the commercial arena—that have been experimenting with nonhierarchical modes of governance, sometimes even without authoritative structures.[5]

Among the novel forms of organizing—those having goals comparable to traditional organizations but relying on self-organization in at least one of the 4+1 domains[6]—the most radically decentralized forms have received the most attention. In the community of practice sometimes also referred to as TEAL organizations, a term coined by Frederic Laloux,[7] these are organizations that seek to minimize managerial intervention and to self-organize as much as possible. For us, they are interesting in that they provide a proof of existence that ***(quasi-)decentral decision-making can work in all the 4+1 domains***—and potentially beat a traditional form of organizing. One of the most illustrative comparisons in that regard is that between Wikipedia and Encyclopaedia Britannica.

Wikipedia

Wikipedia is the largest online encyclopedia and is operated by the nonprofit Wikimedia Foundation. It is free for everyone to use, contains no advertising, and is funded mainly through donations.[8] The project was launched in 2001 by Jimmy Wales and Larry Sanger as a complement of Nupedia[9] and today is among the most visited sites on the internet.[10] Articles are created and edited by a community of volunteer contributors.

Anyone can contribute to Wikipedia. Once registered, users can edit articles they find interesting or feel driven to work on and even create new articles on topics of interest.[11] There is no chief editor who defines goals or allocates tasks to these volunteers. Nevertheless, certain authorities called "administrators" and "bureaucrats" have the power to block users, apply page protection, or delete pages.[12] Because the project relies on free, user-generated reference work, Wikipedia does not pay its contributors, administrators, or bureaucrats. Through its "Talk Pages," Wikipedia offers contributors a platform for collaborating and sharing information.[13] The platform also serves other means, since a loose task structure like Wikipedia's often comes with exceptions regarding the content of articles. When such conflicts arise, Wikipedia relies on the use of an advice process and lateral authority. In practice, if there is disagreement over an edit, the editing process continues until consensus is reached. Bigger decisions are often made through a voting process that includes several contributors.[14]

Encyclopaedia Britannica, Inc.

Encyclopaedia Britannica is a former print encyclopedia, first published in 1768 in Edinburgh, Scotland,[15] the brainchild of Colin Macfarquhar and Andrew Bell, who, in collaboration with William Smellie, published the first edition.[16] As of 2012 Encyclopaedia Britannica Inc. announced that it would no longer publish in print and would instead focus on the online edition.[17] Today, Encyclopaedia Britannica concentrates on providing high-quality educational services, partnering with schools and libraries around the world, rather than pure reference work.[18]

The encyclopedia works with a team of editors, subject experts, freelancers, and an editor-in-chief who oversees the whole operation.[19] They also used to employ the so-called answer girls who researched and answered any request concerning an article via phone.[20] Taking a look into the editorial teams that determine the content of an *Encyclopaedia Britannica* edition, one can spot a

(*continued*)

> (continued)
> hierarchical structure consisting of copy editors, senior editors, associate editors, supervisors, and coordinators.[21] As soon as the content is defined, the execution is up to the contributors. Because the company is a for-profit organization, most of the people are working for a salary. Encyclopaedia Britannica relies on traditional ways of collaboration supported by information technology. When exception and conflicts arise, these are managed and resolved by senior management.[22]

As the comparison shows, Wikipedia relies on de-facto decentralized decision-making in all those domains in which its most reputed traditional competitor, the Encyclopaedia Britannica, invokes traditional command structures. As a simple comparison of one of an encyclopedia's key performance indicators—the number of articles it provides—also demonstrates, Wikipedia has long emerged from the shadow of being a cheap, open substitute of dubious quality to an editorially managed lexicon.

So what Wikipedia shows is that it is ***possible*** to delegate decision rights with regard to task division, allocation, rewards distribution, information exchange, and exception management to peers—and have them jointly run a successful organization. In fact, the resulting form of organizing may even be more powerful than its traditional counterpart.

Naturally, this outcome is not a given. Many conditions need to come together, and we will study them over the following chapters. Just one condition is not required, as one might prematurely come to suspect, though. The fact that Wikipedia is a ***nonprofit does not mean that high delegation along several or all of the 4+1 domains would not also work in the for-profit sector***. A beautiful example dismissing these doubts stems from the company "Valve"—producing blockbuster video games and competing successfully in a fiercely fought for market.

> **Valve Corporation**
> Valve was founded in 1996 by former Microsoft employees Gabe Newell and Mike Harrington. The company's mission is to "make games, Steam, and hardware."[23] As their slogan suggests, they're most famous for being the developer behind the software distribution platform Steam and the creator of computer games such as *Half-Life, Counter-Strike,* and *Dota*. The Washington-based company employs around 360 people[24] and generates over 4 billion dollars in sales from Steam alone.[25]
> What distinguishes them from most other companies involved with game development is how work is organized at Valve. Despite a growing number of
>
> (continued)

> (continued)
> employees, the company operates with a flat structure, having no middle management, and leaving CEO Gabe Newell as the only person with authority.[26] There are no specific job descriptions when hiring; employees choose the projects they want to work on depending on what they like or think might be the most promising.[27] Further, employees are welcome to initiate projects themselves and to get involved in any decisions made around the company.[28] Valve also strives to ensure internal transparency. The company encourages its employees to talk to each other about projects and decisions and provides moveable desks to further enable collaboration. Also, all contemporary projects are listed transparently, and there are no secret decision-making cabals.[29] When conflicts arise they are resolved within the project teams without involving management.[30]

As the example illustrates, Valve's CEO has successfully run the organization and scaled it without introducing mid-levels of management. While perhaps not as decentralized as Wikipedia, Valve also clearly operates without a hierarchy—making Gabe Newell the ultimate decision-maker on literally every matter that can't be organized or resolved differently. No one below him can take away this burden, and there's no one above him to pass the responsibility on to. Strictly speaking, his span of control extends to all employees within Valve.

Naturally, this could not work unless either one of the following was true, or both.

First: Gabe Newell being superhuman and able to manage more subordinates than anyone else.

Second: his way of informally delegating[31] responsibility to his staff setting free time of his elsewhere.

Notwithstanding the undisputed skills of Valve's CEO, it would appear that the second aspect was key. Which brings us back to this chapter's last question.

(Where) Does High Delegation Save Managerial Time?

So far, in this chapter, I have drawn on organizational examples from both the commercial and noncommercial sector that would take us to the extremes of (informal) decentralization. The intention was to convey what's possible in terms of working with flat structures. At the same time, it becomes difficult

2 What Managers Can Effectively and Efficiently Delegate   27

with such vanguard organizations to parse out exactly which effect the different delegation decisions had. Overall they seem to be working well, which could not be the case if they created an exaggerated workflow for remaining managers, to the extent that they still hold on to them at all. Just where exactly the flattening of the structure saves managerial time becomes difficult to disentangle. Is it because employees map corporate goals to tasks themselves and management no longer needs to do so? Or because peers self-select into projects without managerial guidance? Because employees themselves pick the remuneration that's right for them? Talk to one another directly? Resolve their conflicts by themselves?

Taking a closer look at some companies that are a little more selective about where they grant autonomy to their folks helps answer these questions in somewhat greater detail.

Let's focus on some organizations that have been covered extensively in the media, and on which we have sufficient information with regard to two questions: how exactly are they structured at the time they operate a flat structure,[32] and is there (reported) evidence that informal decentralization saved them time? Let's take a closer look at Atlassian, Atos, Buurtzorg, Gore, Patagonia, Ryan, Smarkets, Squarespace, and Sun Hydraulics. Jointly, they cover a spectrum of industries, and show variation in both size and focus of informal decentralization.[33]

Atlassian, a relatively young company in the software sector, marks the start.

Atlassian Corporation Plc

Atlassian was founded in 2002 by the two college friends, Mike Cannon-Brookes and Scott Farquhar, to avoid working in an "environment where they had to conform rather than be who they authentically are."[34] Beginning with JIRA 1.0, they now provide a broad portfolio of software tools that help people working as a team and therefore compete with companies such as Microsoft.[35] Despite the company growing to over 4900 employees and generating 1.6 billion dollars a year,[36] the founders' spirit still can be witnessed in the way work is organized at Atlassian. What stands out are the ShipIT Days, a 24-hour hackathon that takes place on a regular basis at all company offices.[37] During that time, employees are encouraged to come up with their own ideas and projects of either a technical or a nontechnical nature, organize in teams, and resolve barriers and conflicts themselves. Everyone can join the projects they would like to work on; at the end, the most creative ideas are awarded. Among other things, employees report, ShipIT days have seen the origin of the JIRA ServiceDesk feature, changing all the lightbulbs in the phone-booth rooms of the offices, and fixing software bugs.[38] Apart from ShipIT, Atlassian is known as a very open company and ensures that information is shared well across the company.[39]

Another company in the software and IT sector more broadly that had garnered interest by organizations scholars is Atos. Considerably larger, and operating out of France, it shows marked differences in terms of where it informally decentralizes decision-making.

> **Atos SE**
>
> Atos is a French multinational IT company founded in 2000, with headquarters in Bezons, generating over 11 billion in revenue per year.[40] Their product portfolio covers, among other things, cloud services and cybersecurity, which makes them a direct competitor to firms such as Sopra Steria.[41] Having over 105,000 employees across 71 countries comes with a high need for collaboration, which in turn produces massive communication data and interferes with employees' personal lives.[42] In 2011 Atos acted to counter this trend by introducing the "Zero Email Policy."[43] As the name suggests, the initiative aimed for Atos to become a company in which employees will no longer communicate via email. Instead, the companywide enterprise social network (ESN), "bluekiwi," was introduced, which basically allowed Atos employees to communicate via threads, to share thoughts as posts, to have access to the profiles of all their colleagues, to have discussions with multiple employees about various topics, to collaborate live on documents and archives, and to set up and hold virtual meetings.[44] By 2013 they had reduced email traffic by 60%.[45] As a result of the declining use of bluekiwi, Atos implemented the more advanced ESN "Circuit" in order to further drive the zero-email policy.[46]

Moving from software and IT to nursing, but staying within Europe, let's now visit Netherlands-based Buurtzorg.

> **Buurtzorg**
>
> Buurtzorg is a 2006-founded non-profit organization providing holistic home healthcare services for elderly people and people in need of help.[47] Following its mission, "humanity over bureaucracy," the company adapted rather unusual management practices compared with its competitors, such as Amedisys.[48] The unique approach paid off, as the organization has grown into a 10,000-nurse network operating in more than 25 countries, making it the biggest healthcare provider in the Netherlands.[49] Rather than in a traditional hierarchy, people at Buurtzorg are organized in autonomous teams without a leader. Nurses within those teams organize their work themselves and decide for themselves what might be the best care for their patients.[50] Employees at Buurtzorg are encouraged to build their own network including social workers, volunteers, other nurses, and so forth, and have the opportunity to stay updated about the organization's developments such as client data and financials via the IT system "Buurtzorgweb."[51] The platform not only serves information-sharing purposes but also helps give everyone a say in how to handle arising problems.[52] When issues come up on a team level and there is disagreement among nurses, the team brings in a "regional coach" who helps find a consensus decision through an advice process.[53]

2 What Managers Can Effectively and Efficiently Delegate 29

Considerably older, operating out of the US, and in an entirely different industry is W. L. Gore & Associates. Again, where they allow for informal decentralization differs.

> **W. L. Gore & Associates, Inc.**
>
> Gore was founded in 1958 in Newark, Delaware, employs over 11,000, and exceeds 3.8 billion dollars in revenue.[54] The firm competes in the markets of aerospace, land, automation, and energy applications against organizations such as Bard[55] and is best known for its breathable Gore-Tex fabrics. In order to drive innovation and productivity, founders Bill and Vieve Gore installed rather unusual management practices that still very much define the contemporary modus operandi.[56] Employees, or associates as they are called at Gore, can commit to whatever they wish to work on instead of being allocated to projects by their bosses.[57] Additionally, their compensation design is influenced by peer-review mechanisms. Each employee is ranked by colleagues on their work and on whether they execute their tasks in alignment with Gore's values. These evaluations ultimately influence salaries.[58] Also, the company operates with a network approach rather than hierarchical structures, which encourages its associates to interact with the relevant people regarding information or decisions in case they are in need of those.[59]

Moving from Delaware to the West Coast of the US, to a company that uses some of Gore's fabrics in its products, takes us to Patagonia.

> **Patagonia, Inc.**
>
> Patagonia operates in the outdoor sports apparel industry along with firms like The North Face and Jack Wolfskin.[60] The company was founded in 1973 as a successor to Chouinard Equipment and, as of this writing, employs over 1500 and generates total sales of 1 billion dollars a year.[61] Because of its mission to "build the best product, cause no unnecessary harm, and use business to inspire and implement solutions to the environmental crisis," Patagonia hires primarily outdoor enthusiasts and people wishing to make an environmental impact.[62] This unfolds in progressive ways when it comes to compensating employees. There is the "let my people go surfing policy," which allows employees to take time off during the workday without asking permission, in order to go for a surf, go skiing, or simply pick their kids up from school.[63] After a tenure of one year working for Patagonia, employees are allowed to take two months off to volunteer with an environmental organization while they receive full salary.[64] Further, the company even pays for employees' bail if they're arrested while demonstrating peacefully for an environmental cause.[65] Further compensation perks include onsite childcare and an organic cafeteria in their headquarters in Ventura, California, various insurance and pension benefits, and so forth.[66]

For the next corporate example, we stay in the US, but move to the services sector.

Ryan, LLC

Operating from Dallas, Texas, Ryan serves over 18,000 clients in more than 60 countries with federal, state, local, and international tax services.[67] The 3000-employee organization generates an annual revenue of over 0.5 billion dollars.[68] Founded in 1991 under the name Collis & Ryan, P.C., the company adopted working principles that embrace flexibility and autonomy from early on.[69] In practice, those values are anchored in the "MyRyan Program," which shifts the focus away from working hours and toward results. In general, the program has two essential features. First, it allows Ryan employees to execute their work wherever they like, hence freeing them from the obligation of attending the office every day.[70] Second, the company does not determine working hours, so scheduling worktime is totally up to the employees themselves.[71] But flexibility does not end with the MyRyan Program. According to an employee review, the company doesn't track vacation days, and it's up to employees when and for how long they take vacation time.[72] Employees also report that compensation is flexible at Ryan, depending on how much work they want to put in.[73] Internally, the company is described as totally transparent with financials, strategy, and initiatives in order to ensure that employees have all the information they need to perform their jobs properly.[74] It is those practices that would appear to distinguish Ryan's structure, at least in part, from that of other successful companies operating in the same sector, such as H&R Block.[75]

Smarkets, the example of a relatively young venture, takes us back to Europe, but we stick to the services sector.

Smarkets, Ltd.

The online betting company Smarkets was founded in 2008 and employs over 100 people with annual sales of over 16 million pounds.[76] The London-based organization offers trading on sports, politics, and current affairs, similar to its competitors such as Tipico or Mr. Green.[77] However, what sets Smarkets apart is how work is organized. The company operates with self-organized teams. Although the teams have certain business objectives, they decide for themselves how to reach those goals.[78] Employees select in teams or projects voluntarily depending what they'd like to work on.[79] What really stands out is how the company compensates its employees. People can set their own salaries at Smarkets, and whether a certain pay will be granted or not is determined by peer review by their colleagues.[80] Additionally, employees don't need to seek approval for vacation time; they can take time off whenever they want, and there's no official limit on vacation days, either.[81] The company's transparency does not stop at publishing salaries internally; CEO and management have a true open-door policy.[82]

Finally, the last two examples take us back to the US. The two companies, Squarespace and Sun Hydraulics, not only operate in different sectors, software versus engineering products; they also differ in terms of vintage and the ways in which managers pass on high degrees of autonomy to their employees.

Squarespace, Inc.

Squarespace was founded in 2003 by Anthony Casalena. What began as one man working from his dorm room evolved into a 1100-person organization serving millions of customers.[83] Squarespace is in the business of website-building and hosting and competes with firms such as WordPress.[84] However, what sets Squarespace apart from its rivals is how work is organized within the company. In general, employees at Squarespace enjoy significant autonomy in order to foster creativity. They report being free to come up with their own ideas and encouraged to push them further in the company.[85] Moreover, projects are seldom assigned; instead, employees report deciding for themselves what to work on.[86] The company culture is described as characterized by transparency: all departments are open to collaborate, management is proactive in sharing information, and colleagues are happy to help each other with whatever concerns.[87]

Sun Hydraulics, LLC

The company was founded in 1970 in Sarasota, Florida, and produces hydraulic cartridge valves and manifolds.[88] Sun Hydraulics' founders, Bob Koski and John Allen, believed that operational success comes from establishing a "culture of curiosity and collaboration."[89] This belief is deeply rooted in the company's DNA and ultimately translates into unique management practices that differentiate Sun Hydraulics from its more traditional competitors such as the Delta Power Company.[90] Projects, for instance, are initiated by employees without management constantly interfering.[91] Also, employees are granted the freedom to work on what "they sense is the most important, most urgent, or most fun to do."[92]

The above brief corporate profiles provide the relevant summary information on the companies' structures which we will make use of below. When it comes to the evidence on delegation saving managerial time, the quotes we receive from the different managers cluster into three groups.

In the case of Atos and Gore, it would appear that the decentralization of information was perceived as the main time-saver for management. As Thierry Breton, Atos CEO at the time of implementing the zero-email policy, put it: "The volume of emails we send and receive is unsustainable for business. [...] Managers spend between five and 20 hours a week reading and writing emails."[93] And this is what Jan Krans, Director of Enterprise Collaboration, said after an initial period of abandoning email as a means of conversation: "In the beginning I had to do some extra effort in converting email conversations to the ESN, but now the colleagues I interact with on a regular basis are also adopting this new way of working. Why? They are also benefiting from the same time savers and see a rise in quality of the output and everything gets done in a faster pace."[94] Similarly, Terri Kelly, CEO of Gore at the time, stated: "The job of leadership has changed a lot in terms of context setting. […] The more we can expose our associates to the tensions that are in the system of balancing one thing at the expense of something else. In many organizations the leaders may be very aware of that tension but I found that actually having 10,000 associates understanding these tensions and understand that what we are trying to do is keep them in balance it's gonna much better prepare them. […] So I think what's changed over the years is how much we try to articulate and paint that broad picture in context for the whole organization not just for leadership."[95]

In the case of Patagonia and Smarkets, the C-officers report that their time is freed up by delegating rewards distribution to their staff. As Dean Carter, Head of HR, reported at the time: "Now HR is providing a tool that people can use and opt into, that they feel is helping their performance, and that they can lean into based on their needs and the needs of their manager. And that frees up the HR organization to look for insights and other interesting pieces of data that can help us continue to improve the system and structure. It also frees up time for the employee and the manager to lean in and do better work—or in Patagonia's case, maybe go catch a surf."[96] These sentiments are echoed by Jason Trost, CEO of Smarkets, and ideator of the decentralized rewards system: "As somebody that is used to keep salaries secret […] giving up that responsibility was something that I spend a lot of time worrying about but a lot of my worries have been unfounded."[97] It seems that the process of delegation had not resulted in extra trouble—to the contrary.

Finally, the interviews with Buurtzorg's and Squarespace's top management suggest that delegating task division, and in parts task allocation, freed their agenda and allowed them to concentrate on other issues compared with before. As Jos de Blok, CEO of Buurtzorg, stated: "We didn't have one management meeting since we started […] My former jobs were only about meetings, from one meeting to another. I think now we just have time to solve the problems."[98] And Squarespace's CEO, Anthony Casalena, sounds similar when he describes his experience operating a flat structure in his company: "Which is completely different from how Squarespace operates today, where I go into meetings people present their product ideas they are working on and I am like 'I have little to say.' This is just great […] I try to be very low level and try to get involved and also be very high level but I am really only controlling who is in the room."[99]

Table 2.1 attempts to summarize the above information.

It not only provides a summary, however.

Table 2.1 Dimensions of structural decentralization for our sample corporations. Unless a narrow scope is mentioned explicitly, de-facto decentralization refers to the corporate-wide structure

Company	Informally decentralized with regard to …										
	… task division		… task allocation		… rewards distribution		… information exchange		… exception management		Time-saving mentioned explicitly?
	Y/N	Scope	Y/N	Scope	Y/N	Scope	Y/N	Scope	Y/N	Scope	
Atlassian	Y	Narrow (initiative-based)	Y	Narrow (initiative-based)	N		Y		Y	Narrow (initiative-based)	N
Atos	N		N		N		Y		N		Y (through decentralized information exchange)
Buurtzorg	Y		Y	Narrow	N		Y		Y		Y (through decentralized task division and allocation)
Gore	N		Y		Y		Y		N		Y (through decentralized information exchange)
Patagonia	N		N		Y		Y		N		Y (through decentralized rewards distribution)
Ryan	Y		Y		Y		Y		N		N
Smarkets	Y		Y		Y		Y		N		Y (through decentralized rewards distribution)

(continued)

Table 2.1 (continued)

Company	Informally decentralized with regard to ...									Time-saving mentioned explicitly?
	...task division		...task allocation		...rewards distribution		...information exchange		...exception management	
	Y/N	Scope	Y/N	Scope	Y/N	Scope	Y/N	Scope	Y/N	Scope	
Squarespace	Y		Y		N		Y		N		Y (through decentralized task division and allocation)
Sun Hydraulics	Y		Y		N		?		N		N

Note: Y = we know for sure that they delegate along a given dimension; N = we either know for sure that they don't delegate (in most instances) or we don't know for sure. The information on the companies is as accurate as was possible to tell from publicly available accounts, and we conservatively assume that the companies traditionally approach those dimensions of organizing unless we had information to the contrary. © Markus Reitzig 2021

In fact, a superficial inspection suggests that delegating decision rights along any of the 4+1 dimensions of organizing is equally helpful in saving managerial time. If that were so, we'd have learned little beyond what Wikipedia and Valve have already taught us.

Upon closer inspection, however, we observe that ***quasi-decentralized information exchange is observed on its own*** (e.g., at Atos), whereas an ***informal decentralization of the rewards distribution or task division and allocation always cooccurs together with decentralized information exchange***. I argue that this finding, obtained on an admittedly small sample of selected cases, is no artifact. On the contrary, I argue that it reflects a systematic necessity that managers should be aware of. Unless employees can freely exchange information, it would be naïve to assume that they can successfully engage in dividing tasks and engaging in a functioning process of self-selection for work, let alone discuss each other's salaries. High delegation in one domain is a prerequisite for the other, and unless managers get this part right, they will never be able to save time—because they will end up with a messy organization.

So, while it appears that quasi-decentralization along all dimensions can save time, certain patterns of delegating authority will have to be combined in order to avoid chaos.

This, in turn, has an important consequence: depending on what you want to achieve (see Chaps. 7 and 9 for more detail), you may find yourself needing to delegate decision rights along more than one dimension. Clearly, this creates significant extra work for your staff.

How realistic is that? Asking this question is equivalent to asking what would motivate folks to self-organize for task division and allocation, rewards distribution, information exchange, and exception management. The next chapter is devoted to providing an answer.

Notes

1. Puranam, Alexy, and Reitzig, "What's 'New' about New Forms of Organizing?"
2. March and Simon, *Organizations*; Lawrence and Lorsch, "Differentiation and Integration in Complex Organizations."
3. Simon, "A Formal Theory of the Employment Relationship."
4. The idea of having people self-organize as a collective, like almost all ideas in social science, has been around for a long time. Hailing forms of organizing with a (partly) decentralized structure as a globally novel phenomenon would be a vast overstatement. Yet, clearly, these companies show novelty compared

with their traditional counterparts (i.e., those pursuing similar goals) along at least selected dimensions of organizing, and at a minimum along one of them.

5. Recall that we refer to a hierarchy as a system of stacked positions of authorities (e.g., managers). An authoritative structure has only one layer of management above the peers. This distinction may seem picky; however, as we shall see, it matters a great deal.
6. Puranam, Alexy, and Reitzig, "What's 'New' about New Forms of Organizing?"
7. Laloux, *Reinventing Organizations*.
8. Philiposa, "Why is Wikipedia Seeking Donations from its Users."
9. Kock, Jung, and Syn, "Wikipedia and e-Collaboration Research."
10. Alexa, https://www.alexa.com/siteinfo/wikipedia.org (accessed February 27, 2021).
11. Puranam, Alexy, and Reitzig.
12. Constantino, "Infomaven 2: How Wikipedia Works."
13. Ibid.
14. Ibid.
15. Kearney, "Encyclopaedia Britannica."
16. "Encyclopedia Britannica: All the World at Your Fingertips."
17. Kearney, "Encyclopaedia Britannica."
18. "Britannica, the 250 Year Old Encyclopedia Still Lives, Adapts and Thrives."
19. "Encyclopedia Britannica: All the World at Your Fingertips."
20. Ibid.
21. "Encyclopædia Britannica."
22. "Encyclopedia Britannica: All the World at Your Fingertips."
23. Valve website, https://www.valvesoftware.com/de/ (accessed February 27, 2021).
24. Chalk, "Valve Denies Wrongdoing in Skin Gambling Legal Rumblings."
25. Statt, "Valve's New Steam Revenue Agreement Gives More Money to Game Developers."
26. *The Valve Handbook*, https://assets.sbnation.com/assets/1074301/Valve_Handbook_LowRes.pdf (accessed February 27, 2021).
27. Ibid.
28. Ibid.
29. Ibid.
30. Ibid.
31. "Gabe Newell." Legally speaking, a CEO will always remain responsible for the actions taken by delegates. Thus, Gabe Newell cannot formally delegate responsibility to any of his team. If push comes to shove, he will have to respond to the authorities. It is in this sense that I use the word "informal" in the context of his delegating of decision-making rights to his colleagues.
32. Note that some companies may have changed their structure between the time they were covered in the media and the time of this writing. I seek to

ensure that the information we attribute to the decentralized structure in Chaps. 2 and 3 is synchronized accordingly.

33. Academic colleagues may, at this point, wonder about sample selection, sample size, measurement error, etc. And even though this book is dedicated to practicing managers, I believe a few words may be useful—as I will be drawing on these cases again in Chap. 3.

    First, the chosen examples are instances in which high degrees of delegation lead to functional corporations. Thus, all inference drawn from these cases suffers from a so-called survivor bias. I must not rule out that under different conditions, informal delegation might not work well. To study these conditions, we would have to examine very closely many companies that weren't able to implement high delegation, too. This is practically impossible, however. Companies just talk far less about their failures than about their successes. Barring this, all we can do is be careful with our conclusions, particularly in Chap. 3.

    Second, we must not rule out that results might change if we added more companies to our sample that successfully decentralized informally along one or more of the 4+1 dimensions. This is an inevitable problem when working with incomplete data, and this is what we do. Companies that operate such high delegation as the ones described in this chapter are on the verge of emerging. We will have more data in the future, but at present it seems that our sample captured a fair amount of the existing variation when it comes to delegation patterns along the 4+1 dimensions. This is the most crucial point for this book. Being able to parse out effects for industries and company size is something that must be left to future researchers.

    Third, let's not forget that the cases complement theory—they do not substitute for it. I'll make sure to draw a clear line between what we've come to know from decades of research and what we can infer from combining theory and anecdotal evidence.

34. "Who We Are," *Atlassian,* https://www.atlassian.com/company (accessed February 25, 2021).
35. "About: Our Company," *Microsoft,* https://www.microsoft.com/en-us/about/company (accessed February 25, 2021).
36. Atlassian Investor Relations Data Sheet, 2021, https://s2.q4cdn.com/141359120/files/doc_financials/2020/q4/TEAM-IR-Data-Sheet-Q4'20_vF.pdf (accessed February 25, 2021).
37. "ShipIt," *Atlassian,* https://www.atlassian.com/company/shipit (accessed February 25, 2021).
38. Atlassian employee review, "A genuinely excellent company to work for," *Glassdoor,* January 5, 2021, https://www.glassdoor.at/Bewertungen/Bewertungen-Atlassian-RVW40111931.htm (accessed February 25, 2021).
39. Atlassian employee review, "Overall Pretty Good," *Glassdoor,* January 17, 2021, https://www.glassdoor.at/Bewertungen/Bewertungen-Atlassian-RVW40890877.htm (accessed February 25, 2021).

40. "Company Profile," *Atos,* https://atos.net/en/company-profile (accessed February 24, 2021).
41. https://www.soprasteria.com (accessed February 24, 2021).
42. "Company Profile," *Atos.*
43. Burkus, "Why Atos Origin Is Striving to Be a Zero-Email Company."
44. "Atos—Zero Email—Social Collaboration—Business Technologist"; Oettl et al., "Zero Email Initiative."
45. Burkus, "Why Atos Origin Is Striving to Be a Zero-Email Company."
46. Oettl et al., "Zero Email Initiative."
47. https://www.buurtzorg.com (accessed February 24, 2021).
48. https://www.amedisys.com (accessed February 24, 2021).
49. https://www.buurtzorg.com (accessed February 24, 2021).
50. "Jos de Blok on Organizational Structures."
51. Ibid.
52. Ibid.
53. "Buurtzorg—Coaches not Managers."
54. "About Gore: The Gore Story," *Gore,* https://www.gore.com/about/the-gore-story (accessed February 25, 2021).
55. "Company," CR Bard, https://www.crbard.com/medical/about-us (accessed February 25, 2021).
56. Kelly, "The End of Hierarchy."
57. Ibid.
58. Ibid.
59. T. Kelly, "W.L. Gore's Original Management Model."
60. "Our Story: Behind the Brand," *North Face,* https://www.thenorthface.com/about-us/our-story.html (accessed February 25, 2021); Jack Wolfskin website, https://www.jack-wolfskin.com/company/ (accessed February 25, 2021).
61. Chouinard, *Let My People Go Surfing*; "100 Best Companies to Work For: Patagonia."
62. Chouinard, *Let My People Go Surfing.*
63. Ibid.
64. Anderson, "5 'Ridiculous' Ways Patagonia Has Built a Culture That Does Well and Does Good."
65. Chouinard, *Let My People Go Surfing.*
66. Ibid.
67. "About Ryan," *Ryan,* https://www.ryan.com/about-ryan/ (accessed February 25, 2021).
68. Womack, "Ryan Acquiring European Company to Expand after $317 M Investment."
69. "About Ryan: Our History," *Ryan,* https://www.ryan.com/about-ryan/our-history/#All (accessed February 25, 2021).
70. Ryan website, https://ryan.com/careers/people%2D%2Dculture (accessed February 25, 2021).

71. Ibid.
72. Ryan employee review, "Great place to work," *Indeed,* May 4, 2018, https://at.indeed.com/cmp/Ryan,-LLC/reviews/great-place-to-work?id=d096b5371387b7b9 (accessed February 25, 2021).
73. Ryan employee review, "Make your own living while having complete work-life balance," *Indeed,* August 19, 2020, https://at.indeed.com/cmp/Ryan,-LLC/reviews/make-your-own-living-while-having-complete-work-life-balance?id=61e7c982d2ff6a90 (accessed February 25, 2021).
74. Ryan employee review, "Flexibility, Growth and Trust, how it should be!!," *Glassdoor,* January 22, 2021, https://www.glassdoor.at/Bewertungen/Bewertungen-Ryan-LLC-RVW41259230.htm (accessed February 25, 2021).
75. https://www.hrblock.com/filing-options-and-products/ (accessed February 25, 2021).
76. "About Smarkets," *Smarkets,* https://smarkets.com/about/ (accessed February 24, 2021); Smarkets, *Annual Report 2018.*
77. Tipico website, https://www.tipico-group.com/en/about-tipico/ (accessed February 24, 2021); Mr. Green website, https://www.mrgreen.com/about-us (accessed February 24, 2021).
78. "Life at Smarkets," *Smarkets,* https://smarkets.com/culture/ (accessed February 24, 2021).
79. Ibid.; "Self-Management at Smarkets."
80. "Setting Your Own Salary."
81. "Life at Smarkets"; "Self-Management at Smarkets."
82. "Life at Smarkets"; Smarkets employee review, "Amazing Company," *Glassdoor,* September 14, 2018, https://www.glassdoor.at/Bewertungen/Bewertungen-Smarkets-RVW22484003.htm (accessed February 24, 2021).
83. "Helping Creative Ideas Succeed," *Squarespace,* https://www.squarespace.com/about/company (accessed February 25, 2021).
84. "Our Mission," *WordPress,* https://wordpress.org/about/ (accessed February 25, 2021).
85. Squarespace employee review, "Relaxed workplace with freedom to innovate," *Indeed,* June 29, 2012, https://at.indeed.com/cmp/Squarespace/reviews/relaxed-workplace-with-freedom-to-innovate?id=2ae83e54a6ff077f (accessed February 25, 2021).
86. Squarespace employee review, "A terrific environment with smart, friendly, enthusiastic people," *Indeed,* February 27, 2013, https://at.indeed.com/cmp/Squarespace/reviews/a-terrific-environment-with-smart-friendly-enthusiastic-people?id=0465366752b0a886 (accessed February 25, 2021).
87. Squarespace employee review, "Squarespace is a great organization for anyone passionate about tech or social equality," *Indeed,* September 24, 2018, https://at.indeed.com/cmp/Squarespace/reviews/squarespace-is-a-great-organization-for-anyone-passionate-about-tech-or-social-equality?id=864a36df8c522bfb (accessed February 25, 2021); Squarespace employee review,

Overall postivie [sic] work environment, with tons of amenities and good "vibes." May have changed over the last year." *Indeed,* August 25, 2016, https://at.indeed.com/cmp/Squarespace/reviews/overall-postivie-work-environment-with-tons-of-amenities-and-good-vibes-may-have-changed-over-the-last-year?id=424466d331bb8dbf (accessed February 25, 2021).
88. "About Sun Hydraulics," *Sun Hydraulics,* https://www.sunhydraulics.com/about (accessed February 25, 2021).
89. "Company History," *Sun Hydraulics,* https://www.sunhydraulics.com/about/company-history/1970–1979 (accessed February 25, 2021).
90. https://www.delta-power.com (accessed February 25, 2021).
91. Laloux, *Reinventing Organizations.*
92. Ibid., p. 84.
93. Burkus, "Why Atos Origin Is Striving to Be a Zero-Email Company."
94. Krans, "Zero Email, How to Get Things Done! Part 3."
95. Kelly, "The End of Hierarchy: Natural Leadership at W.L. Gore."
96. Rock, "The NLI Interview: Patagonia's Dean Carter on How to Treat Employees Like People."
97. "Setting Your Own Salary."
98. "Jos de Blok on Organizational Structures."
99. "Foundation 39 // Anthony Casalena."

Bibliography

"100 Best Companies to Work For: Patagonia." *Forbes*, n.d. https://fortune.com/best-companies/2019/patagonia/ (accessed February 25, 2021).

Anderson, Bruce. "5 'Ridiculous' Ways Patagonia Has Built a Culture That Does Well and Does Good." *LinkedIn Talent Blog*, https://business.linkedin.com/talent-solutions/blog/talent-connect/2019/5-ways-patagonia-built-ridiculous-culture (accessed February 25, 2021).

"Atos—Zero Email—Social Collaboration—Business Technologist." *Atos Group,* December 11, 2013. https://www.youtube.com/watch?v=Mv6zKh8Jq70 (accessed February 24, 2021).

"Buurtzorg—Coaches not Managers." *Buurtzorg Britain & Ireland,* November 27, 2018, https://www.youtube.com/watch?v=vO9zhGWDcr4 (accessed February 24, 2021).

"Britannica, the 250 Year Old Encyclopedia Still Lives, Adapts and Thrives." *Phoenix Rotary 100*, June 7, 2019. https://www.youtube.com/watch?v=pqp7jIQzGrU (accessed February 27, 2021).

Burkus, D. "Why Atos Origin Is Striving to Be a Zero-Email Company." *Forbes,* July 12, 2016. https://www.forbes.com/sites/davidburkus/2016/07/12/why-atos-origin-is-striving-to-be-a-zero-email-company/?sh=240b04368d0f (accessed February 22, 2021).

Chalk, Andy. "Valve Denies Wrongdoing in Skin Gambling Legal Rumblings: 'No Factual or Legal Support for These Accusations.'" *PC Gamer*, October 18, 2016. https://www.pcgamer.com/valve-misses-deadline-to-respond-to-washington-state-gambling-regulator-but-says-its-coming-soon/ (accessed February 27, 2021).

Chouinard, Yvon. *Let My People Go Surfing*. New York: Penguin Books, 2016.

Constantino, Joe. "Infomaven 2: How Wikipedia Works." February 25, 2016. https://www.youtube.com/watch?v=xt4X80TcJlM (accessed February 27, 2021).

"Encyclopædia Britannica." *Wikipedia*, n.d. https://en.wikipedia.org/wiki/Encyclopædia_Britannica#Contributors (accessed February 27, 2021).

"Encyclopedia Britannica: All the World at Your Fingertips." *CBS Sunday Morning*, December 30, 2018. https://youtu.be/d2g4oXAtIlU (accessed February 27, 2021).

"Foundation 39 // Anthony Casalena." *Foundation 39*, July 8, 2014. https://www.youtube.com/watch?v=wIuHaHjpKIM (accessed February 24, 2021).

"Gabe Newell." *Forbes*. https://www.forbes.com/profile/gabe-newell/?sh=75980e7da074 (accessed February 27, 2021).

"Jos de Blok on Organizational Structures." *RSA*, December 30, 2014. https://www.youtube.com/watch?v=BeOrNjwHw58 (accessed February 18, 2021).

Kearney, Christine. "Encyclopaedia Britannica: After 244 years in Print, Only Digital Copies Sold." *Christian Science Monitor*, March 14, 2012. https://www.csmonitor.com/Business/Latest-News-Wires/2012/0314/Encyclopaedia-Britannica-After-244-years-in-print-only-digital-copies-sold (accessed February 27, 2021).

Kelly, T. "The End of Hierarchy: Natural Leadership at W.L. Gore." *Management Innovation eXchange*, n.d.-a https://www.managementexchange.com/video/terri-kelly-wl-gores-original-management-model-0 (accessed February 22, 2021).

———. "W.L. Gore's Original Management Model." *Management Innovation eXchange*, n.d.-b https://www.managementexchange.com/video/end-hierarchy-natural-leadership (accessed February 25, 2021).

Kock, N., Y. Jung, and T. Syn. "Wikipedia and e-Collaboration Research: Opportunities and Challenges." *International Journal of e-Collaboration* 12, no. 2 (2016): 1–8. http://cits.tamiu.edu/kock/pubs/journals/2016JournalIJeC_WikipediaEcollaboration/Kock_etal_2016_IJeC_WikipediaEcollaboration.pdf (accessed February 27, 2021).

Krans, J. "Zero Email, How to Get Things Done! Part 3." *Atos*, November 25, 2013. https://atos.net/en/blog/zero-email-how-to-get-things-done-part-three-the-last-mile-becoming-zero-email (accessed February 22, 2021).

Laloux, F. *Reinventing Organizations: A Guide to Creating Organizations Inspired by the Next Stage of Human Consciousness*. Brussels, Belgium: Nelson Parker, 2014.

Lawrence, P. R., and J. W. Lorsch. *Organization and environment: Managing differentiation and integration*. Boston: Harvard University Press, 1967.

March, J. G., and H. A. Simon. *Organizations*. New York: Wiley, 1958.

Oettl, Christian Albert, Katharina Beck, Franziska Marie Raufer, Anja Teresa Priglmeir, Markus Böhm, and Helmut Krcmar. "Zero Email Initiative: A Critical Review of Change Management during the Introduction of Enterprise Social

Networks." *Journal of Information Technology Teaching Cases* 8, (2018): 172–83. https://doi.org/10.1057/s41266-018-0033-y.

Philiposa, Rahel. "Explained: Why Is Wikipedia Seeking Donations from its Users?" *Indian Express,* August 9, 2020. https://indianexpress.com/article/explained/explained-why-wikipedia-one-of-worlds-most-popular-websites-is-asking-users-for-donations-6546982/ (accessed August 08, 2021).

Puranam, P. O., Alexy, and M. Reitzig. "What's 'New' about New Forms of Organizing?" *Academy of Management Review* 39, no. 2 (2014): 162–80.

Rock, D. "The NLI Interview: Patagonia's Dean Carter on How to Treat Employees Like People." Forbes, January 9, 2020. https://www.forbes.com/sites/davidrock/2020/01/09/the-nli-interview-patagonias-dean-carter-on-how-to-treat-employees-like-people/ (accessed February 18, 2021).

"Self-Management at Smarkets", *Smarkets,* August 16, 2018, https://youtu.be/VdV0a2OiMO8 (accessed February 24, 2021).

"Setting Your Own Salary." *Smarkets,* December 16, 2016. https://www.youtube.com/watch?v=zwFMMJpTfbM (accessed February 17, 2021).

Simon, H. A. "A Formal Theory of the Employment Relationship." *Econometrica* 19 (1951): 293–305.

Smarkets. *Annual Report 2018.* http://files.smarkets.com/pdf/Smarkets-annual-report-2018.pdf (accessed February 24, 2021).

Statt, Nick. "Valve's New Steam Revenue Agreement Gives More Money to Game Developers." *The Verge,* November 30, 2018. https://www.theverge.com/2018/11/30/18120577/valve-steam-game-marketplace-revenue-split-new-rules-competition (accessed February 27, 2021).

The Valve Handbook. https://assets.sbnation.com/assets/1074301/Valve_Handbook_LowRes.pdf (accessed February 27, 2021).

Womack, Brian. "Ryan Acquiring European Company to Expand after $317M Investment." *Dallas Business Journal,* December 12, 2018. https://www.bizjournals.com/dallas/news/2018/12/12/ryan-llc-vat-systems.html (accessed February 25, 2021).

3

Why Would Employees Ever Assume Extra Work in a Decentralized Organization?

While it is undisputed that the above examples provide evidence of high delegation potentially saving managers time, they still raise the question of why employees would ever pick up the tab and do the extra work.

One answer might be that they are being paid extra to do so. However, there are no systematic indications that this is what happens across organizations adopting an informally decentralized approach. Which changes the initial question in an important way: ***why would employees voluntarily engage in additional work***?

If five decades of academic research and numerous practitioner interviews provide one simple answer, it's that humans greatly ***enjoy autonomy at work***. And in exchange for such autonomy, they may be willing to exert greater effort for their corporation.[1]

But autonomy where? Along which of the 4+1 dimensions? Clearly it should make a difference if I let my subordinates decide which projects to work on, as opposed to whom they talk to about their work. And how does the degree to which I grant them autonomy have an impact? Just for selected initiatives or projects? Or always?

Eventually, these are the questions we'll need to answer in order to understand where leadership can (most) promisingly delegate to subordinates. In the second part of this chapter, we will turn to these issues. Then we'll also revisit our corporate examples from Chap. 2 and a few more.

Addressing any of the above questions, however, requires us to first understand better why autonomy—the right to govern oneself—can act as a stimulus for peers within organizations at all. In which ways exactly does autonomy unleash greater effort on the part of subordinates? Only if we know which different psychological mechanisms link autonomy to effort will we be able to map out which options and challenges high delegation along any of the 4+1 dimensions can bring.

Embarking on this journey can easily become confusing. Applied psychologists and management scholars more broadly have conducted countless studies over the last half-century, and they have unearthed an extremely nuanced understanding of why, when, and how much autonomy employees appreciate at work. Some of these nuances are important for practicing managers to know when they seek to move to flatter structures; others are less important.

In the first part of this chapter, I try to separate the wheat from the chaff and guide you through the scientific jungle, making sure that you don't lose sight of the forest for the trees.[2]

How Exactly Autonomy Motivates Staff—Nailing the Psychological Mechanisms

So why is there a jungle, and why should you care?

The answer is that science did not start out to pursue the managerial questions directly that we care about in this book: along which of the 4+1 dimensions can we delegate decision rights, and how much, if we want to motivate our staff? The bits and pieces we seek are hidden in different places. We need to turn over the leaves to find them, and to puzzle our findings together to arrive at final answers. Admittedly, this approach is both tedious and imperfect. But it still yields more robust evidence than we could obtain if all we did were to get inspired by half a dozen corporate cases and nothing else.

So where should we begin our search for wisdom?

Our basic tree of knowledge is self-determination theory (SDT), a term coined by Richard Ryan and Edward Deci. SDT is not restricted to workplace settings. Instead, it proclaims and empirically finds that humans—no matter whether they engage in sports, education, or work—need to be motivated either extrinsically or intrinsically to exert effort. Here "extrinsic motivation refers to the performance of an activity in order to attain some separable outcome"—like getting a job done, receiving a salary increase, or obtaining a promotion. It "thus, contrasts with intrinsic motivation, which refers to doing an activity for the inherent satisfaction of the activity itself,"[3] where such inherent satisfaction can stem from "natural inclination toward assimilation, mastery, spontaneous interest, and exploration."[4] Importantly, research on SDT shows that conditions of autonomy lead to higher motivation irrespective of its extrinsic or intrinsic nature, however. As a consequence, therefore, Ryan and Deci proclaim autonomy to be an innate psychological need—the satisfaction of which will always lead to higher self-motivation.[5] For the purpose of this book, the insights we gain from SDT appear fundamental but also insufficient on their own to answer our questions. They are fundamental in that they suggest that irrespective of the particular motivation an employee may bring to her job, receiving greater autonomy should make her exert greater effort. In turn, this means that granting autonomy along any of the 4+1 dimensions of organizing should potentially unleash extra effort: if autonomy is an innate need of each of us, we should embrace it no matter where. It's this type of grand statement that, on one hand, makes SDT the tree of knowledge on which all other branches of wisdom may grow but, on the other hand, the least specific in helping us understand exactly how informal decentralization unleashes energy.

Three narrower branches of literature help address the latter challenge.

First is the literature on job (re)design. From its early days in the 1960s[6] and 1970s[7] until today, a key question in this vein has been how jobs—set bundles of tasks—should be designed to increase employee satisfaction and, in turn, help a company reach higher-level goals. A key factor shown to influence employees' job happiness and performance—next to, say, the variety of skills needed for a job or the perceived significance of a task—has been autonomy at work. Here, autonomy more narrowly refers to the right of employees to decide how to execute certain tasks, how to prioritize them, and sometimes which tasks to pick from a bundle of alternatives. Half a century of empirical work has yielded interesting insights about why this limited autonomy appeals to workers so much. More specifically, three mechanisms seem to be recurring across different studies.

The first one, we'll refer to as ***self-actualization***. Building on the insights of self-determination theory, employees can use the choice to prioritize or pick certain tasks from predefined bundles to better attain their personal goals—whatever these may be.[8] Returning to our example of the fictious furniture company, imagine that carpenters enjoy some discretion on which doorframe designs they want to work on on a given day—allowing them to better follow their instantaneous artistic inspirations. Reported effects of how much such autonomy releases extra effort differ across studies, but they can be substantial in terms of their effect size.[9] Unleashing similar amounts of effort through financial compensation—by paying employees rather than granting them the liberties mentioned above—might in fact be an expensive proposition.[10]

The second one, we'll call **perceived control**.[11] Among employees granted the right to make decisions on their own behalf, job autonomy instills a sense of control over their actions within the company—a feeling that leads them to exert greater effort and to take their fate and that of their firm into their own hands. In our fictitious company, the carpenter may also enjoy the fact that he is in charge of his daily schedule, irrespective of his preference for certain tasks over others. This second mechanism is related to but different from self-actualization—an employee may appreciate a sense of control irrespective of how well she can realize her own goals within a given job. Admittedly, however, it may be difficult to disentangle self-actualization and perceived control at all times. And, again, the effects can be meaningful.[12]

Third, and finally, there is **engagement**. Autonomy can lead to engagement, "a state in which employees 'bring in' their personal selves during work role performances, investing personal energy and experiencing an emotional connection with their work."[13] Distinctively, engagement is tied to the *performance of work tasks*. Whereas self-actualization or perceived control may represent an *attitude toward features* of the job, engagement speaks to the joy of seeing something work out[14]—much like in John "Hannibal" Smith's classic line "I love it when a plan comes together" from the *A-Team* television series, for those of you who can remember it still. Overall, the effects of engagement on job performance and satisfaction seem to be moderate.[15]

The second literature branch that holds interesting insights is that of organizational commitment. Focusing on the overall organization rather than the job itself, it demonstrates how employee motivations as well as corporate consequences—intent to leave, turnover, and absenteeism—depend on job-level and organizational-level characteristics. Again, autonomy speaks to the freedom of employees to select from predefined tasks or to prioritize them, and again it is associated positively with organizational commitment.[16] The original contribution of this literature is that autonomy can create a sense of **attachment** with a group of people; notably, decentralized information exchange fosters a sense of psychological attachment to the workplace.[17] Put simply, in our fictitious furniture company, letting carpenters and locksmiths communicate autonomously and in the open with one another would bind them to the corporation more strongly. Overall, the effects of attachment on job performance and satisfaction seem to be small, but they substantially reduce the intent of individuals to leave the company.[18]

Third, and finally, the broader (interdisciplinary) managerial literature provides some relevant findings for practicing managers. Some of these would, at this stage, mechanistically be mere reconfirmations of what we've covered above: for example, the fact that more job autonomy—in terms of prioritizing and selecting tasks—facilitates self-actualization and leads to more employee satisfaction.[19] Or the insight that perceived control may lead employees to detach less from corporate goals.[20] Additionally, however, this literature also suggests and confirms that autonomy can lead to reduced **evaluation apprehension**, or less fear of making a visible mistake, and lead employees to embark on potentially more risky projects than they would otherwise.[21] In plain English: the less carpenters and locksmiths, in our exemplary company, had to report to their superiors, the more likely they would be to also engage in uncertain or novel activities—activities they might otherwise not even touch as they seem too risky.

In summary, it would appear that autonomy could lead to increased motivation and extra effort by employees in very different ways. Pursuing one's own interest, perceiving greater control, feeling engaged, feeling attached, or sensing less fear of making a visible mistake—all of these may be ways in which autonomy can manifest itself.

The question now is: how do they play out depending on where we de-facto decentralize?

Why and to What End Does Quasi-decentralization Motivate Employees? A Conceptual Map

Let's reflect on where we stand and what we've come to learn.

Managers, when working in structures that lack interim layers of hierarchical positions, need to free up some of their own time and delegate parts of their traditional work to subordinates (Chap. 2). This works if—and only if—the autonomy granted to employees leads them to pick up the extra work that is left to do. There are different ways in which autonomy can motivate subordinates to do so, as we've uncovered above.

Which of these would still matter when autonomy is being granted much more comprehensively, as in the case of near decentralization? And how do the different autonomy-related mechanisms map onto which of the 4+1 domains of informal decentralization, however? Answering these questions will be important for a variety of reasons.

First, we want to know which form of high delegation releases (most) energy among employees.

Second, and related, we want to ensure that we know which type of staff will be maximally motivated and should thus be recruited for a flat organization (Chap. 4), depending on where we intend to delegate decision rights eventually (Chaps. 7 and 9).

So what we really need is a map that connects the 4+1 dimensions of high delegation to the different effects that autonomy can have. Seeking to create such a map by returning to the academic literature would seem futile at this stage—as scholars still have little to say on this question so far. Instead, in this instance, generating our own case-based evidence seems more promising, much like we did in Chap. 2 when we wondered where high delegation could free up managerial time.

To that end, let's revisit the companies we had featured in the previous chapter. In alphabetical order, our sample includes Atlassian, Atos, Buurtzorg, Gore, Patagonia, Ryan, Smarkets, Squarespace, and Sun Hydraulics.

Table 2.1 in the preceding chapter had already provided a summary along which of the 4+1 dimensions the companies had chosen to grant their employees autonomy.

To create the conceptual map we are after, let us now complement the structural information with **data on employee motivation from three other sources**. The first is a collection of corporate videos featuring **employee testimonials**. The second and third are publicly accessible data from Glassdoor.com and Indeed.com. According to information published by the companies themselves, both organizations belong to the largest job sites operating globally, boasting of millions of company ratings and employee reviews—including those pertaining to the companies listed in Table 2.1.[22]

Several statements from employees of the above companies confirm that *self-actualization* motivates them to work within the decentralized structures their organizations offer. At Atlassian, employees report on their experience with the ShipIT days, a contest designed to come up with new business ideas for the company. As one employee puts it: "It is really fun, when you get up there and you present and people really appreciate it. And you are like, 'That was really cool in a sense of recognition'"[23]—echoing academic studies showing that peer recognition provides an important extrinsic incentive to creative staff.[24] Similarly, employees at Gore report having the "opportunity to choose opportunities that interest you. Regardless of job, always able to openly share your opinion and it will be heard,"[25] and that "we were able to solve some great problems."[26] About Squarespace, one member of staff described it as "a collaborator's dream" because "it's easy to take the initiative to add features or improve the product, easy to find collaborators, and easy to get support and guidance from management. My favorite place to work so far."[27] Taking the initiative, pursuing one's own interest, is equally visible at Sun Hydraulics. One employee offered: "The sky is the limit at Sun. They recognize employees not only for the work they do, but also for the impact they have on their co-workers. Leaders are very trusting in their employees, so employees can tackle projects in which they are interested. Employees are friends in and out of work."[28] Thus, clearly, we find evidence of personnel being extra-motivated by the liberties they are granted to realize their own ambitions at work through the freedom of choice, or even designing that choice.

Equally clear are indications of employees enjoying a certain degree of **perceived control** over their work and their company's future among our focus companies. A voice from Atlassian put it this way: "I feel empowered within Atlassian to make decisions to make life better for Atlassian and our customers. Along with the amazing culture, the benefits are the best I've ever had!"[29] About Gore, another person offers: "Great place to Work for. Real possibility to own your development and understand how you can contribute for the Enterprise."[30] Ryan employees use the term "control" explicitly and repeatedly in their reviews: "The compensation plan allows you to essentially control your earnings"[31] or "the 'MyRyan' program is an amazing feature and allows you to work when and where is most productive for you and your work style. This allows you the flexibility to take control of your work/life success."[32] Similarly, Squarespace employees mention their ability to make an impact and be in charge: "I think when I came in, I realized, 'this is where I get to make an impact,'"[33] "I feel I have more of a voice and also I can do more with my voice," or "data scientists on the Strategy team work on fascinating business problems, develop pretty cool machine learning models, and have real influence on decision making across the organization."[34] And finally, at Smarkets, Jason Trost, CEO and company founder, believes that letting people set their salaries creates a sense of control among them that unleashes extra energy: "It makes people feel that they are not an employee, they are not a cog in a machine. They have some autonomy about the path they take in this company and that is really important to us."[35]

What about **engagement**? Apparently, the joy of working on projects that perform is a motivator for some employees in our sample corporations. "A feeling that we are really making a difference in the world"[36] is what a Gore staffer writes. Tackling problems that are challenging but to which solutions can be found stimulates employees at Squarespace: "The intellectual challenge. I love digging into these problems we encounter every day and solving them for our customers. I think that's really really stimulating."[37]

Not surprisingly, a sense of **attachment** to their organization shines through in the testimonials or reviews of many employees. A co-worker of Atlassian, for example, speaks of the trust she feels in her top management: "CEOs and exec team [...] are open and trusting with information."[38] Similarly, at Atos an employee praises the "full immersion in a motivated team focused on passing knowledge and support[ing] your journey."[39] Gore employees mention that "Gore's culture and commitment to all Associates makes this a fantastic place to work"[40] and feel connected to the company because of the "supportive atmosphere where you are encouraged to build your network and leverage others."[41] Interestingly, with Patagonia, the attachment still prevailed for an individual even after she had left the company: "Loved working for Patagonia. They actually take care of their employees, which is a step up from 80% of companies in the workplace currently. The company ethos of durability and functionality makes it easy to see why there is such a strong following of people who love Patagonia."[42] Transparency and collegiality at Smarkets lead to positive reviews by their employees: "Not only are salaries public, but the CEO and Management truly have an open door policy. I have found this incredibly refreshing and helpful as it feels like you truly know what is going on behind the scenes."[43] Another stated: "This attitude of engaging constructively is embedded at all levels in the company, with those in the leadership team holding 'drop-in' office hours and showcasing company strategy to all employees."[44] And finally, Jos de Blok, CEO of Buurtzorg, is convinced that attachment really keeps his company together: "The teams work very solistic. [...] But because of the platform they feel like one, they feel like a part of Buurtzorg."[45]

Finally, employee voices from several companies confirm that staffers perceive a **reduced fear of being evaluated**. Probably the most pronounced statements come from Patagonia staff: "Patagonia work culture is the BEST of the BEST! Relaxed, no micromanagement, extreme product knowledge, friendly, paced, LOTS of management and co-worker support. You can't find a better place to work!"[46] and that "the management is beyond amazing. They never yell or belittle you. Always finding a way to teach you rather than correct you"[47] or that the company has a "great workplace culture and business environment. Everyone was so friendly and management did not micromanage. Great benefits and makes you appreciative of the workplace."[48] This lack of micromanagement, potentially leading to subordinates' anxiety, is also mentioned in a Sun Hydraulics review: "Great place to work the hours are reasonable for the shift that you work. You also don't have to worry about being micro managed all day."[49] Finally, Jos de Blok, CEO of Buurtzorg, believes that his employees "don't feel Buurtzorg as an organization that gives them trouble, but only as a network that gives them presence."[50]

Reflecting on the above, it seems undisputed that across our focal firms we find evidence of employees feeling highly motivated by the ability to pursue their own needs, being in control of their work lives, feeling engaged, having a sense of belonging, and experiencing little fear of making visible mistakes. And it is equally obvious from the quotes that it is the workplace autonomy that acts a key stimulus for the staffers who went on record. Thus, in a way, our case inspection suggests that the general psychological mechanisms linking autonomy to motivation also matter in the context of flat organizations—which is reassuring.

In order to tell which dimensions of informal decentralization trigger which autonomy mechanism, we must eventually merge our findings from the employee review inspection with our structural analysis of our sample companies (Table 2.1) and conduct preliminary qualitative comparative analysis and complement by additional plausibility considerations. The methodological approach is described in the Appendix to this chapter for those readers who are interested. For the others, let me jump straight to the findings:

- *Attachment is visible when information exchange is informally decentralized*; there are instances in which, despite information exchange being informally decentralized, employees do not report attachment; however, that can be due to other reasons. Importantly, attachment also arises in the presence of centralized task division, task allocation, and rewards distribution. The inference is that attachment can be created by decentralized information exchange on its own. This finding would be consistent with those of prior studies in the field of organizational commitment.
- *Engagement seems to require high delegation with regard to task allocation*; this makes sense theoretically: employees can decide which tasks they want to work on; therefore, they can also decide to pick those tasks that perform well. To that end, it helps if they can communicate directly with others.
- *Self-actualization and perceived control both require informal decentral task allocation*, at least of a narrow type. By that, I mean employees' choice to self-select into certain roles, at least for certain projects. ***De-facto decentralized task allocation usually requires informally decentralized information exchange***. The effect of high delegation with regard to task division on self-actualization and perceived control is difficult to disentangle from the current data. It seems plausible, however, that the more people can determine what the company should work on (task division), the more they should feel in control, even when the scope is limited to certain project-related activities; and the more employees can choose which activities to work on, the higher their chance of satisfying extrinsic or intrinsic needs.

- With respect to the reduced fear of evaluation apprehension, there is simply no conclusive picture as of this writing. It seems to be a relevant mechanism irrespective of where corporations de-facto decentralize, reflecting a general sense of disapproval of micromanagement. Theoretically, the result for Buurtzorg is particularly plausible in that traditional managerial involvement in disputes among subordinates is often found to be a distraction.[51]

Table 3.1 summarizes our very first inference for the purpose of this book. It should be read line-by-line. With all disclaimers in place, it provides some preliminary guidance about which structural features may be helpful, required, or sufficient to implement to increase the chances of triggering a certain type of motivation among your employees.

Coming to the end of this chapter, we can conclude the following.

Our analysis above of both the academic literature and selected case companies provides an explanation for why employees would be willing to walk the extra mile and assume some of the burdens originally reserved for managers. Autonomy through informal decentralization *can (!)* motivate employees by allowing them to pursue their own interests, making them feel in control of their fate and that of their company, making them feel engaged, attached, and not unnecessarily fearsome. Depending on where companies decentralize, different mechanisms *can (!)* be triggered. Table 3.1 provides an interim summary of our—admittedly imperfect—knowledge at this point.

Our analysis in this chapter bears one additional insight and raises—at least—one further question, which leads to a disclaimer that cautions us to treat our findings with care.

Table 3.1 A conceptual map linking motivational mechanisms to dimensions of informal decentralization

Mechanism to trigger	De-facto decentralized with regard to ...				
	... task division	... task allocation	... rewards distribution	... information exchange	... exception management
Self-actualization	Helpful	Required		Required	
Perceived control	Helpful	Required		Required	Somewhat helpful
Engagement		Required	Helpful	Helpful	
Attachment			Helpful	Sufficient	
Reduced evaluation apprehension			Helpful		Helpful

Note: © Markus Reitzig 2021

First, the insight: our examples may hint not only that the extra effort unleashed by subordinates in exchange for autonomy compensates for the time managers saved but that the de-facto delegation of responsibility to peers may actually improve results such that they beat alternative structural setups. Patagonia is a category leader in its domain, and some of our sample companies do significantly better than their competition, too. As we will see later, these are the hidden benefits that managers—often prematurely—aspire to when flattening. As we discuss in the following chapters (Chaps. 5 and 6), some of these benefits do not arise unless we put other measures in place, however.

Then, the question: if the mechanisms described above held for everyone within every company, why wouldn't all organizations be fully decentralized? The answer is that not all employees are equal and that the success of decentralization depends on the staff we hire (Chap. 4) and on how we treat them (Chap. 5).

Which leads to the disclaimer: our sample of cases represents a selection in which the above mechanisms unfolded because the companies both hired a particular type of employee and treated them in a specific way. As we shall see, the effects of granting autonomy to different types of employees may have very different effects, and failing to adjust other design parameters next to informal decentralization can create havoc within the organization. This forces us not to overgeneralize our findings from this chapter: Table 3.1 provides good guidance to those companies that ensure that they get both hiring and the organizational support right as well. Hence my stressing of the word "can" above.[52]

Appendix

To create the conceptual map presented in Table 3.1, I depart from the structural information provided on our sample companies summarized in Table 2.1. I add five more columns that summarize for which companies we witness which type of autonomy-related motivation (see Table 3.2). To draw an admittedly preliminary first inference, I follow the principles of fuzzy set logics,[53] even though I cannot and will not execute it with excessive academic rigor at this point. The basic idea is conveyed rather easily, however: when, for a given company, I see a joint occurrence of, say, de-facto decentralized task division and, say, attachment, I seek to disentangle whether this is an indication that attachment always requires informal decentralized task division (necessary condition), only requires informal decentralized task division

Table 3.2 Dimensions of informal quasi-decentralization and reported motivations among employees of our sample corporations

	De-facto decentralized with regard to ...											Motivational mechanism				
	...Task division		...Task allocation		...Rewards distribution		...Information exchange		...Exception management			Self-actualization	Perceived control	Engagement	Attachment	Reduced evaluation apprehension
Company	Y/N	Scope	Y/N	scope	Y/N	scope	Y/N	scope	Y/N	scope						
Atlassian	Y	Narrow (initiative-based)	Y	Narrow (initiative-based)	N		Y		Y	Narrow (initiative-based)		Y	Y		Y	
Atos	N		N		N		Y		N							
Buurtzorg	Y		Y	Narrow	N		Y		Y						Y	Y
Gore	N		Y		Y		Y		N			Y	Y	Y	Y	
Patagonia	N		N		Y		Y		N						Y	Y
Ryan	Y		Y		Y		Y		N				Y			
Smarkets	Y		Y		Y		Y		N				Y		Y	
Squarespace	Y		Y		N		Y		N			Y	Y	Y		
Sun Hydraulics	Y		Y		N		?		N			Y				Y

Note: © Markus Reitzig 2021

(sufficient condition), or can occur irrespective of task division (no condition). When I see no such occurrence, I seek to clarify whether attachment may require there to be centralized task division (not condition). Skimming the data this way, and complementing it with additional theoretical considerations, the pattern described in Table 3.1 emerges.

Notes

1. One question readers may immediately have is: does this really hold for all individuals? Are there not those who appreciate no autonomy at all? The answer, for what we can tell from science is: to some extent, every individual appreciates the right to selfgovern her activities. This degree may vary, however, as we elaborate on throughout this chapter and the next two.
2. Note that I refer to the academic literature parsimoniously. This is not a book for fellow researchers that seeks to pay tribute to each and every contribution made by my peers. I ask for their forgiveness. Instead, I point you to selected references—some older, some more recent—that make the point I'm trying to highlight.
3. Ryan and Deci, p. 71.
4. Ibid., p. 70.
5. These views are supported by experimental findings in the field of behavioral economics. See, for example, Bartling, Fehr, and Herz, "The Intrinsic Value of Decision Rights."
6. Turner and Lawrence.
7. Hackman and Oldham.
8. See Morrison, E. W., "Role Definitions and Organizational Citizenship Behavior"; Hofmann, Morgeson, and Gerras, "Climate as a Moderator of the Relationship between LMX and Content Specific Citizenship." Essentially, if employees can pick the tasks they find interesting, this is what I refer to as selfactualization. Note that the original papers may use different terminology.
9. I urge readers to view these results with caution. To get a sense of the order of magnitude, see, for example, Morgeson, Delaney-Klinger, and Hemingway, "The Importance of Job Autonomy, Cognitive Ability, and Job-Related Skill for Predicting Role Breadth and Job Performance." They find that an increase of 1 unit on a 5-point scale for autonomy increases role breadth, the total number of tasks employees cater to in their function, by 0.24. So employees who perceive to have a lot of autonomy would, on average, add more than a task more to their role than those who perceive to have none.
10. Hard data on the wage compensation equivalent for autonomy at work is notoriously difficult to find. Probably to this day some of the most robust results stem from Scott Stern's study of why scientists pay to be scientists.

Among other things, he can show that scientist job offers that permit employees to publish their results in academic journals are, on average, 14,000 US$ lower in annual compensation than other offers. Clearly, scientists represent a very particular part of the workforce, notoriously known to be driven by other motivations in addition to their salaries, and generalizing such figures should therefore be taken with caution. Sauermann and Roach provide a more nuanced account of how these figures vary even within the population of scientists. See Sauermann and Roach, "Not All Scientists Pay to Be Scientists."

11. The first related meta studies were available as early as 1986; Spector, "Perceived Control by Employees." In his work, Spector already draws on the cumulated findings of 88 related individual scientific investigations. Few findings seem as robust in social science.
12. Most interestingly for this book are perhaps the results found by Brockner et al., "Perceived Control as an Antidote to the Negative Effects of Layoffs on Survivors' Organizational Commitment and Job Performance." In this study, the authors find that individuals who are concerned with their future well-being after a potential layoff perform 21 percent better when they feel they are in control. As delayering, see Chap. 1, may also entail the perspective of job losses, this finding highlights how important job autonomy triggering perceived control may be in decentralization scenarios.
13. See Christian, Garza, and Slaughter, "Work Engagement," referring back to insights by Kahn, "Psychological Conditions of Personal Engagement and Disengagement at Work."
14. Maslach, Schaufeli, and Leiter, "Job Burnout."
15. See Christian, Garza, and Slaughter, "Work Engagement."
16. For a meta study comparing the results of a series of prior academic studies, see Mathieu and Zajac, "A Review and Meta-analysis of the Antecedents, Correlates, and Consequences of Organizational Commitment."
17. See, for example, Rousseau, "Why Workers Still Identify with Organizations"; Soupata, "Engaging Employees in Company Success."
18. See Mathieu and Zajac, "A Review and Meta-analysis of the Antecedents, Correlates, and Consequences of Organizational Commitment."
19. See, for example, Ivancevich, and Donnelly, "Relation of Organizational Structure to Job Satisfaction, Anxiety-Stress, and Performance," showing in a study of 295 trade salesmen that "salesmen in flat organizations (1) perceive more satisfaction with respect to self-actualization."
20. Reitzig and Maciejovsky, "Corporate Hierarchy and Vertical Information Flow Inside the Firm—A Behavioral View."
21. Cottrell; ibid.
22. Naturally, listening to selected employees sharing their experiences on video can never paint a conclusive picture of what drives staff inside a given organization; neither can inspecting their reviews on a job site. Many employees

may never choose to write a review; others may vent their anger and be unfair to management. Our goal is hence not to make general statements about how well these companies listed in Table 3.1 treat their staff, or to draw similar inferences. Our intentions are far less judgmental. In fact, the only purpose that perusing the reviews serves for us is to see whether we can spot indications as to why (!) selected employees feel motivated to work for the above companies, and how (!) this relates to their structure. And such indications, we find plenty of! Also, importantly, we find only a very few indications that such autonomy would also demotivate selected employees in the companies we portray.

23. "ShipIt - Inside the Atlassian Ritual."
24. Lakhani and Wolf, "Why Hackers Do What They Do."
25. Gore employee review, "Great place to work with unique culture," *Glassdoor,* August 25, 2020. https://www.glassdoor.at/Bewertungen/Bewertungen-W-L-Gore-and-Associates-RVW35288152.htm (accessed February 27, 2021).
26. Gore employee review, "Great team," *Glassdoor,* December 22, 2020. https://www.glassdoor.at/Bewertungen/Bewertungen-W-L-Gore-and-Associates-RVW39733663.htm (accessed February 25, 2021).
27. Squarespace employee review, "Relaxed, focused work ethic, freedom to innovate," *Indeed,* March 1, 2013. https://at.indeed.com/cmp/Squarespace/reviews/relaxed-focused-work-ethic-freedom-to-innovate?id=0e751563d9cfcde4 (accessed 23 February 2021).
28. Sun Hydraulics employee review, "Excellent place to work," *Glassdoor,* December 6, 2014. https://www.glassdoor.at/Bewertungen/Bewertungen-Sun-Hydraulics-RVW5492701.htm (accessed February 27, 2021).
29. Atlassian employee review, "AMAZING Company!," *Glassdoor,* November 16, 2020. https://www.glassdoor.at/Bewertungen/Bewertungen-Atlassian-RVW38376956.htm (accessed February 23, 2021).
30. Gore employee review, "Great company with room for improvement," *Glassdoor,* December 19, 2016. https://www.glassdoor.at/Bewertungen/Bewertungen-W-L-Gore-and-Associates-RVW13044120.htm (accessed February 23, 2021).
31. Ryan employee review, "Ryan, LLC Director Review - Make your own living while having complete work-life balance," *Indeed,* August 19, 2020. https://www.indeed.com/cmp/Ryan,-LLC/reviews/make-your-own-living-while--having-complete-work-life-balance?id=61e7c982d2ff6a90 (accessed February 23, 2021).
32. Ryan employee review, "Ryan, LLC Consultant Review - Flexible Work Schedules," *Indeed,* December 4, 2019. https://www.indeed.com/cmp/Ryan,-LLC/reviews/flexible-work-schedules?id=ee705b50881c142b (accessed February 23, 2021).
33. "Squarespace | Year End Final."

34. Squarespace employee review, "Real(!) Cutting-edge Work," *Glassdoor*, November 7, 2017. https://www.glassdoor.at/Bewertungen/Bewertungen-Squarespace-RVW17773807.htm (accessed February 23, 2021).
35. "Setting Your Own Salary."
36. Gore employee review, "My Animal Care Technician Review," *Glassdoor*, February 4, 2018. https://www.glassdoor.at/Bewertungen/Bewertungen-W-L-Gore-and-Associates-RVW19070421.htm (accessed February 23, 2021).
37. "Squarespace | Year End Final."
38. Atlassian employee review, "Values driven, a company who cares for its people," *Glassdoor*, January 6, 2021, https://www.glassdoor.at/Bewertungen/Bewertungen-Atlassian-RVW40190423.htm (accessed February 23, 2021).
39. Atos employee review, "Successful experience in a tormented context," *Glassdoor*, November 11, 2020. https://www.glassdoor.at/Bewertungen/Bewertungen-Atos-RVW38228089.htm (accessed 23 February 2021).
40. Gore employee review, "Great company to work for," *Glassdoor*, January 24, 2021. https://www.glassdoor.at/Bewertungen/Bewertungen-W-L-Gore-and-Associates-RVW41319396.htm (accessed 23 February 2021).
41. Gore employee review, "Making money and having fun!," *Glassdoor*, December 11, 2019. https://www.glassdoor.co.uk/Reviews/Employee-Review-W-L-Gore-and-Associates-RVW30819325.htm (accessed February 23, 2021).
42. Patagonia employee review, "Greatwork [sic] place for a company that actually respects and treats their employees right," *Indeed*, August 17, 2019. https://at.indeed.com/cmp/Patagonia/reviews/greatwork-place-for-a-company-that-actually-respects-and-treats-their-employees-right?id=458bd1471262f546 (accessed February 23, 2021).
43. Smarkets employee review, "Amazing Company," *Glassdoor*, September 14, 2018. https://www.glassdoor.at/Bewertungen/Bewertungen-Smarkets-RVW22484003.htm (accessed February 23, 2021).
44. Smarkets employee review, "Building great products with people who care," *Glassdoor*, January 21, 2021. https://www.glassdoor.at/Bewertungen/Bewertungen-Smarkets-RVW41147202.htm (accessed February 23, 2021).
45. "Jos de Blok on Organizational Structures."
46. Patagonia employee review, "The Best company you can work for ever!," *Indeed*, January 18, 2020. https://at.indeed.com/cmp/Patagonia/reviews/the-best-company-you-can-work-for-ever?id=0a01e01014f3827b (accessed February 23, 2021).
47. Patagonia employee review, "It truly is amazing," *Indeed*, May 10, 2019. https://at.indeed.com/cmp/Patagonia/reviews/it-truly-is-amazing?id=c15db4cd79532b48 (accessed February 22, 2021).
48. Patagonia employee review, "Great and fun workplace," *Indeed*, May 31, 2018. https://at.indeed.com/cmp/Patagonia/reviews/great-and-fun-workplace?id=957809a2d0b90d10 (accessed February 22, 2021).

49. Sun Hydraulics employee review, "Sun Hydraulics Valve Technician Review - Great place to work regret leaving," *Indeed,* January 31, 2021. https://www.indeed.com/cmp/Sun-Hydraulics/reviews/great-place-to-work-regret-leaving?id=16dce7c738149b0e (accessed February 22, 2021).
50. "Jos de Blok on Organizational Structures."
51. Klapper and Reitzig, "On the Effects of Authority on Peer Motivation."
52. Academically speaking, our sample suffers from a bias in that we only focus on companies that continue to work with flat structures of some sort. These are firms that managed to avoid mistakes in hiring and failing to support their staff adequately. Hence, strictly speaking, our inference cannot be generalized to companies that make mistakes in the latter two departments. Then again, this book is written for those who seek to get these issues right and want to influence their choices.
53. Ragin, *Fuzzy-Set Social Science.*

Bibliography

Bartling, B., Fehr E., and H. Herz. "The Intrinsic Value of Decision Rights." *Econometrica* 82, no. 6 (2014): 2005–39.

Brockner, J., G. Spreitzer,, A. Mishra,, W. Hochwarter,, L. Pepper, and Weinberg, J. "Perceived Control as an Antidote to the Negative Effects of Layoffs on Survivors' Organizational Commitment and Job Performance." *Administrative Science Quarterly 49,* no. 1 (2004): 76–100.

Christian, M. S., A. S. Garza, and J. E. Slaughter. "Work Engagement: A Quantitative Review and Test of Its Relations with Task and Contextual Performance." *Personnel Psychology* 64, no. 1 (2011): 89–136.

Cottrell, N. B. "Social Facilitation." In *Experimental Social Psychology,* edited by C. McClintock, 185–236. New York: Holt, Rinehart and Winston, 1972.

Hackman, J. R., and G. R. Oldham. "Motivation through the Design of Work: Test of a Theory." *Organizational Behavior and Human Performance* 16, no. 2 (1976): 250–79.

Hofmann, D. A., F. Morgeson, and S. Gerras. "Climate as a Moderator of the Relationship between LMX and Content Specific Citizenship: Safety Climate as an Exemplar." *Journal of Applied Psychology* 88 (2003): 170–78.

Ivancevich, J. M., and J. H. Donnelly. "Relation of Organizational Structure to Job Satisfaction, Anxiety-Stress, and Performance." *Administrative Science Quarterly* 20, no. 2 (1975): 272–80.

"Jos de Blok on Organizational Structures." *RSA,* December 30, 2014. https://www.youtube.com/watch?v=BeOrNjwHw58 (accessed February 23, 2021).

Kahn, W. A. "Psychological Conditions of Personal Engagement and Disengagement at Work." *Academy of Management Journal* 33, no. 4 (1990): 692–724.

Klapper, H., and M. Reitzig. "On the Effects of Authority on Peer Motivation: Learning from Wikipedia." *Strategic Management Journal* 39, no. 8 (2018): 2178–203.

Lakhani, K., and R. Wolf. "Why Hackers Do What They Do: Understanding Motivation and Effort in Free/Open Source Software Projects." In *Perspectives on Free and Open Source Software*, edited by J. Feller, B. FitzGerald, S. Hissam, and K. Lakhani, 3–21. Cambridge, MA: MIT Press. (2005)

Maslach, C., W. B. Schaufeli, and M. Leiter. "Job Burnout." *Annual Review of Psychology* 52 (2001): 397–422.

Mathieu, J. E., and D. M. Zajac. "A Review and Meta-analysis of the Antecedents, Correlates, and Consequences of Organizational Commitment." *Psychological Bulletin* 108, no. 2 (1990): 171–94.

Morgeson, F. P., K. Delaney-Klinger, and M. A. Hemingway. "The Importance of Job Autonomy, Cognitive Ability, and Job-Related Skill for Predicting Role Breadth and Job Performance." *Journal of Applied Psychology* 90, no. 2 (2005): 399–406.

Morrison, E. W. "Role Definitions and Organizational Citizenship Behavior: The Importance of the Employee's Perspective." *Academy of Management Journal* 37 (1994): 1543–67.

Ragin, C. C. *Fuzzy-Set Social Science.* Chicago: University of Chicago Press, 2000.

Reitzig, M., and B. Maciejovsky. "Corporate Hierarchy and Vertical Information Flow Inside the Firm—A Behavioral View." *Strategic Management Journal* 36, no. 13 (2015): 1979–99.

Rousseau, D. M., "Why Workers Still Identify with Organizations," *Journal of Organizational Behavior* 19, no. 3 (1998): 217–33;

Ryan, R. M., and E. L. Deci. "Self-Determination Theory and the Facilitation of Intrinsic Motivation, Social Development, and Well-Being." *American Psychologist* 55, no. 1 (2000): 68–78.

Sauermann, H., and M. Roach. "Not All Scientists Pay to Be Scientists: PhDs' Preferences for Publishing in Industrial Employment." *Research Policy*, 43, no. 1 (2014): 32–47.

"Setting Your Own Salary." *Smarkets,* December 16, 2016. https://www.youtube.com/watch?v=zwFMMJpTfbM (accessed February 23, 2021).

"ShipIt—Inside the Atlassian Ritual." *Atlassian,* February 16, 2018. https://www.youtube.com/watch?v=zgFNTNYJlUk (accessed February 27, 2021).

Soupata, L. "Engaging Employees in Company Success: The UPS Approach to a Winning Team." *Human Resource Management* 44, no. 1 (2005): 95–98.

Spector, P. E. "Perceived Control by Employees: A Meta-analysis of Studies Concerning Autonomy and Participation at Work." *Human Relations* 39 (1986): 1005–16.

"Squarespace | Year End Final." *Squarespace,* December 24, 2018. https://youtu.be/9r_DHYcv-2s (accessed February 23, 2021).

Turner, A. N., and P. R. Lawrence. *Industrial Jobs and the Worker: An Investigation of Response to Task Attributes.* Harvard University, Graduate School of Business Division of Research, Cambridge, MA, 1965.

Part II

What Managers Can Do to Make Flat Structures Work Well

4

What Type of Persons Should You Take on the Journey?

Chapters 2 and 3 provided examples of organizations in which informal decentralization along one or more organizational dimensions had positive consequences. Managerial time was saved and the effort delegated to subordinates was (over)compensated by their increased motivation levels.

But why would some organizations then still be dissatisfied with moving to flatter structures as highlighted in Chap. 1?

The answer is threefold.

One reason is that unless you have the "right" people embark on the structural transition, you need to put a series of other design measures in place to avoid failure—and doing so can become quite cumbersome (see Chap. 5). So, ***picking suited personnel*** from the beginning helps.

The second reason is that even when taking many of the right people along on the journey, ***treating employees appropriately*** is key. Organizations need to avoid mistakes on that front, too, in order to leverage the maximum potential of a flat structure.

The third reason is that flat structures ***will only work*** well at all ***for certain corporate challenges*** and not for others.

We will address the second challenge of treating staff adequately in the next two Chaps. 5 and 6, and we will tackle the third one in Chaps. 7 and 8. For the rest of this chapter, let's concentrate on mastering the first one: having the right employees participating in a high-delegation environment and recruiting suited staff from the outset.

Who Is Truly Willing to Embark on a Journey Toward More Decentralization?

Who are the right people to run a de-facto decentralized structure largely on their own? These would be people who are both particularly ***willing and able*** to take over more responsibilities, including arduous ones, when moving to a flatter structure.

Let's discuss desired abilities in the next section, and focus on above-average willingness first. Here, two aspects appear important.

First, the psychological effects described in Chap. 3 differ between personalities, and they also depend on the conditions employees find themselves in. For example, the motivational boost released through autonomy in the form of, say, self-actualization is more prominent for some personality types than for others. Understanding which personality traits—"stable patterns of emotion, motivation, cognition, and behavior"[1]—are particularly responsive to autonomy will thus be key. And even for the same type of person, this boost may differ depending on the situation in which she finds herself—for example, at the beginning, in the middle, or in the second half of her working life. So, above-average willingness in terms of being extra motivated to work autonomously will arise from the interplay between the personality trait, the conditions an employee finds herself in, and the precise way in which autonomy will stimulate her—the latter being a function of where exactly we give the employee the right to make her own decisions (see Chap. 3, Appendix Table 3.2).

Second, organizing without a supervisor requires employees to self-coordinate on picking up laborious tasks as well. A more decentralized setup will likely fail when peers merely let their extra motivation from autonomy guide them in what they work on—their pure self-interest. Boring, tiring, or strenuous tasks may be left unattended-to when self-selection is based solely on maximizing individual motivation. The willingness of personnel to protect their joint autonomous workplace and invest in its setup is important, too. Certain prosocial personality traits will facilitate achieving this goal, notably agreeableness and honesty-humility, which we will discuss below. Importantly, however, not all people who enjoy autonomy have these traits. And, equally importantly, they are also formed and manifested over extended periods—so it's best to look for people who have shown them for a while, ideally since joining the company, but definitely before moving to a flat structure.

Let's take a closer look at the two aspects of employees' willingness—extraordinary motivation and willingness to invest in an informally decentralized structure—and see how they are related.

Extraordinarily Motivated by Autonomy

Should you, when reading the first part of Chap. 3, ever have wondered whether you learn more about personnel psychology than you would like to, then hopefully by the time we reached the end of the last chapter you appreciated our attention to detail. When tasked with actual decisions about how to design a company, it makes a difference whether a manager understands what exactly autonomy triggers within an employee or not.

At this point, our attention to detail in Chap. 3 will pay off once again. You may recall that we identified five key mechanisms that link autonomy at work to the release of extra effort on the part of the employee: self-actualization, perceived control, engagement, attachment, and reduced evaluation apprehension.

Equipped with this understanding, we are now in a good position to understand which type of staff would show an above-average willingness to work in a flat structure. Simply put, these are people who are *particularly responsive* to one or several of the above mechanisms.

What do we know about who these are? The same scientific literatures we already drew on in Chap. 3 provide some guidance. This time, their findings may not be as robust and unambiguous as in Chap. 3, but the following seems helpful.

When it comes to self-actualization, scholarship has long suggested that employees with a **high need of achievement** should be particularly prone to appreciating job autonomy.[2] And there is some empirical evidence for this. **Conscientiousness**, one of the Big Five personality traits likely known to most human resource officers and described in Table 4.1, and capturing a person's achievement orientation among other things, has been shown to increase the effect of autonomy on a person's job performance. Put simply: the higher a person rates on conscientiousness, the likelier autonomy helps her do well in her job. The effects are quantitatively significant as well.[3]

Perceived control granted through autonomy should matter most to employees who have a strong belief that they can affect the outcomes in their lives more generally speaking. People with such a high "***locus of control***"[4] personality should obviously appreciate autonomy more than others, as it allows them to take better charge of the professional part of their lives than

Table 4.1 Personality traits associated with extra motivation gained from autonomous work

Personality trait	What it refers to
Need for achievement	… an intense and enduring concern to accomplish something difficult[a]
Conscientiousness	… the "propensity to be self-controlled, responsible to others, hardworking, orderly, and rule abiding"[b]
Locus of control	… a person's belief to be in control over her own fate[c]
Proactive	… the tendency to be unconstrained by situational forces and effects environmental change[d]

[a] The trait was originally introduced by Alexander Murray. H. A. Murray, *Explorations in Personality* (New York: Oxford University Press, 1938), 164
[b] See B. W. Roberts, J. J. Jackson, J. V. Fayard, G. Edmonds, and J. Meints, "Conscientiousness," in *Handbook of Individual Differences in Social Behavior*, edited by M. Leary and R. Hoyle (New York: Guilford Press, 2009), 369–81
[c] See Thomas W. H. Ng, Kelly I. Sorensen, and Lillian T. Eby, "Locus of Control at Work: A Meta-Analysis," *Journal of Organizational Behavior* 27 (2006): 1057–87, p. 1057
[d] See Thomas S. Bateman and J. Michael Crant, "The Proactive Component of Organizational Behavior," *Journal of Organizational Behavior* 14, no. 2 (1993): 103–18

before. Empirical evidence supporting the logic is scarce, however.[5] At the same time, and maybe counterintuitive on first sight to some of us, there are indications that *age* has an impact on how folks appreciate autonomy. More specifically, seasoned employees between the ages of 55 and 65 seem to disproportionally appreciate autonomy to follow their own interests at work.[6] While their general willingness to work seems to decrease, allowing them to follow their intrinsic motivation by granting them more control over their own work can offset these negative effects. Upon reflection, this seems quite intuitive. What's known about personnel in that age bracket is that many of them have paid off their mortgages or are close to doing so, and that their children are usually off to college or are working. Admittedly, some of these senior employees may still feel the need to save up for their retirement, but what really motivates them to go to work each morning is the joy of doing what they like best.

Finally, there is evidence that ***proactive personalities*** will be particularly engaged when offered autonomy. Proactive personalities are those said to have a "stable disposition to take personal initiative in a broad range of activities and situations."[7] Compared with other individuals, their work engagement increases more when they're offered similar freedom to govern their own work, and so does their job performance. Again, the few studies available report quantitatively significant results.[8]

Overall, the literature would thus suggest the following:

- Persons with a need for achievement, a sense of proactiveness, and more senior employees should appreciate high delegation the most.
- More specifically, when consulting Table 3.1, any of the above should particularly appreciate the possibility of self-selecting into tasks and projects, and they should—to varying degrees—appreciate a flat informational structure. Allowing them to carve out their own tasks should be the icing on the cake for them.
- Proactive staff are probably those who would be most energized by the possibility to create and discuss their own compensation schemes the most.
- Folks with a high locus of control might appreciate autonomy in conflict resolution with peers the most.

These findings have implications for both recruiting new employees and selecting existing personnel for work in informally decentralized (sub)structures. We will discuss them in more depth towards the end of this chapter.

First, though, let's recall that ensuring that employees' self-interests are best met through a flat structure is just one part of the equation. The second part is ensuring that they're willing to invest in the autonomous workplace they're being offered and to act as gardeners of their own backyard. Which brings us to the next section.

Willing to Put Up with the Costs

High degrees of delegation leading to anarchical structures in which employees merely work on what they individually like best are prone to result in failure. Picking the right people for a journey towards more decentralization therefore also means picking people who are aware of the above problem themselves—and who will self-coordinate to avoid later chaos. Their challenge, making sure that peers pick tasks they like but also give to the organization where needed, is well-known and has been studied in different fields of academe. Two disciplines have produced the most valuable practical insights for managers.

The first is the field of behavioral economics. In their lingo, and one that may sound familiar to some of you, perhaps, the challenge that peers eventually face in a de-facto decentralized structure is to ensure coordination and guarantee that the public good—their joint autonomous workplace, which everybody benefits from within the company—is maintained.[9] This type of autonomous work environment is particularly endangered if the company begins to become dysfunctional—and eventually fails to make the profits it takes to keep it alive.[10] But what exactly are the dangers to its proper workings? There are two connected ones.

I invite you to think about it this way. Profits result when the company manages to divide labor and integrate effort effectively and efficiently. So, peers, whether or not they are being supervised by managers, need to make their individual specialized contributions. Remember the case of the hypothetical furniture company we drew on in Chap. 2? Imagine they move to a more decentralized structure and you allow employees to decide which tasks they want to work on (= you entirely delegate task allocation, maybe even task division). Here, the locksmith still has to do his work, and so must the carpenter; otherwise, there won't be a door for the corporation to sell in the end. But whereas in the traditional company setup, the locksmith can rely on the carpenter being pushed by the manager to meet his responsibilities, in the decentralized setup this is no longer the case. This poses the risk that the locksmith provides idle work as the other party, here the carpenter, no longer lives up to his part of the deal. Imagine that with the new autonomy the carpenter was offered, he suddenly decided to devote his time to decorating window frames, as this is what he likes best. The carpenter may be happy in the short run, but the company will run into trouble. And if the locksmith realizes that his work for the door is not being complemented by other specialized contributions, he will likely quit the company or just work on whatever he likes best—which may accelerate the process of corporate failure.

So, the locksmith and the carpenter have to coordinate on both doing what it takes to get some sort of product delivered to the client that generates a profit. For that, they have to be able to trust one another in general terms.

Absent such trust, the workings of the decentralized setup are endangered.

So, **trusting each other to achieve coordination** in that all parties continue to provide their specific inputs is the first challenge to be tackled.

If you think about it, the only alternative to keeping the company alive would be for the locksmith to pick up the entire tab of the move towards a flatter structure. While the carpenter would continue to enjoy his newly gained freedom of decorating window frames, the locksmith would struggle to keep the company afloat, maybe working on the door frames himself on overtime to deliver some product to the client—a highly unfair and likely unstable situation.

As if this weren't enough, the situation gets even more complicated. Speaking of unfairness, we mustn't forget that extra time will be required to pick up some of the work the manager was doing before. In the above example, the locksmith and the carpenter, at a bare minimum, will have to speak

4 What Type of Persons Should You Take on the Journey?

more often to one another than before, when they could rely on the manager to facilitate the cooperation. And there may be other tasks left over, depending on what the manager chose to delegate. Who takes care of those issues that, on first sight, seem equally alien to the job of a locksmith or a carpenter? Like, say, drafting production plans, talking to suppliers, and so forth? Clearly, if one party has to do it all, this will be perceived as unfair, so it's better if ***all chip in*** to those activities.

As a manager, when delegating responsibility to your employees and having them self-coordinate, you want to reduce related dangers of failure.

So, ideally, you pick people who (1) are ***trustworthy*** to make their co-specialized contributions and (2) ***avoid cherry-picking*** but rather "take one for the team"[11]—as they say in sports.

Table 4.2 provides an overview of what we know from a series of experimental studies about which types of personalities particularly help with establishing a reputation for trust and achieving fair allocations of wealth.[12]

Key traits are ***agreeableness, politeness,*** and ***honesty-humility***.

Table 4.2 Personality traits associated with cooperation in relevant games in behavioral economics

Personality trait	What it refers to
Agreeableness[a]	… the perception of being kind, considerate, likable, cooperative, helpful[b]
Politeness[c]	… the tendency to be courteous and civil[d]
Honesty-humility	… the tendency to be fair and genuine in dealing with others[e]

[a] The trait "agreeableness" features in two canonical categorizations of personality traits, the so-called Big Five model and the so-called HEXACO model. Depending on the categorization, the role agreeableness has played in the emergence of trust and fair distribution of wealth differs. For the purpose of this book, we discard these nuanced findings
[b] See William G. Graziano and Nancy Eisenberg, "Agreeableness: A Dimension of Personality," in *Handbook of Personality Psychology,* edited by Robert Hogan, John Johnson, and Stephen Briggs, 795–82 (San Diego, CA: Academic Press, 1997)
[c] Politeness is often seen as a narrower aspect of agreeableness more broadly
[d] See Zhao, K., E. Ferguson, and L. D. Smillie, "Individual Differences in Good Manners rather than Compassion Predict Fair Allocations of Wealth in the Dictator Game," *Journal of Personality* 85 (2017): 244–56
[e] This trait is characteristic of the so-called HEXACO model by Ashton and Lee and is, more elaborately, defined as "the tendency to be fair and genuine in dealing with others, in the sense of cooperation with others even when one might exploit others without suffering retaliation." M. C. Ashton and K. Lee, "Empirical, Theoretical, and Practical Advantages of the HEXACO Model of Personality Structure," *Personality and Social Psychology Review* 11, no. 2 (2007): 150–66, p. 156

These results are echoed by scholarship in personnel and social psychology, the second discipline that has made important contributions to our understanding of which behaviors and personalities facilitate self-organization.

In their lingo, organizational citizenship behavior is what is required to maintain the functionality of the informally decentralized organizational setup.[13] Of the nuances they add to the above, two appear most interesting for practicing managers.

First, when it comes to the aforementioned traits, a person's **trustworthiness** really seems to hinge on **honesty-humility** rather than on agreeableness.[14]

Second, **prosocial behavior may, in part, be learned**, albeit only over long periods. Being exposed to certain cultural norms can lead persons to learn reciprocal behavior,[15] which facilitates prosocial behavior.[16]

Notwithstanding the richness of investigations conducted in the domain of what it takes for employees to self-coordinate in setups without managerial control, it would appear to be a stretch to link the study results to specific domains of decentralization at this point. There simply isn't enough robust knowledge out there that would allow us to draw conclusions such as "if you want to let your people choose their own tasks, pick those who rank high on agreeableness, but if you want them to resolve their own disputes, pick those who are polite"—just to give an example.

That said, I believe simple reasoning would suggest that it would be particularly helpful to draw on highly prosocial staff if the intention was to let employees set their own salaries and resolve their own disputes.

Again, we'll elaborate more on the implications for hiring towards the end of this chapter. But not before we've taken a closer look at the abilities employees should bring when working in an informally decentralized structure, and the information they require.

And Who Is Capable (Enough)?

Where there's a will, there's a way—so they say. Possibly, but in our situation, most certainly only if folks bring certain abilities, too.

Which are these?

What's required in terms of knowledge, competence, and skills by employees, again, depends on where exactly they're supposed to autonomously engage in work.

Task division—understanding **what needs to be done**—requires peers to be **aware of the organizational goals**, to be **able to map them onto subgoals** and divide them into tasks. Depending on the type of breakdown into tasks, both generalist and specialist competence pertaining to the company's modes of production (technology, market) will be inevitable. Not telling people what the company stands for, and/or having untrained staff draw up a plan, is merely naïve.

In task allocation—understanding **who should do what**—matching pieces of work to persons with skill is key. In an informally decentralized setup, this **requires employees to identify** not only what they're interested in but also **what they're skilled at doing**. Task-related interests and skills are often related, particularly when folks' motivation is intrinsic or when they are engagement-driven. They need not always match, however. Think of tasks that are perceived as shiny and prestigious and that constitute an incentive for peers to engage in them; these incentives may take precedence over fit-related considerations. Employees must have the ability to understand that their self-interest in being seen as associated with such tasks is secondary to the corporate's overall functionality. And they must have the **discipline to stick to this insight**.

To fully delegate the distribution of rewards—deciding **who gets what**—employees need much more information than they would usually have in a traditional company. Essentially, they need the same **information** that **management accounts would normally have** access to: how did a peer's effort translate into profits? Individually? At the team level? What leeway does the company have to distribute excess revenue at all? And they need to have the competence to talk sense into that information. And finally, it will help a great deal if they have a **sense of fairness** (see also Table 4.2).

A co-worker's ability to communicate effectively is key when decentralizing information exchange—putting the decision about **who needs to know what** into the hands of employees. Aside from the personal skills in doing so, a prerequisite is for employees to have **knowledge of the overall task architecture**, or at least access to it whenever they want. Employees need to be able to see the big picture in order to decide which channel of communication to choose with whom, at what frequency, about which topic.

And finally, when it comes to exception management—how to **resolve a conflict**—it takes information about the nature of the conflict, the competence to assess it, and the skills to resolve it.

Some of you, when perusing the last lines, may think to yourselves: sure, I have such people. But you know what? They're all in managerial positions already!

If that's so, that's great news for you—it means you've chosen your managerial staff wisely.

What it doesn't mean, however, is that these are the only people in your company who have the competence and skills it takes. Eventually, you'll find out, by trying, who else among your staff brings these requirements to the table. You may, in many cases, already have an intuition, or your mid-level managers may. I encourage you to take a close look at individuals who have proven records of adapting to prior (organizational) changes; co-workers who have demonstrated independence and skill in searching for information, who have the cognitive ability to filter it, and learn.

Truth be told; however, you may also encounter a lower bound in your company below which the (cognitive) abilities required to engage in successful self-coordination are no longer salient enough among your personnel to delegate many decision rights to them. Your efforts towards decentralizing your structure may end at the layer above this ultimate layer of subordinates who continue to receive instructions from members of the teams operating above them. Whether such a barrier to further delegation exists, and, if so, at which level in the corporate hierarchy it surfaces, is a highly idiosyncratic question for each company, but an important one to assess (see also Chap. 9).

So, What's the Practical Takeaway in Terms of Who We Should Bring to the New Structure?

Having come thus far, there's only one question left for this chapter, but an important one for all practical purposes: How do we find those folks we'd ideally like to have? How do we reach the relevant part of the labor market and identify suited staff in interviews?

Now, I'm not in a position to make recommendations pertaining to a company's specific approaches for presenting itself to potential hires, and I won't. I believe it's evident that corporates should only market themselves based on information that withstands the reality test. In other words, it would be foolish to recommend that your company pitch itself as a highly creative and autonomy-supporting company in the labor market if how you're really structured is very different. So how you reach out and which candidates you appeal to will be constrained by how you run your firm.

Ensuring that you choose the right people is something we can take a somewhat more prescriptive stance on, however. It applies both to hiring staff at the outset and to selecting certain individuals for a decentralized subpart of the organization—if your company's large enough to entertain the latter. Still, we should be careful at this stage.

The information on potentially helpful personality traits summarized in Tables 4.1 and 4.2, and the list of desirable abilities that employees should bring, provides a starting point. A simple, but likely overly simplistic recommendation would be to bring only those individuals who excel along all dimensions. This appears overly simplistic for at least two reasons.

First, there may be very few individuals who meet this criterion in the first place. So trading off between different personality traits and abilities of candidates may become inevitable. What if, let's say, agreeable candidates all had lower ability to screen information than others? The manager responsible for hiring would have to decide what's more important to her company, or she would end up with no candidates at all.

Second, what if there were complicated interdependencies between personality traits and abilities that affect a person's performance, absenteeism, and so forth, in an informally decentralized structure that we are still ignorant of today? What if, say, the effect of agreeableness on work engagement was much stronger when the person was, at the same time, also proactive? For as long as we don't know, all recommendations for staffing the decentral organization must remain imperfect, and requiring a person to rank high on all dimensions might be counterproductive.

Given the above, I believe there are two practical ways forward to bringing the best possible people in to work in the decentralized setup—a simple way, and a more sophisticated one. No matter which you opt for, the first two steps are identical.

1. For all the people you consider bringing into the flat structure, collect data on the potentially relevant traits, attitudes, and abilities discussed in this chapter:

    - Measure the following traits (through either self-assessments or observation) using readily available tests:

        – ***Need for achievement.*** The thematic apperception test (TAT) allows for a person's self-assessment of that trait.[17]
        – ***Conscientiousness***. There are several offers in the marketplace that allow for (the self-)testing (of) a person's tendency to be careful and diligent.[18]
        – ***Locus of control.*** Tests are readily available.[19]
        – ***Proactive personality***. Again, tests are available.[20]
        – ***Agreeableness and honesty-humility*** using, for example, the HEXACO test, no matter whether you assess them as an observer or whether candidates rate themselves.[21]

    - Measure ***substance matter competence***, ***communication skills***, and ***work discipline*** in a way suitable to your company.

2. Narrow in on candidates who rank high on the traits and abilities discussed in this chapter and *that you deem most important for your structure*. This will depend on where you seek to delegate (also see Chaps. 6 and 8)!

When you opt for the simple method, this is where the scientific approach ends.

Should you feel that you'd like to walk the extra mile to find out how to improve your hiring strategy in the future and select even more effectively from the outset, I recommend that you bring in your big-data experts and have them do the following for you:

3. *Track performance* of your employees at the individual and team levels over time. Potentially, repeat measurements for some of the *skills and competences*, as they may vary over time. *Use state-of-the-art machine learning algorithms* to uncover, over time, which people are most important to the success of your organization, by linking performance to the information gathered in Step 1, so you can adjust your hiring approach in the future.[22]

At this point we must ask ourselves one critical question: What do we do if, despite following the above approach of selecting co-workers for the new structure, we end up with less than ideal personnel for creating and operating a flat structure? Can we kiss the idea goodbye straightaway?

The answer is: not quite, although the air will get thinner when you still want to beat a traditional corporation with a flat structure. What we can do in addition to hiring or selecting the right people from within is what we cover in Chap. 5.

Notes

1. DeYoung, "Cybernetic Big Five Theory."
2. Oldman and Hackman (1980) originally spoke of a person's "growth need strength," which refers to her need for personal accomplishment, learning, and development. Evans, Kiggundu, and House, in "A Partial Test and Extension of the Job Characteristics Model of Motivation," suggest that the need for achievement "appears to be a more stable personality trait than growth need strength which appears to be more developmental" (377).

3. Barrick and Mount, "Autonomy as a Moderator of the Relationships between the Big Five Personality Dimensions and Job Performance." In their study, a 30 percent increase in conscientiousness leads to an improvement of 13 percent per performance in a scenario in which autonomy is being perceived as high compared with a scenario in which autonomy is being perceived as low, where the same increase in conscientiousness leads to only a 2 percent increase in performance. They also find similar results for extraversion, another personality trait.
4. The term was coined by Rotter. See Rotter, "Generalized Expectancies for Internal versus External Control of Reinforcement."
5. Kristof-Brown, Zimmerman, and Johnson, in "Consequences of Individual's Fit at Work," are generally skeptical that there are many moderators affecting the person–environment fit. Ng, Sorenson, and Eby, in "Locus of Control at Work: A Meta-Analysis," find that internal locus of control correlates with job autonomy; however, they do not report moderating effects of autonomy on the link between locus of control and performance. So recommendations with regard to selecting people with a high locus of control come with a bit of a disclaimer.
6. Van Den Berg, "Characteristics of the Work Environment Related to Older Employees' Willingness to Continue Working."
7. See Seibert, Kraimer, and Crant, "What Do Proactive People Do?"
8. See Shin and Jeung, "Uncovering the Turnover Intention of Proactive Employees." They find that a person scoring high on a proactive personality scale experiences an 18 percent increase in work engagement when offered high job autonomy (as opposed to an increase of only 7 percent for people with low proactivity scores). So for proactive persons, job autonomy matters significantly more when it comes to work engagement. See also Fuller, Hester, and Cox, "Proactive Personality and Job Performance."
9. The word *public* does not imply that the infrastructure would be available to persons outside the company. In keeping with standard vocabulary in economics, it just denotes that the good, here the infrastructure, is accessible to everyone within the company (and not just parts of it), and that it is nonrivalrous in consumption—meaning that one person's use of the good does not reduce a peer's ability to use it.
10. In a nonprofit organization, the equivalent situation would be one in which the organization no longer meets its noncommercial goal.
11. Note that there is a difference between picking persons who are naturally disposed to contribute to a common good and inducing altruism by trying to make people feel empathy for others. The latter approach may backfire, as has been shown in related experiments. See Batson et al., "Two Threats to the Common Good."

12. I adapted this table from Zhao et al.'s (2016) more elaborate synopsis (Zhao, Ferguson, and Smillie, "Prosocial Personality Traits Differentially Predict Egalitarianism, Generosity, and Reciprocity in Economic Games," 4). The authors provide an excellent overview of the topic, and I strongly recommend their paper as further reading for those who are interested in learning more about the details we covered in this section.
13. Penner, Midili, and Kegelmeyer, "Beyond Job Attitudes."
14. See Thielmann and Hilbig, "The Traits One Can Trust." It seems important to note that personality traits alone do not account for a person's trustworthiness: her being perceived as truthful, reliable, and honest (Cummings and Bromiley, '"The Organizational Trust Inventory (OTI)"). Importantly, competence, integrity, and benevolence have also been shown to matter in the assessment of whether a person is perceived as trustworthy, just as much as trustworthy person's ability to trust others in turn (see Ferrin, Bligh, and Kohles, "It Takes Two to Tango").
15. Note that reciprocal behavior is also associated with personality traits that do not vary over time. See Zhao et al., "Prosocial Personality Traits," 4.
16. Mayr and Freund, "Do We Become More Prosocial as We Age, and If So, Why?" Of particular importance to the functioning of large decentralized collectives may by exchanges that my co-authors Inna Smirnova, Hitoshi Mitsuhashi, and I describe as nonequivalent indirect reciprocity. Essentially, two members within an organization both make specialized contributions, so the exchange is not of the same kind, but nonequivalent. And they do not exchange these indirect services with one another directly, but indirectly via third persons in the system. This type of exchange would appear to require a high interest among members in the organization succeeding, and a high level of trust among peers. For details, see Smirnova, Reitzig, and Mitsuhashi, "OSS Communities as Complementary Assets."
17. For a version of the text, see, for example, https://www.utpsyc.org/tatintro/.
18. See, for example, https://www.truity.com/test/big-five-personality-test. If you wanted to compare how well they actually map onto the original scales that researchers use, I encourage you to review Mount and Barrick, *Manual for the Personal Characteristics Inventory*.
19. See, for example, https://my-personality-test.com/locus-of-control.
20. See, for example, https://www.hiresuccess.com/help/reactive-vs-proactive-personality-types-at-work.
21. See, for example, https://hexaco.org/.
22. By now, these approaches belong to the standard canon of what data scientists do within companies. For further information, see https://hbr.org/2016/10/how-to-hire-with-algorithms.

Bibliography

Ashton, M. C., and K. Lee. "Empirical, Theoretical, and Practical Advantages of the HEXACO Model of Personality Structure." *Personality and Social Psychology Review* 11, no. 2 (2007): 150–66.

Barrick, M. R., and M. K. Mount. "Autonomy as a Moderator of the Relationships between the Big Five Personality Dimensions and Job Performance" *Journal of Applied Psychology* 78, no. 1 (1993): 111–18.

Bateman, Thomas S., and J. Michael Crant. "The Proactive Component of Organizational Behavior." *Journal of Organizational Behavior* 14, no. 2 (1993): 103–18.

Batson, C. D., N. Ahmad, J. Yin, S. J. Bedell, J. W. Johnson, C. M. Templin, and A. Whiteside. "Two Threats to the Common Good: Self-Interested Egoism and Empathy and Empathy-Induced Altruism." *Personality and Social Psychology Bulletin* 25, no. 1 (1999): 3–16.

Cummings, L. L., and P. Bromiley. "The Organizational Trust Inventory (OTI): Development and Validation." In Trust in Organizations: Frontiers of Theory and Research, edited by R. M. Kramer and T. R. Tyler, 302–30. Thousand Oaks, CA: Sage, 1996.

DeYoung, C. G. "Cybernetic Big Five Theory." *Journal of Research in Personality* 56 (2015): 33–58. https://doi.org/10.1016/j.jrp.2014.07.004.

Evans, M. G., Kiggundu, M. N., and House, R. J. (1979). "A Partial Test and Extension of the Job Characteristics Model of Motivation." *Organisational Behaviour and Human Performance* 24, 354–81.

Ferrin, D. L., M. C. Bligh, and J. C. Kohles. "It Takes Two to Tango: An Interdependence Analysis of the Spiraling of Perceived Trustworthiness and Cooperation in Interpersonal and Intergroup Relationships." *Organizational Behavior and Human Decision Processes 107*, no. 2 (2008): 161–78.

Fuller, J. B., K. Hester, and S. Cox. "Proactive Personality and Job Performance: Exploring Job Autonomy as a Moderator." *Journal of Managerial Issues* 22 (2010): 35–51.

Graziano, William G., and Nancy Eisenberg. "Agreeableness: A Dimension of Personality." In *Handbook of Personality Psychology,* edited by Robert Hogan, John Johnson, and Stephen Briggs, 795–824. San Diego, CA: Academic Press, 1997.

Kristof-Brown, A. L., R. D. Zimmerman, and E. C. Johnson. "Consequences of Individual's Fit at Work: A Meta-Analysis of Person-Job, Person-Organization, Person-Group, and Person-Supervisor Fit." *Personnel Psychology* 58, no. 2 (2005): 281–342.

Mayr, U., and A. Freund. "Do We Become More Prosocial as We Age, and If So, Why?" *Current Directions in Psychological Science* 29, no. 3 (2020): 248–54.

Mount, M. K., and M. R. Barrick. *Manual for the Personal Characteristics Inventory.* Libertyville, IL: Wonderlic Personnel Test, 1995.

Murray, H. A. *Explorations in Personality.* New York: Oxford University Press, 1938.

Ng, Thomas W. H., Kelly l. Sorensen, and Lillian T. Eby. "Locus of Control at Work: A Meta-Analysis." *Journal of Organizational Behavior* 27 (2006): 1057–87.

Penner, L. A., A. R. Midili, and J. Kegelmeyer. "Beyond Job Attitudes: A Personality and Social Psychology Perspective on the Causes of Organizational Citizenship Behavior." *Human Performance* 10, no. 2 (1997): 111–31.

Roberts, B. W., J. J. Jackson, J. V. Fayard, G. Edmonds, and J. Meints. "Conscientiousness." In *Handbook of Individual Differences in Social Behavior,* edited by M. Leary and R. Hoyle, 369–81. New York: Guilford Press, 2009.

Rotter, Julian B. "Generalized Expectancies for Internal versus External Control of Reinforcement." *Psychological Monographs: General and Applied* 80, no. 1 (1966): 1–28.

Seibert, S. E., M. L. Kraimer, and J. M. Crant. "What Do Proactive People Do? A Longitudinal Model Linking Proactive Personality and Career Success." *Personnel Psychology* 54, no. 4 (2001): 845–74.

Shin, I., and C. Jeung. "Uncovering the Turnover Intention of Proactive Employees: The Mediating Role of Work Engagement and the Moderated Mediating Role of Job Autonomy." *International Journal of Environmental Research and Public Health* 16, no. 5 (2019): Article 843.

Smirnova, I., M. Reitzig, and H. Mitsuhashi. "OSS Communities as Complementary Assets." Working paper, University of Vienna / Waseda University of Tokyo, 2020.

Thielmann, I., and E. Hilbig. "The Traits One Can Trust: Dissecting Reciprocity and Kindness as Determinants of Trustworthy Behavior." *Personality and Social Psychology Bulletin* 41, no. 11 (2015): 1523–36.

Van Den Berg, P. T. "Characteristics of the Work Environment Related to Older Employees' Willingness to Continue Working: Intrinsic Motivation as a Mediator." *Psychological Reports* 109, no. 1 (2011): 174–86.

Zhao, K., E. Ferguson, and L. D. Smillie. "Prosocial Personality Traits Differentially Predict Egalitarianism, Generosity, and Reciprocity in Economic Games." *Frontiers in Psychology* 7 (2016): Article 1137.

Zhao, K., E. Ferguson, and L. D. Smillie. "Individual Differences in Good Manners rather than Compassion Predict Fair Allocations of Wealth in the Dictator Game." *Journal of Personality* 85 (2017): 244–56.

5

How to Enforce and Foster Effective Self-organization?

There are instances in which flat organizations not only work but even outcompete traditional structures. Notably, this is the case when, among other things, managers can delegate important work to their subordinates (Chap. 2) because the latter not only appreciate (Chap. 3) but thrive on the autonomy they're being granted (Chap. 4).

Therefore, one important lever of excelling with a flat organization, as we discussed in the preceding chapter, is selecting the right people—by hiring from the labor market or recruiting from within the company. But is there *anything else we can or must do?*

The answer is *yes*, once we allow for *three very realistic complications*.

The first complication is that we may find ourselves in *situations where we need to draw on personnel who do not*, at least in part, *look like* an *ideal* match for work in a high-delegation environment. Can we still make the flat organization work in such instances? And make it work well?

The second complication lies in the fact that even those *employees* who are ideally suited to work in a flat structure, let alone other staff, still *require some managerial support* to make the flat structure work. What do they need?

And the third complication is that all employees, to make the flat structure work really well, benefit from *management foresight and guidance* when it comes to creating the general setup or *framework within which employees can enjoy their autonomy*.

Addressing the first two complications appears essential to prevent the flat structure from collapsing. Addressing the third complication seems critical to set the flat structure up to be competitive with a traditional one.

The rest of this chapter is devoted to dealing with the first two complications. Chapter 6 will address the third.

Preventing the Breakdown of the Flat Structure

In Chap. 4, we discussed the need for staff to be willing to maintain their largely decentralized workplace in order to keep the flat structure from collapsing. In an ideal world where we can hire employees suited to a quasi-decentralized organization from scratch, smart recruiting can mostly resolve this challenge. In a situation where we need to staff the flat structure with existing employees, we must ***consider*** complementary ***means of securing*** that a rather ***decentralized infrastructure*** survives.

Also, in Chaps. 3 and 4 we highlighted what motivates individuals to work in flat structures and which cognitive abilities employees should ideally bring. However, the truth of the matter is that even motivated ***employees*** require reassurance, let alone other people, and that even smart employees require information. Put simply—all employees ***require support from the organization***.

The two subsections below address the two challenges above in turn.

Ensuring Collaboration among Existing Staff in a Quasi-decentralized Structure

Startups, at least in the early stages of their growth, can often attract conscientious and proactive people, who expect to work in a team-based environment where they need to assume arduous tasks when necessary. Quite obviously, working in a flat structure not only comes easily to many of them but is not seldomly one of the reasons they join a company in the first place.

However, as organizations grow, their hiring pattern may change, for a variety of reasons. Jobs become more specialized and individual accountability narrows in scope. People join less frequently with the goal of becoming part of the corporate family; instead, salary considerations and other traditional perks such as corporate retirement plans or institutionalized sabbaticals begin to determine the decision whether to accept a job offer or not.[1]

By the time organizations have grown to a size where they feel the need to delayer their multilevel hierarchies, a fair share of their employees may be there for reasons other than the hope of flourishing in an autonomous workplace. Being ***delegated managerial work*** may come as a welcome surprise to some of them at best, but others may eye the developments critically, and yet others may even **oppose such informal decentralization openly or in a hidden manner**.

Such criticism, and potential unwillingness, can become detrimental to the company's ambition to move to a flatter setup, particularly when current employees seem uninterested in engaging in the critical parts of the self-management, housekeeping, or maintenance of their more decentralized workplace.

Even if the faction of such individuals is smaller than those who are, in principle, keen on working in a more autonomous manner and willing to put up with the related costs (see Chap. 4), the freeriding of the unwilling on the efforts of the motivated, and the formers' shirking of investments in the public good, may lead the latter to resign, too.

So what can be done?

In the fields of organizational behavior and economics, related problems have been studied for a long time. Even though these studies were not conducted in the exact context of commercial organizations that delegate much decision-making to their employees, practicing managers can take important insights from science.

If, as in Chap. 4, we consider the quasi-decentralized workplace as a public good to which all employees should contribute in order to guarantee the longevity of their newly gained autonomy, then basic reasoning would suggest that **both reward and sanction mechanisms** could be remedies to avoid shirking and freeriding.

And when it comes to empirical evidence on the efficacy of these mechanisms, social **scientists do agree on the viability of sanctions**. Studies on their effectiveness abound across a plethora of settings related to the one we care about.[2] Perhaps one of the most interesting nuances this vein of research has carved out is that *(even imperfect) sanctioning systems can be quite effective*. To that end, some of my colleagues have provided evidence that sanctioning, **when perceived as a social norm**, leads members of an organization to contribute to the public good irrespective of whether detection of misbehavior and the enforcement of the sanction is likely to affect them in the future.[3] Critically, in certain scenarios, the viability of the sanctioning mechanism **depends on the number of individuals "adverse to advantageous inequity"**[4]—that is, employees who do not appreciate receiving more than others absent a visible reason. Identification with the group would appear to be a potential driver for the emergence of adversity to such inequity.[5]

Interestingly, the **results on the usefulness of incentivization approaches are more mixed**. While some studies suggest that rewarding people in order to encourage them to contribute to a common good may help sustain the latter, others do not.[6]

What appears to hold for both sanction and reward systems is that they foster "instrumental" rather than "elementary" cooperation.[7] Importantly, such ***instrumental cooperation tends to break down as soon as the supporting structure***—institutionalized penalties or incentives—***is removed***. Also, the danger of gaming the supporting structure may increase when the nature of cooperation is purely instrumental.[8]

Against the backdrop of the above, some of the actions taken by the companies described in Chaps. 1 and 2 become even more comprehensible than they might already have been otherwise.

At Treehouse, for example, "employees are asked to evaluate colleagues' judgment, communication, working style and skill level. Good reviews are the key factor in deciding who gets raises. Consistently bad reviews start a process that can lead to firing."[9]

Similarly, W. L. Gore & Associates use peer-review systems to help determine an employee's salary, in which alignment between corporate values and co-worker behavior plays an important role.[10]

So, companies, when granting autonomy to their employees, do at times install systems that allow on-the-ground assessment of employee behavior, with the explicit goal of rewarding contributions and sanctioning misbehaviors if they become excessive. Interestingly, the monitoring process itself is also decentralized.

Providing Support

Systems for incentivizing good citizenship behavior, let alone systems for sanctioning deviations from the latter, are by themselves insufficient to enable employees to operate with the autonomy they're given in a flat structure, however. Even employees who one would expect to flourish in a de-facto decentralized environment need the support of their remaining superiors along two different dimensions: access to information and psychological "empowerment."

Access to Information

When employees are authorized to decide—at least in part—which tasks the company should work on in order to achieve its goals (task division); who should be working on which tasks (task allocation); who should receive which type of compensation for it (rewards distribution); and who should talk to whom about what, at which frequency, in which manner (information exchange), and how conflicts shall be resolved (exception management), they can't proceed by guesswork. They need information.

Providing such information, or ensuring that it's accessible, is a task you should address as the designer of the flat structure. Making sure employees have the information they need to get the job done is a necessary condition for every flat structure to work. So, depending on where you seek to delegate to a high degree, employees should know about

- *Corporate goals*
- *The overall task architecture*
- *(Other) Employees' skills and preferences*
- *The nature of individual tasks*
- *Effort and outcome of their peers' actions*
- *The cause and nature of conflicts*

Irrespective of where exactly formerly managerial work is being delegated to employees, it appears useful to communicate corporate goals very clearly in a high-delegation regime. Assessing whether lower-level actions ultimately help meet these goals is the one test that seems applicable at all stages of the process. To conduct it, at least qualitatively, information on the desired outcome is crucial.

Employees also need information about the overall task architecture. The level of knowledge they require depends on whether they're involved in the process of task division, and on whether they're being granted the right to self-select into tasks.

To the extent that **employees participate in designing the task structure** of the organization, they **need** full information about which different tasks exist at all, how they depend on each other, how they're being composed (or bundled), and which constraints these compositions raise.[11] Creating **common "architectural knowledge"**[12] is crucial in delegating task division, for a variety of reasons. To the extent that employees are autonomous in the process of task division by means of delegation, they become responsible for designing an architecture that helps match people to tasks optimally, gain benefits from parallelizing efforts where possible, and so forth. Meeting this responsibility is impossible in the absence of architectural knowledge. This imperative also holds, albeit in a reduced form, where employees only participate in devising the task architecture and co-create it with management. As an example in this vein, think of open-source software development (OSSD). In

OSSD, the initial formulation of the problem by a project founder influences task division, but it's elaborated and developed significantly as others join and contribute to the project.[13] Wikipedia, discussed in Chap. 2, is a similar case in point. Jimmy Wales and Larry Sanger, by formulating the goal of creating an encyclopedia to which anyone could contribute, influenced the task structure of Wikipedia as we know it today. Just think of the elements they fixed by design—the article pages. That said, which article pages precisely would emerge, on which topics, of what length, and so on, was something they delegated entirely to the community. Depending on the degree of delegation pertaining to task division, employees may not need to have full architectural knowledge eventually, just parts of it. This, then, depends very much on the individual design.

To the extent that **employees** (only) receive **authority to self-select into tasks**, the knowledge they **require** extends to the nature of the tasks. *A transparent task architecture*—one that allows employees to determine the fine-grained structure of what they're supposed to work on exactly—helps them pick tasks that map onto their skills and preferences.[14]

When it comes to delegating the integration of effort, additional information may need to be made accessible to **employees** when they are to ***autonomously distribute rewards among themselves***. In essence, to successfully engage in a quasi-decentralized determination of compensation packages, peers ***must have access to what managers and HR departments would usually have***. Effort and outcome data at the individual level must be available to ensure that incentives are set in line with corporate expectations and constraints. The corporation's contractual obligations to the individual must be factored in. To the extent that autonomy in rewards is autofocused—meaning that an individual can simply put together her own compensation package but does not determine that of her peers—the above information need not be shared.

Delegating information exchange, on the other hand, requires little additional information beyond the ***transparent task architecture*** mentioned above. All that's required on top is information about ***who does what***.

Finally, to ***delegate exception management*** successfully, managers must enable their employees to understand the nature of conflicts that can arise, whether task-related or interpersonal. In addition to a ***transparent task architecture***, employees require ***procedural process data*** on the cases they are supposed to decide on.

Organizations that successfully operate a quasi-decentralized structure along one or several of the 4+1 dimensions of organizing meet these information provision requirements. Let's highlight a few observations.

Table 5.1 High delegation and decentral information requirements

Where to delegate	What information needs to be accessible to employees
Task division	Information required to build architectural knowledge—elements of the task architecture, their interdependencies, their bundling, and constraints
Task allocation	Information on the nature of individual tasks
Rewards distribution	Information on peer effort and performance, corporate constraints (not needed when autofocused)
Information exchange	Tasks, task interdependence, and task allocation to individuals
Exception management	As above, + procedural data on conflict cases

Note: © Markus Reitzig 2021

At Atlassian, teams participating in the ShipIt hackathons create their own projects from scratch. Common architectural knowledge required for the decentralized task division engenders and facilitates self-selection.

At W.L. Gore, employees gain firsthand impressions of the effort and performance of their teammates through their joint work, enabling them to rate their peers. It's company policy that "you only rank who you know, you do not rank based on perception,"[15] as former CEO Terri Kelly puts it.

At Smarkets, employees need to articulate their demands for salaries, which are then either approved or rejected by their peers. To help with that process, peers can access to all salary data through an internal wiki, allowing them to put such demands into perspective for each individual.[16]

At Patagonia, where employees autonomously choose how they want to be compensated, this information need not be shared.

And at Buurtzorg, resolving conflicts entails a lengthy process in which all relevant data are revealed.

Table 5.1 summarizes the above.

Psychological "Empowerment"

Employee access to relevant information in a more decentralized structure is critical. But we shouldn't forget that employees are more than information processors. As human beings, they have ambitions, ***doubts, fears***—and to the extent that these are ***exacerbated by granting more autonomy***, managers are well advised to take them seriously to ensure that they succeed in setting up flat structures.

Exaggerated ambitions, the ruthless pursuit of self-interest—we discussed these issues above. Doubts and fears arising from being thrown into the pond of self-determined work is an aspect we haven't yet touched on but must engage with now.

Thinking back to Chap. 3, you might recall that autonomy can unleash energy among employees in a variety of ways. You might also recall from Chap. 4 that differences in certain personality traits and other factors across individuals may lead to some employees enjoying such autonomy more than others. So, variation in autonomy orientation is no longer novel to us at this point.

So it should come as no surprise that you'll find among your staff some people with less enthusiasm for working in a flat structure than others. For these less-motivated individuals, the potential carrot of determining their own workday in a flat environment more than before may not be large enough to eliminate the doubts and fears that accompany novel accountability. What may be a bit bigger surprise is that these doubts and fears can also be substantial among those who are actually eager to move to a flatter structure.

To alleviate these concerns, management is well advised to provide organizational support, more specifically, *autonomy support*, to all employees.

Self-determination theorists Deci and Ryan, whose work we touched upon in Chap. 3, propose that management best supports employees in embracing autonomy by "taking their perspective, encouraging initiation, supporting a sense of choice, and being responsive to their thoughts, questions, and initiatives,"[17] and they find *evidence* for their suggestions *across several workplace settings*.

Important *nuances* that are both *managerially relevant and actionable* are found in the literature on perceived organizational support more broadly—the scientific literature that would come closest to capturing phenomena that are colloquially often referred to as "empowerment."

In this domain, studies showed that *custom-tailoring autonomy support* to individual co-workers is key in reaching them. Rather than broadcasting a generic pep talk, these findings suggest, managers must sit down with key employees individually and make an effort to understand their concerns. Done correctly, this *can actually lead to reduced turnover*.[18]

Also, a trust-engendering *humble leadership style* can help a great deal. Loud-voiced managers neither signal a willingness to listen to their employees; nor will employees believe in their forbearance when spotting mistakes. Highly humble leaders, by contrast, *increase employees' feeling of being trusted* by management, an effect that appears to become stronger and more relevant the more autonomy employees are offered.[19]

In terms of who would be *particularly susceptible to autonomy support*, it appears that it makes *conscientious and emotionally stable individuals* thrive the most; the rationale here being that goal-driven individuals, by ascribing humanlike characteristics to an organization and feeling supported in terms of reaching their goals, may reciprocate more often.[20]

What psychologists tested in the lab and in the field seems to map quite nicely onto the anecdotal evidence that our case companies provide.

When important decisions need to be made within Reaktor, employees can seek the advice of top management. Former CFO Hannu Terävä views the executive group as a "sparring partner [that] helps people look at things from different angles."[21]

Also, when Atos banned emails as a communication tool internally, they did not leave their employees to themselves. Instead, they "built a social network for the entire enterprise [and] organized the network around 7,500 open communities representing the various projects that required collaboration."[22]

Finally, Buurtzorg not only operates a rather transparent approach when it comes to conflict management, as illustrated before, but also supports its self-managing teams with so-called regional coaches. Their job is to "give advice or share how other teams have solved similar problems"[23] without their having actual decision-making authority. As an employee said, "Leaving it up to us as a team, we really feel empowered to take our own decisions."[24]

The Important Takeaways

This chapter showed which setscrews management can adjust to prevent the flat structure from collapsing, particularly—but not solely—in situations where employees were not initially selected to work in an informally decentralized setup.

To ensure the longevity of a rather decentralized workplace, it seems advisable to *put sanctioning systems in place. Even an imperfect system* may foster an overall understanding that everyone is expected to contribute, and that *freeriding is not tolerated*. But sanctioning won't be sufficient. *Enabling personnel* to flourish in a high-delegation environment is equally critical. *Providing detailed information* where needed (see Table 5.1) is key. Access to such information has to be easy—internal wikis and other representations can help. For all practical purposes, avoiding information overload also appears to be key in this scenario. Some communication tools have features built in to avoid such overload in the first place.[25] *Empowering your staff* is also key, whether employees are open to or critical of working in a high-delegation environment. This may include specific training initiatives to help people deal with their new responsibilities more broadly. Eventually, leaders must not underestimate that even when they delegate formal decision rights, they might still be regarded as higher-status individuals by their (former) subordinates, and that leaders still influence their peers' behaviors in subtle ways.[26] Also, ***credibility is crucial***—reflected in the appreciation of the individual's needs and a nonauthoritative leadership style.

When we succeed with all of the above, is our work done?

Clearly, our ambition was not just to ensure the mere workings of a flat structure. We also want it to be as efficient as possible in order to make it truly competitive with a traditional hierarchy. Which other design measures can we implement to improve the workings of a flat structure so that it offers the playing field best-suited to delegating decisions and actions?

Chapter 6 takes up these questions in detail.

Notes

1. My colleagues Mike Roach and Henry Sauerman made some very interesting related observations in the context of maturing startups. See Roach and Sauerman, "Founder or Joiner?"
2. For some of the earliest contributions, see Yamagishi, "The Provision of a Sanctioning System as a Public Good." For a rather recent overview of the work conducted since, see, for example, Chen, Pillutla, and Yao, "Unintended Consequences of Cooperation Inducing and Maintaining Mechanisms in Public Goods Dilemmas."
3. See Vyrastekova, Funaki, and Takeuchi, "Sanctioning as a Social Norm."
4. See Engel, "Social Preferences Can Make Imperfect Sanctions Work."
5. Readers who feel intrigued by this kind of reasoning may enjoy following up on the works in sociobiology. Of particular relevance seems a domain called multilevel selection theory. It seeks to reconcile the seemingly contradictory observations that humans behave both selfishly and altruistically in groups. Its basics go back to Darwin's original writings, in which he suggests that natural selection occurs at different levels—the individual and the group—where selfish behavior fosters individual selection and cooperative and altruistic behavior fosters group survival. For a recent review of this field, see Wilson and Wilson, "Rethinking the Theoretical Foundation of Sociobiology."
6. See Chen et al., "Unintended Consequences of Cooperation Inducing and Maintaining Mechanisms in Public Goods Dilemmas," for an overview of studies suggesting that incentive systems can ensure collaboration in settings related to ours. See Sefton, Shupp, and Walker, "The Effects of Rewards and

Sanctions in Provision of Public Goods," for an example of a study questioning the viability of reward schemes to sustain cooperation on public goods.
7. See Yamagishi, "The Provision of a Sanctioning System as a Public Good."
8. Groups of employees may form cartels or coalitions and engage in undesired bargaining with one another.
9. Rogoway, "Portland Startup Treehouse Eliminates the Boss, Tells Workers to Manage Themselves."
10. Kelly, "The End of Hierarchy: Natural Leadership at W.L. Gore."
11. This definition leans heavily on Shaw and Garlan, *Software Architecture: An Emerging Discipline*. It was adapted to organizational structures by Carliss Baldwin and her co-authors. See, for example, Baldwin and Clark, "The Architecture of Participation."
12. See Henderson and Clark, "Architectural Innovation."
13. See Puranam, Alexy, and Reitzig, "What's 'New' about New Forms of Organizing?," citing MacCormack, Rusnak, and Baldwin, "Exploring the Structure of Complex Software Designs."
14. See Puranam et al., "What's 'New' about New Forms of Organizing?" See MacCormack et al., "Exploring the Structure of Complex Software Designs." See also MacCormack, Baldwin, and Rusnak, "Exploring the Duality between Product and Organizational Architectures."
15. Kelly, "The End of Hierarchy: Natural Leadership at W.L. Gore," at 20:14.
16. Bernard, "What Happens When You Let Employees Pick How Much They Want to Be Paid?."
17. See Deci and Ryan, "Self-Determination Theory.", 18.
18. See Liu, Zhang, Wang, and Lee, T. W., "The Effects of Autonomy and Empowerment on Employee Turnover."
19. See Cho, Schilpzand, Huang, and Paterson, "How and When Humble Leadership Facilitates Employee Job Performance." The authors provide several studies, the first of which at least suggests that autonomy and humble leadership complement each other in instilling a sense of being trusted among employees.
20. See Sears and Han, "Do Employee Responses to Organizational Support Depend on Their Personality?"
21. Terävä, "How Reaktor Grew without Hierarchy."
22. Burkus, "Some Companies Are Banning Email and Getting More Done."
23. Laloux, *Reinventing Organizations*, 69.
24. Buurtzorg—Coaches not Managers.
25. For example, the @ sign in a Slack™ channel allows self-organization of attention.
26. See also Chap. 8 and the usefulness of distinguishing between different sources of social influence in hierarchies.

Bibliography

Baldwin, C. Y., and K. B. Clark. "The Architecture of Participation: Does Code Architecture Mitigate Free Riding in the Open Source Development Model?" *Management Science* 52 (2006): 1116–11.

Bernard, Zoë. "What Happens When You Let Employees Pick How Much They Want to Be Paid? This Company Decided to Find Out." *Business Insider*, September 23, 2018. https://www.businessinsider.com/smarkets-employees-pick-salary-jason-trost-2018-9?r=DE&IR=T.

Burkus, D. "Some Companies Are Banning Email and Getting More Done." Harvard Business Review, June 8, 2016. https://hbr.org/2016/06/some-companies-are-banning-email-and-getting-more-done.

Buurtzorg—Coaches not Managers." *Buurtzorg Britain & Ireland*, November 27, 2018, https://www.youtube.com/watch?v=vO9zhGWDcr4 (accessed February 24, 2021).

Chen, X.-P., M. M. Pillutla, and X. Yao. "Unintended Consequences of Cooperation Inducing and Maintaining Mechanisms in Public Goods Dilemmas: Sanctions and Moral Appeals." *Group Processes & Intergroup Relations* 12, no. 2 (2009): 241–55.

Cho, J., P. Schilpzand, L. Huang, and T. Paterson. "How and When Humble Leadership Facilitates Employee Job Performance: The Roles of Feeling Trusted and Job Autonomy." *Journal of Leadership and Organizational Studies* 28, no. 2 (2021). https://doi.org/10.1177/1548051820979634.

Deci, E. L., and R. M. Ryan. "Facilitating Optimal Motivation and Psychological Well-Being Across Life's Domains." *Canadian Psychology* 49, no.1 (2008): 14–23.

Engel, C. "Social Preferences Can Make Imperfect Sanctions Work: Evidence from a Public Good Experiment." *Journal of Economic Behavior & Organization* 108 (2014): 343–53.

Henderson, Rebecca M., and Kim B. Clark. "Architectural Innovation: The Reconfiguration of Existing Product Technologies and the Failure of Established Firms." *Administrative Science Quarterly* 35, no. 1 (1990, Special Issue: Technology, Organizations, and Innovation): 9–30.

Kelly, T. "The End of Hierarchy: Natural Leadership at W.L. Gore." *Management Innovation eXchange*, n.d. https://www.managementexchange.com/video/terri-kelly-wl-gores-original-management-model-0 (accessed February 22, 2021).

Laloux, F. *Reinventing Organizations: A Guide to Creating Organizations Inspired by the Next Stage in Human Consciousness.* Brussels: Nelson Parker, 2014.

Liu, D., Zhang, S., Wang, L., & Lee, T. W. "The Effects of Autonomy and Empowerment on Employee Turnover: Test of a Multilevel Model in Teams." *Journal of Applied Psychology* 96, no. 6 (2011): 1305–16.

MacCormack, A., C. Baldwin, and J. Rusnak. "Exploring the Duality between Product and Organizational Architectures: A Test of the 'mirroring' Hypothesis." *Research Policy* 41 (2012): 1309–24.

MacCormack, A. D., J. Rusnak, and C. Y. Baldwin. "Exploring the Structure of Complex Software Designs: An Empirical Study of Open Source and Proprietary Code." *Management Science* 52 (2006): 1015–30.

Puranam, P., O. Alexy, and M. Reitzig. "What's 'New' about New Forms of Organizing?" Academy of Management Review 39, no. 2 (2014): 162–80.

Roach, M., and H. Sauerman. "Founder or Joiner? The Role of Preferences and Context in Shaping Different Entrepreneurial Interests." *Management Science* 61, no. 9 (2015): 2160–84.

Rogoway, Mike. "Portland Startup Treehouse Eliminates the Boss, Tells Workers to Manage Themselves." *Oregon Live*, December 19, 2013, updated January 10, 2019. https://www.oregonlive.com/silicon-forest/2013/12/portland_startup_treehouse_eli.html (accessed February 4, 2021).

Sears, G. J., and Y. Han. "Do Employee Responses to Organizational Support Depend on Their Personality? The Joint Moderating Role of Conscientiousness and Emotional Stability." *Employee Relations* 43, no. 5 (2021): 1130–46.

Sefton, M., R. Shupp, and J. M. Walker. "The Effects of Rewards and Sanctions in Provision of Public Goods." *Economic Inquiry* 45 (2007): 671–90.

Shaw, Mary, and David Garlan. *Software Architecture: An Emerging Discipline.* Upper Saddle River, NJ: Prentice-Hall, 1996.

Terävä, Hannu. "How Reaktor Grew without Hierarchy." *Reaktor*, September 3, 2015. https://www.reaktor.com/blog/how-reaktor-grew-without-hierarchy/ (accessed February 4, 2021).

Vyrastekova, J., Y. Funaki, and A. Takeuchi. "Sanctioning as a Social Norm: Expectations of Non-strategic Sanctioning in a Public Goods Game Experiment." *The Journal of Socio-Economics* 40, no. 6 (2011): 919–28.

Wilson, D. S., and E. O. Wilson. "Rethinking the Theoretical Foundation of Sociobiology." *Quarterly Review of Biology* 82, no. 4 (2007): 327–48.

Yamagishi, T. "The Provision of a Sanctioning System as a Public Good." *Journal of Personality and Social Psychology* 51, no. 1 (1986): 110–16.

6

How to Design the Playing Field for Efficient Quasi-decentralization?

Chapter 5 dealt with two important complications you'll (almost) inevitably encounter in practice when seeking to design a flat structure. You'll (almost) always depend ***on some personnel who do not look like*** an ***ideal*** match for work in a high-delegation environment. And you'll have to provide ***managerial support*** to all your employees in order to make the flat structure work. Failing to meet these challenges will likely lead to the collapse of the quasi-decentralized workplace.

But merely ensuring the survival of a flat structure is hardly a goal worth pushing for, or reason enough to read an entire book on the subject. Eventually, we'd like to understand what it takes for these structures to beat traditional hierarchies—and what we can do to make the most of them.

So let us, for the remainder of this chapter, assume that we've successfully addressed the above two complications. ***Which additional measures*** can we still put in place ***to maximize the performance of the flat structure***?

Asking this question begs for two related answers. How can we ***increase the gains*** from operating with a flat structure? And how can we ***reduce the costs***—financial, time-wise, in terms of confusing employees or clients, and so forth—of running a more decentralized organization?

The first-answer part can be kept rather brief. Asking how to ramp up the gains from working with a flat structure is identical to asking what else it is we can do to make the high performers in that structure perform even better. And on that there's little to share, at least as far as current scholarship goes. High performers within a flat structure, as we discussed in Chap. 4, are those who rank high on the personality traits presented in Tables 4.1 and 4.2: people with a high need for achievement, proactive employees, conscientious employees, honest and trustworthy peers. Little is known about what else motivates them beyond autonomy and money. Having discussed the effects of autonomy in Chaps. 3 and 4, what remains to be said is that pay-for-performance schemes seem more attractive to employees who seek to achieve. Whether the implication is to introduce such payment schemes or not, however, really depends on whether the expected positive effects outweigh the challenges of enabling solid self-organization among peers (see Chap. 5), a question to which there is no universal answer that would hold for all organizations alike.

The second-answer part—***how to reduce the costs*** of operating a flat structure—***requires more elaboration***. Here, as so many times before by now, we must consider more carefully along which of the 4+1 dimensions of organizing we seek to implement a high-delegation regime.

Reducing Costs of Task Division and Allocation Through Modularization

As mentioned above, delegating decisions pertaining to task division—allowing employees to break corporate goals down into work packages—requires that people have access to information that allows them to build architectural knowledge: knowledge of the different tasks, their interdependence, their bundling, and the accompanying constraints. Obviously, this process can become quite demanding, even for those employees who bring the cognitive skills in general (see Chap. 4). Notably, task interdependence and constraints require coordinating the different activities being initiated by different individuals or teams within the company. The effort to achieve such coordination may push even smart employees beyond their cognitive limits—at least if these activities can suddenly happen everywhere, at any time, with no clear guidelines whatsoever.

One ***extremely powerful and popular approach to reducing*** these ***costs of coordination*** for employees and to providing them a frame for working in a quasi-decentralized manner ***is modularization***. As my colleague and leading modularity expert Carliss Baldwin neatly summarizes in her book, "under this approach, different parts … could be designed by separate, specialized groups working independently of one another. The 'modules' could then be connected and (in theory at least) would function seamlessly, as long as they conformed to a predetermined set of design rules."[1] At the heart of this approach lies the idea of defining units, or modules, of tasks that are "powerfully connected among themselves but relatively weakly connected to elements of other units."[2]

Management, by predefining (placeholders for) such units and the interfaces between them, **can create a work architecture** in which different teams can then concentrate on working on different modules, thereby massively reducing their ultimate coordination efforts across individuals and teams. Key considerations in this process relate to the breaking down of a complex organizational goal into smaller pieces, tracking the complexity of these smaller pieces, stopping at a point where expected complexity within a module seems manageable, and defining the interfaces between these modules.

Whether modularization leaves room for **decentralized task division or** merely for decentralized **task allocation is a matter of degree**. Modular task architectures that allow employees to add new modules and shape their contents would involve peers in mapping corporate goals to problems. Modular task architectures that prespecify the number and nature of modules would merely leave room for employees to self-select into their work.

Designing any such modular architecture can undoubtedly be challenging, most certainly works better in some settings than in others, but in any case requires in-depth engagement of management with the approach to conduct it successfully. As my describing of the underlying principles would not only blow the scope of this book but likely result in an explanation that pales in comparison to that provided by Carliss Baldwin and Kim Clark, I refer interested readers to the original works, but not without highlighting how frequently modularity—in both task division and allocation—might also play a role in the examples of the companies portrayed in this book, however.

Take the example of Atlassian. The ShipIt hackathons are isolated events that occur outside the day-to-day production process within the company. While they may impose some constraints on other activities—ShipIt participants can't attend to other duties while the hackathon is underway—there are hardly other immediate interdependences visible. Importantly, the results of the hackathon need not immediately be integrated into the work routines of Atlassian. If the outcomes appear interesting enough to be scaled, traditional management will again be involved.

Similarly, Ryan operates in an industry where the rather standardized nature of the product facilitates modularization. Tax returns, for example, tend to consist of different sections that can be worked on separately by different employees if needed. So, in theory, different experts can work on separate aspects of a complex declaration without having to interact too frequently. However, the business also allows for a different type of modularity. In essence, each tax service, while following standard procedures, is a customized good offered to an individual client. So, in terms of task allocation, it's feasible to define individual client–advisor relationships that can, for the most part, operate independently of other client–advisor relationships within the firm. Thus, it seems entirely feasible that Ryan does well as a company while also allowing its staff to operate from wherever and whenever.

Sun Hydraulics works in an industry that's quite susceptible to the concept of modularity—the origins of which go back to complex industries such as computing. Across such industries, the products—or artifacts—that companies produce have both a structure and a function. The design process describes how the artifact has to be constructed to obtain its structure and function. In complex industries, such as hydraulic engineering, this design process can easily become highly complicated. It is for this reason that companies in these industries often resort to the use of design structure matrices (DSM) or similar representations that map out the relationship between the tasks required to design a particular artifact. The more complex a product, the more it benefits from such representations, which highlight the need for coordination and the related constraints. Importantly, however, the use of such DSMs, or similar representations, can in turn foster the emergence of mental maps capturing the design process—maps that employees eventually share and that help them coordinate with each other.

The computer game producer Valve operates in an industry that gave rise to many of the original ideas behind modularity theory. Ultimately, computer games are software code, and so it makes sense that code-related modularity reduces some of the coordination costs that employees face across teams within the company. Within teams, on the other hand, frequent coordination is required—which is why Valve employees are heavily collocated.

And, finally, Wikipedia serves as a case in point. While the system architecture is set up to allow maximum contributor participation, the modular architecture of independent article pages also reduces coordination costs across subcommunities working on different topics of the encyclopedia.

Slack as a Means to Allow for Frictionless Autonomous Rewards Distribution

If setting up modular task architectures is a means to reduce coordination costs for employees working in quasi-decentralized structures, ***building in*** slack, more specifically ***human resource slack***, is the grease that ***helps*** *company* engines ***run without frictions when granting*** employees ***autonomy*** to select from a menu of ***rewards***.

More than 60 years ago, organizations masterminds Richard Cyert and Jim March introduced the then radical idea of slack as a pool of excess resources that helps firms adjust to unexpected fluctuations. In essence, they proposed that holding more resources—whether cash, machinery, or whatever—than needed to sustain daily operations could be a good thing for companies to do, notably in order to have a buffer in times of turmoil. Going straight against modern teachings in finance and economics, which all so often focus far too naïvely on short-term corporate efficiency, the concept of slack created uproar at first. Today, more than seven decades later, we have ample empirical evidence that ***slack can indeed increase firms' long-term performance*** in many ways. To this base of knowledge, my former student Ramon Lecuona Torras and I several years back contributed a study in which we showed that holding more personnel than is needed to sustain daily operations—referred to as human resource slack—might also benefit companies under certain conditions.[3] In more detail, we argued and showed that certain types of staff, notably those holding knowledge about very specific processes within a firm that are difficult to capture in a simple manual, are so important to the firm that it may be useful to keep more of them on the payroll than needed on a sunny day. The ***logic*** being that such ***personnel cannot be easily re-recruited*** from the labor market when there is a need for their competences, and so ***keeping them in the firm at all times is ultimately cheaper***. Intuitively, such slack should be most valuable to those firms facing external pressures.

Patagonia is a fantastic example to highlight all the above. The "let my people go surfing"[4] approach puts a certain pressure on the company to organize for a steady workflow while also granting individual members of staff enormous freedom at the same time. Clearly, clients will expect to be served and catered to at all times, irrespective of whether individual employees are off work. The key to managing such constraints, so it would appear, is to operate with a certain level of human resource slack that can help act as a buffer.

Are there any indications that Patagonia would have such slack? With the disclaimer that computing such a measure from public data is notoriously difficult, the answer is: absolutely. Notably, with an estimated ratio of around 1.9 corporate employees per million US$ in sales for the year 2020, the rate of (nonretail) personnel to sales is among the highest of the established competitors in the industry. The measure is a key ingredient of capturing the human resource slack within an industry.[5]

But does it pay off for the company? Absent observable profit figures, we are unable to tell with certainty. In order for it to pay off eventually, holding such slack would have to reduce costs for the company in other places. Notably, if Patagonia could afford to attract talent similar to its competitors by offering lower salaries and keeping costs down, or if savings on recruiting and redundancy packages due to low fluctuation had a positive impact on performance.

Structured Processes in Exception Management—Voting, Lateral Authority, and Arbitration

When it comes to *managing unforeseen problems* in the workflow or conflicts among peers, *employees can easily lose enormous amounts of time* when left to self-organize. In few domains of organizing would high delegation hold similar potential for delays in decision-making and frustration among peers as in exception management. Anecdotal evidence abounds. If you think about it, that's actually quite understandable. As humans, in most parts of the world, we're accustomed to conflicts being settled by someone with authority, ideally paired with competence, viewing a given matter impartially. Our legal systems build on this principle, and our norms reflect it every so often.

It's for this reason that almost all approaches to teams-based organizing feature some elements of guidance/support when it comes to delegation in the area of exception management. They broadly fall into three categories: *(1) voting rules, (2) provision of limited authority, and (3) installation of arbitration mechanisms*.

While these approaches differ in several ways, from a practical standpoint we'd ideally distinguish their efficacy from their efficiency. Unfortunately, the comparative studies we'd need to do so aren't available as of this writing. Given this lack of data, perhaps the next best criterion for ranking them is their costliness—something we can assess at least qualitatively.

Voting procedures—guidelines on which peers have how much of a voice on which subject—are probably *cheapest to operate* for sizeable groups of peers, at least once the general design is implemented. Admittedly, the *challenge with this approach lies in presenting a case on which peers can meaningfully cast a vote*, that is, a case for which they have the information they require and the competence to assess it. Voting unfolds its comparative *advantage when involving large groups* of employees in the decision-making process; at the same time, such group sizes are often rather heterogeneous in their understanding of a given problem—which limits the scope of voting to certain types of problems. For some time, the English football club Ebbsfleet United, once acquired by MyFootballClub, operated such a voting system. It extended to many domains that were important to club life at the time. Many (micro)shareholders regularly made decisions about how joint capital was to be spent. When asked what exactly shareholders could decide on, former CEO David Davis gave the example of "the kit that the team is wearing at the moment, […] selling John Akinde, […] ticket pricing."[6] Whether Ebbsfleet United separated from MyFootballClub because the shareholder decision-making did not work effectively or efficiently is a question that remains for others. To this day, the club is an example of an attempt to democratize decision-making on a large scale using voting procedures.

Arbitration approaches, by contrast, seem **extremely costly**. By its very nature, the arbitration process is one in which the key person, the arbitrator, holds no rights. The ultimate decision-making, once again, redounds to the conflicting parties. The great **advantage of arbitration lies in its sheer unlimited applicability** to interpersonal problems. Buurtzorg, the Dutch nursing company, successfully relies on arbitration processes. Importantly, as in other walks of life, notably negotiations between employers and employees, their arbitrators are externals to a conflict—experienced nurses or healthcare experts, but not involved in a regional chapter of the organization. Therefore, they "are not responsible for team results, […] have no targets to reach and no profit-and-loss responsibility."[7] As Buurtzorg CEO Jos de Blok elaborates, "Coaches shouldn't have too much time on their hands, or they risk getting too involved with teams, and that would hurt teams' autonomy,"[8] but there is no restriction on which kind of conflicts can be arbitrated, really. The Holacracy concept also features a role that has a function one might refer to as an arbitrator-at-large. Here, so-called facilitators are team (or, in Holacracy jargon, circle) members who take over accountabilities such as "tension" removal. Whether the role adds value or makes team work more efficient or not seems unclear from a scientific standpoint at present.

In between voting and arbitration lies the use of interim or reduced forms of authority that corporations retain or, perhaps more importantly, allow particular individuals to acquire in the process of delegating exception management. One of the best-researched concepts in this vein is the concept of—what is known today as—lateral authority, and, as with so many great concepts, its core idea dates back several decades by now.[9] The basic logic is easily summarized: among a group of peers, certain individuals develop an asymmetric influence over others. This influence, when perceived as legitimate by peers because of the superior knowledge, competence, or experience of the influencer, allows the latter to make decisions about crucial issues that are accepted by her peers. This reduced form of authority differs from traditional managerial authority in several ways. Most importantly, however, lateral authority extends to decisions on individual conflict matters only. It's not meant to reward or to sanction particular individuals.

In recent years, the concept has received renewed attention, as it has become a vital mechanism in the governance of large self-organizing collectives, such as OSSD.[10] Part of its current attraction stems from its ***seeming to marry the best of both worlds—the world of traditional and nontraditional organizations—when it comes to conflict management***.

What do I mean by that?

To that end, let us remember that in Chap. 3, we discussed the potentially detrimental effects of hierarchies on employees. Reducing the perceived lack of control among individuals and suppressing evaluation apprehension—a.k.a. the fear of being evaluated—through autonomy seemed important to unleashing energy among employees to assume managerial work.

By introducing (lateral) authority through the back door, so one might fear, these achievements of moving toward a flatter structure might easily be put at risk again. Put differently: employees may again feel set back and fear a superior, this time an asymmetric influencer.

If that were so, however, why would large OSSD collectives work so well? Why would Wikipedia not lose all its contributors in the long run? Here, so-called administrators settle conflicts between Wikipedians on a regular basis.

A few years back my former student Helge Klapper and I published a study that sought to answer these questions. Essentially, what we could show by studying over 1.1 million users on more than 640,000 article–talk-page pairs from 2002 to 2014 is that Wikipedians embrace the authority of their administrators and do not feel set back by it at all. This is, so we argue, because Wikipedia administrators, vetted through a process that selects only those with competence to settle disputes, are perceived as legitimate decision-makers by their peers, the more so the younger the peers are, the fiercer the conflict, and the more competent the administrator.[11]

The Important Takeaways

For a flat structure to stand a chance of beating a traditional hierarchy in terms of efficiency, awareness of the increased coordination effort in teams-based structures is inevitable. In ***defining the work playfield and providing the guardrails***, management can make a major contribution to the success of moving to a flat structure by reducing such coordination costs and enhancing performance. An ***intelligent modular design*** helping employees engage in the cocreation of products and services, a ***smart HR policy going beyond hiring*** to facilitate autonomy in achieving custom-tailored compensation, and ***support schemes to*** prevent deadlocks and accelerate the process of ***decentralized exception management***—through voting schemes, the engendering of lateral authorities, or structured arbitration approaches—will make all the difference.

But how exactly? How does the flat structure, even if it meets all the above criteria, eventually beat the hierarchy? With regard to which performance variable? And is there any large-scale evidence?

These are the questions that will guide us through Chap. 7, the penultimate chapter before we synthesize everything into the guide toward successful decentralization.

Notes

1. Baldwin and Clark, *Design Rules*, 6.
2. Ibid., 63.
3. Lecuona Torras and Reitzig, "Knowledge Worth Having in 'Excess.'"
4. Chouinard, *Let My People Go Surfing*.
5. Lecuona and Reitzig, "Knowledge Worth Having in 'Excess,'" 961.
6. "Ebbsfleet/MyFootballClub—'Inside Out' BBC TV."
7. Laloux, *Reinventing Organizations*, 69.
8. Ibid., 70.
9. Follett et al. (1941/2003) originally introduced the concept of horizontal authority. According to her, (asymmetric) "sideways" influences, as Simon would later put it (Simon, *Administrative Behavior*), are prone to emerge within organizations.
10. See Dahlander and O'Mahony, S., Progressing to the Center." They coined the term *lateral authority*, building on Follett's work.
11. Klapper and Reitzig, "On the Effects of Authority on Peer Motivation."

Bibliography

Baldwin, C., and K. Clark. *Design Rules: The Power of Modularity.* Boston: MIT Press, 2000.

Chouinard, Yvon. *Let My People Go Surfing: The Education of a Reluctant Businessman—Including 10 More Years of Business Unusual.* New York: Penguin Books, 2016.

Dahlander, L., and S. O'Mahony. "Progressing to the Center: Coordinating Project Work." *Organization Science* 22, no. 4 (2011): 961–79.

"Ebbsfleet/MyFootballClub—'Inside Out' BBC TV." *myfctuber*, January 8, 2009. https://www.youtube.com/watch?v=tBz1YMWftBQ (accessed August 1, 2021).

Follett, M.P., H.C. Metcalf and L. Urwick. *Dynamic Administration: The Collected Papers of Mary Parker Follett.* New York: Routledge, 1941/2003.

Klapper, H., and M. Reitzig. "On the Effects of Authority on Peer Motivation: Learning from Wikipedia." *Strategic Management Journal* 39, no. 8 (2018): 2178–203.

Laloux, F. *Reinventing Organizations: A Guide to Creating Organizations Inspired by the Next Stage of Human Consciousness.* Brussels, Belgium: Nelson Parker, 2014.

Lecuona Torras, R., and M. Reitzig. "Knowledge Worth Having in 'Excess': The Value of Tacit and Firm-Specific Human Resource Slack." *Strategic Management Journal* 35, no. 7 (2014): 954–73.

Simon, H. A. *Administrative Behavior: A Study of Decision-Making Processes in Administrative Organization.* Oxford: Macmillan, 1947.

Part III

When, Why, and How Flat Structures Can Beat Traditional Hierarchies

7

When Can Flat Structures Beat More Centralized Structures?

Throughout this book, we've been concerned with making flat structures work as well as possible, the idea being that unless they're truly effective, there's no need to even discuss their comparative advantages over traditional hierarchies.

Toward that end, we began by acknowledging the simple but important fact that avoiding (or removing) middle layers in a classical corporate hierarchy creates extra managerial work for all other members of an organization (Chap. 1). We concluded that such work could not be borne by the remaining leaders alone, but that delegation to the workforce would be critical (Chap. 2). Such delegation, we argued, would require extra effort on the part of co-workers—effort they might happily exert in exchange for the novel autonomy they'd receive and be energized by (Chap. 3)—particularly the conscientious and proactive individuals (Chap. 4) we should try to recruit if they're also capable and willing to work on a team. To ensure that their energy would be well spent and not go to waste, management could and should design structures that facilitate the efficient self-coordination within and among the co-working teams that would inevitably form (Chaps. 5 and 6).

Looking at the above, **we've come a long way**. In fact, it seems **fair to say** that **we now should**, at least theoretically, **be able to design flat structures and staff them** as best as possible.

The critical questions that now remain are: *When do we want to use them? For which purposes can they ever be superior?*

Asking these seemingly naïve questions appears critical for two reasons.

First, because by now, flat structures are often propagated as silver bullets even to those corporate problems they're not suited to help with. Put bluntly: if you believe that de-facto decentralization is your best approach to resolve global quality standardization issues in an international conglomerate, you may be on the wrong track. Just to give an example.

Second, because even those popular management writings that praise flat structures for what they can indeed potentially be superior at—***enhancing corporate creativity, increasing speed to market, and reducing personnel turnover***—seldom reflect on ***why and when*** this can be the case. However, unless we do so and understand these boundary conditions, all our efforts toward designing the flat structure so far are to no avail.

A Yardstick for Comparing the Effectiveness of Flat and More Centralized Structures

So let's step back for a moment and reflect on the flat structures we've discussed in this book so far. What we observed was that our ***case companies differ*** substantially with regard to where they delegate managerial work along the 4+1 dimensions of organizing. That being said, what they all ***have in common is that more decisions are being made by co-workers*** within them than would be made in traditionally hierarchically organized competitors. So, in flat structures, decision-making happens less at the apex, and more at the bottom of the corporate structure.

To ask the question ***where a flat structure can ever be better*** than a more hierarchical one is thus ***equivalent to asking*** the question[1] ***where can the company ever benefit from more decentralized decision-making?***

To answer this question, let's now ***move carefully so that we don't jump the gun*** and arrive at trivia.

More specifically, let's recall the different stages that each decision-making process entails, and compress them—for the purpose of this chapter—into three critical steps.

Step 1: Gathering information
Step 2: Analyzing information
Step 3: Taking action

Notably, doing so now allows us to articulate when quasi-***decentralized structures***—at least those that have been designed and staffed well—should stand a chance to *beat more centralized structures;* namely, **when the advantages in (1) information gathering, (2) information analysis, and (3) taking action** cumulatively ***beat*** those of a traditional **command hierarchy**. If you will, these criteria jointly provide a yardstick we can use to compare the usefulness of flat and more centralized structures for the remainder of this chapter.

The Flat Advantage—When to Delegate Why, Where, and How Much

To understand where the flat structure can beat a steeper hierarchy, we would thus like to apply our novel yardstick to the different domains of organizing in which managers can delegate to their employees. By now, I trust that bucketing design decisions into the 4+1 boxes of (1) task division, (2) task allocation, (3) rewards distribution, (4) information exchange, and (5) exception management has become second nature to you. To determine, for example, whether decentral task division does better than central task division, we'd compare the two structures for their potential to gather information, analyze it, and facilitate related action with regard to mapping corporate goals to work packages.

But *what does "better" mean* here, really?

Is gathering more information always better than collecting less? Is a consensual analysis of such information more desirable than a controversial one? Is the resulting action supposed to be uniform across the corporation, or not?

And, to make matters more complex, how would these considerations differ across the 4+1 dimensions of organizing? Could it be that decisions pertaining to exception management benefit from decentral action, whereas those relating to task division do not?

In other words: How should we apply our yardstick to determine what's better for the company exactly? Do we hold it upwards or downwards? When should we do what?

The answer to these questions, so it would appear, depends on the desired outcome and corporate constraints. In Chap. 8, we'll revisit outcomes and boundary conditions that clearly put flat structures at a disadvantage. For the remainder of this chapter, we'll focus on goals that can potentially be attained better by flat structures.

Finding Innovative Solutions to Business Problems

Few topics have received as much attention in the modern management literature as the one on corporate creativity. No single topic has probably been associated as often with the need to break down traditional structures and move to flat setups. As a result, it appears far easier to get lost in the myriad of related ideas and propositions than to boil the debate down to its core considerations. It's the latter challenge we should tackle, however, in order to get a grip on the problem of deciding where and how we should decentralize to achieve maximum leverage.

Creativity, so scholars would agree, requires the *recombination of diverse pieces of information that need to be gathered*, or aggregated, *first*. So, a creative idea for a new product might benefit from bringing together many thoughts that reside in the heads of very different people within the organization, and then puzzling them together in a new way.

Information gathering (Step 1 of the decision-making process), so research has shown, should thus *benefit from high degrees of interconnectedness between individuals* within an organization. Structures that show such a high degree of interconnectedness are also referred to as *high-density information networks* in which many employees exchange information directly.[2] Intuitively, a quasi-decentralized organization, operating such a high-density information network in which all individuals are connected to one another, should be at an advantage when the goal is to foster corporate creativity. Hierarchies are simply not meant to show high density of informational ties that employees maintain with one another. In fact, hierarchies are supposed to show the lowest degree of interconnectivity between members of an organization that's required to still ensure that information from the boss reaches each employee through the cascade of middle managers.[3] Thus, not surprisingly, there's plenty of *empirical evidence suggesting that* higher-connectivity structures—such as *autonomous teams*[4]—*beat hierarchies when it comes to producing creative ideas.*[5] The *problem* is: *there's equally solid evidence that this isn't the case.*[6] So how come?

It's because *recombining information*—a particular form of analyzing such information (Step 2 of the decision-making process)—*does not only benefit from high levels of connectedness* between members of an organization. First, for a variety of reasons, the *willingness of individuals to exchange information may decrease the more people participate in a decision-making process*; either because they feel they have no new information to add or because they feel their information will no longer make a difference to the outcome of the debate given all that's been said before.[7] Second, because even if information does get exchanged without obstacles, a process of ***mental convergence can lead to a uniformity in the interpretation of information*** that eventually hampers its novel recombination and creativity.[8]

So, whether a flat structure can beat a centralized one in terms of fostering creativity really depends on managing the ***trade-off between gathering*** as much ***information*** as possible and maintaining diversity in perspectives when ***assessing it***.

Taking these findings seriously, it would appear, has ***important consequences*** for how companies may want to set scope or boundary conditions ***for delegating along the 4+1 dimensions of organizing***.

Let's begin with the ***information-exchange dimension***. Against the backdrop of fostering corporate creativity, it may be ***useful to allow every employee to talk to everybody else*** within the company and share their information if they wish (just think of the ATOS solution at the time). However, ***having a corporate-wide discussion to recombine these insights may be less useful*** than having several ones that take place across different teams within the organization on the same overarching topic. So, ***allowing teams to search for new information wherever they want***, to talk to everyone they wish to, ***but to restrict their debate on recombining knowledge to the team level may foster creativity the most***. Such a process should lead to an extended set of ideas for solutions—one of which may plausibly outcompete any single solution that would have emerged from the alternative corporate-wide discussion. Research on team size in brainstorming would appear to support the importance of suppressing cognitive uniformity in the interpretation of information. A large group of individually brainstorming employees produces more and better ideation outputs than a few large teams.

To the extent that such team debates are supposed to transcend the pure ideation phase and translate into tangible ***innovative*** results (Step 3 of the decision-making process)—whether prototypes or small campaigns—top management will need to ponder further how they want to ***delegate decision-making along other dimensions***. Both to motivate (see Chap. 3) and to enable (see Chap. 4) teams, employees will need to be granted authority to break a given problem down into work packages (decentral ***task division***), and team members will need autonomy to decide among themselves who will bear responsibility for which piece of the project (decentral ***task allocation***). In the same vein, such teams will benefit from extended authority to rule on their own conflicts (***exception management***). Naturally, depending on the scope of the teams' output, their ***decision rights shall be capped*** accordingly. Devising a prototype or a small campaign requires them to have some access to the resources needed to ***provide proof of concept for rolling out a new product or service***. However, teams don't need and shouldn't have the authority to engage in decisions that speak to scaling at the corporate level. The latter remains a decision for top management, who can now pick and choose from a canon of candidate solutions. Atlassian's ShipIT days mirror the above approach nicely. Oticon's turnaround approach was based on the same principle.

Only in the rare instances where the need for consensus in finding a corporate-wide solution puts a strong constraint on the search for a solution to a given problem should management consider departing from the teams-based approach and decentralize along all 4+1 dimensions so as to involve all members of the company from the outset. Such cases may involve instances in which the company seeks to find its own new identity and is deeply concerned about bringing everyone on from the beginning. As a case in point, consider the Danish toymaker LEGO. The producer of the iconic plastic bricks has undergone a turbulent history in which the company—after decades of success and expansion—faced serious trouble. In 2003 Lego reported a US$ 300 million loss, attributed in part to ineffective innovativeness. So when Jorgen Vig Knudstorp took over as CEO, part of his restructuring was devoted to allowing and enabling everyone to participate in devising the new vision and trajectory for the company, triggering a somewhat wider corporate debate than usual.[9]

Increasing Speed to Market

Having discussed which flat structure—in terms of direction and scope of delegation—has the potential to beat a hierarchy with regard to fostering corporate creativity enormously simplifies the debate on how flat structures can help corporations to reduce time to market.

Here, ***three scenarios*** appear paramount.

In the ***first***, a company's speed of reacting to market developments is hampered by the time it takes for information to travel from the top to the bottom of the corporation. The move toward a flatter structure merely serves to speed up this transmission.

In the ***second***, a company's speed of reacting to market developments is directly dependent on its release of new products or services.[10] This scenario, particularly relevant to many corporations in high-tech sectors, ***directly maps onto what we discussed in the prior section***. The recommendations thus also apply accordingly. Decentral teams-based task division, allocation, information exchange, and exception management within the scope of using resources required to build and test prototypes appears recommendable. So ideation is decentral. All decisions pertaining to scaling—or to large-scale execution—should remain central. Depending on how important the discovery of novel products or services is to the company, teams should be given more time than the typical 15 to 20 percent of "bootlegging" of their working hours, or the chance to participate in the occasional hackathon.

In the ***third*** scenario, steps 1 and 2 (information gathering and assessment) equally benefit from high delegation as before. However, ***taking action*** (Step 3 of the decision-making process) ***neither requires scaling nor benefits from superior management intervention*** in any other form. As an example, think of a global sales organization within an international conglomerate in which local teams need to make decisions on how to convince their respective customers of the benefits of a given corporate product. While these teams may have no power to change the product specifications per se, they may also not need superior advice on how to design the sales and aftersales process within their regions. In fact, not only may they have all the information they need and be best positioned to assess it given cultural and legal particularities of the territory where they operate, they also won't require levels of resources that justify delaying the decision-making process by playing it back to higher authorities. Thus, ***in these instances, quasi-decentralization along all 4+1 dimensions of organizing seems ideal.*** Notably, given their budget autonomy, these teams may also be best positioned to determine corporate bonus splits among themselves, so decentral decision-making pertaining to rewards distribution is actually feasible.[11]

So, the key difference between the last two scenarios above really lies in the assessment of whether taking action on an idea—that is, executing it corporate-wide (Stage 3 of the decision-making process)—can efficiently be decentralized or not. It's this kind of thinking that also helps explain the different patterns of decentralization between companies like Atlassian or Gore, on the one hand, and Valve, on the other. Whereas Atlassian and Gore grant restricted autonomy in the division of labor, Valve has informally decentralized both task division and allocation. The same holds for the integration of effort.

Attracting and Retaining Talent

Finally, flat structures appear to have the potential to outcompete hierarchies in terms of attracting and retaining personnel.[12]

When it comes to finding and binding staff, the ***mechanisms are predominantly motivational*** and don't require us to compare the quality of decision-making in decentralized versus centralized structures.

Instead, the basic logic can quite simply be put as follows: ***happy employees*** are less likely to leave the company than unhappy ones, leading to less personnel turnover. Employee happiness goes up when people ***feel that they fit with their environment***,[13] and that they ***fit with their job***[14]—including its remuneration. ***Word of mouth*** on such happiness spreads just as much as employer reviews on platforms such as Glassdoor.com, attracting more like-minded candidates to the company.

That quasi-decentralization can increase an employee's attachment to her environment, her direct peers, and the corporation more broadly is an insight we've already discussed, in Chap. 3. Per our summary in Table 3.1, ***decentralizing information exchange*** alone can already help create a ***sense of employee attachment*** to the organization.

Naturally, this sense of attachment can be increased through other measures. ***Self-determination*** in picking from a rewards menu—as in the case of Patagonia—can help foster attachment and simply ***increase the attraction of the job*** to (potential) employees. Dean Carter, Chief Human Resource Officer at Patagonia, is acutely aware of the need to design an overall compensation package that includes more than mere cash incentives. Some of these other incentives may be specific to the people Patagonia seeks to attract and retain.[15] Some of the incentives may well apply across other companies too. As Dean notes, for example, "There is no benefit more powerful than integrated onsite childcare."[16] The measures seem to pay off. According to Carter, the company receives around 9000 applications for every 17 internship positions they advertise.[17] Rose Macario, CEO of Patagonia until recently, estimated the number to be even higher, putting it at around 9000 for each position the company advertises.[18]

Finally, allowing for ***increased motivation through self-actualization and perceived control as a consequence of decentral task division and task allocation*** (see Table 3.1) may also ramp up employee happiness, reduce personnel turnover, and help with the recruiting of new staff.

Importantly, all these decentralization approaches would appear to exert independent effects. So, the "cheapest" way to attract and retain talent may be to decentralize information exchange. After that, companies have the choice of decentralizing rewards distribution as well, and/or task allocation.

What to Take Away

Setting up and staffing a flat organization is one thing (Chaps. 2, 3, 4 and 5); putting it to the right use is another. As we discussed in this chapter, quasi-*decentralized structures* stand a chance to **outperform traditional hierarchies** particularly in those instances where the nature of the **problem** the organization is faced with **benefits from delegating information gathering, information assessment, and potentially also from delegating related action**. Examples of such problems are the enhancement of **corporate creativity, increasing the speed to market, and finding and binding human talent**. So, matching a structure with the right purpose seems essential.

To match the flat structure to the goal of fostering **creativity** in scalable businesses, **delegate decision rights** within the scope of **prototyping** along the dimensions of **task division, task allocation, information exchange**, and **potentially exception management**.

To match the flat structure to the aim of increasing **speed** at the local level, **delegate along all the 4+1 dimensions** of organizing.

To match the flat structure to the goal of **attracting and retaining talent**, delegate rights with regard to **information exchange**, and ponder delegating rights with regard to **task division and task allocation**.

It's this overarching idea of creating a matching structure that has run, by design, like a central thread throughout this book so far. I promised to you in the introduction that this book was meant to help avoid creating

mismatches between the flat structure and the staff you took or take on board (and we devoted Chaps. 3 and 4 to that challenge),
mismatches between the flat structure and how you treat your staff within it (to which we devoted Chaps. 5 and 6), and
mismatches between corporate goal and flat structure (which is debated in this chapter).

So, we've almost reached our goal of becoming smart designers of flat structures, and we could now try to synthesize all our prior deliberations into a **comprehensive but actionable** recipe or **manual** that you can work with in your daily business life. And we'll shortly do so. In fact, **Chap.** 9 is just a stone's throw away now.

Before that, though, I'd like to draw your attention to three other issues that I believe are worth your time.

The first issue relates to the question of when you may not want to consider moving to a flatter structure at all. Chapter 8 will introduce you to a few related thoughts, some of which may be quite surprising to you.

The second is a brief but somewhat more subtle reflection on the ***empirical evidence*** we have on the question of ***when flat structures can beat traditional hierarchies*** in terms of performance. Here, the ***key insight of relevance to executives*** appears to be that in order to succeed with an informally decentralized structure, you really want to ***concentrate on avoiding as many of the above mismatches as you can***. In other words, just picking the right structure for the right purpose will not be sufficient if, at the same time, you fail in recruiting or treating staff correctly—vice versa. Jointly, the many studies we analyzed for this book clearly speak to that effect.[19] There are indications that when decentralized structures do better in terms of fostering creativity, the companies disproportionally often employ staff that are likely proactive;[20] that decentralization is related to lower turnover for those employees who may have a high sense of attachment to their organization;[21] and that flat structures thrive in terms of creativity[22] or speed[23] when employees bring critical cognitive skills. Similarly, when management provides autonomy support to staff, decentralized structures report increases in creativity[24] and speed.[25] Slack can help make a flat structure excel,[26] and modularity may come in handy at times, too.[27] Naturally, these observations have to be treated with care, but they send a strong signal: ***if you want to move to a flatter structure and be successful, you have to work on all aspects—matching the structure to the envisaged goal, designing it so as to treat your staff well, recruiting the right staff for it. These activities are no substitutes!***

The third and final point relates to a question that managers find notoriously important yet difficult to answer in the context of moving to flatter structures, and that's related to the topics we discussed in this chapter. Notably, this is the question of how leadership, during the process of transitioning to a flat(ter) structure, can assess whether they're on the right track. Providing a scientifically sound and elaborate answer on which ***key performance indicators (KPIs)*** to establish for a high-delegation environment is worth a book project in its own right. And yet, so I dare to predict, the ***practical takeaways*** would still very much compare to the brief answer I attempt below; namely, that for lack of comprehensive empirical knowledge, a focus on ***custom-tailoring*** unambiguous key metrics ***to the corporate context*** would appear advisable, focusing on the specific goal achievement of the flat reorganization. More specifically, that moves toward flatter structures with the aim of increasing corporate creativity should be evaluated against the change in the number of reported inventions, potentially patents (and applications thereof) depending on the industry, products in the corporate R&D pipeline, and new services being offered—and that such figures would only become meaningful after months, if not a couple of years, into the transition; that moves toward flatter structures intended to create speedier market responses could be assessed by looking at changes in the time taken for discrete corporate decisions, and for product and service development—ranging from assessment periods of weeks to years depending on context; and that decentralization efforts to attract and retain key personnel should manifest themselves in standard HR data over the course of a few months. Any other, shorter-term indicators, however, would have to be conceptualized and validated within the specific industrial and organizational context in which a company would operate.

Notes

1. At least for as long as organizations are designed and run by human actors, this appears fair to say. As my colleague and friend Phanish Puranam has been arguing, only artificial intelligence may enable flat structures to be massively centralized.
2. Kearns, Suri, and Montfort, "An Experimental Study of the Coloring Problem on Human Subject Networks"; McCubbins, Paturi, and Weller, "Connected Coordination Network Structure and Group Coordination."
3. Puranam, *The Microstructure of Organizations.*
4. Patanakul, Chen, and Lynn, "Autonomous Teams and New Product Development."
5. Damanpour, "Organizational Innovation."
6. Cardinal, "Technological Innovation in the Pharmaceutical Industry."
7. Klapper, Maciejovsky, Puranam, and Reitzig, "Influence Structures and Information Aggregation in Groups."
8. Shore, Bernstein, and Lazer, "Facts and Figuring."
9. See "Innovation Almost Bankrupted LEGO—Until It Rebuilt with a Better Blueprint."
10. Not surprisingly, most of the related empirical studies on speed and decentralization stem from the domain of new product development (NPD) where speed to market is often considered to be one dimension of NPD success. For a recent overview, see Chen, Damanpour, and Reilly, "Understanding Antecedents of New Product Development Speed: A Meta-analysis." Disentangling decentralization in decision-making from other aspects of enabling autonomous teamwork (e.g., empowerment) is not always easy in

this literature. There is a body of research suggesting that high delegation in decision-making increases speed in NPD, however.
11. Note that such an approach not only increases the speed in the domain of responsibility of one individual team. When n teams parallelly pursue such an approach, the overall speed to market of the organization is increased in n places.
12. I am careful when making this claim, as meta-analytical studies conducted in the mid-2000s found no meaningful relationship between job turnover and autonomy. See Humphrey, Nahrgang, and Morgeson, "Integrating Motivational, Social and Contextual Work Design Features." That being said, I believe it seems fair to see that since then, more evidence has emerged that would support the notion that workplace autonomy not only leads to people feeling less exhausted and stress (ibid.) but also reduces personnel turnover (intentions). Also, the type of autonomy awarded in informally decentralized structures may exhibit even stronger effects than the (limited) workplace autonomy hitherto studied in the field of human resources.
13. See Edwards, "Person-Environment Fit in Organizations."
14. See Kristof-Brown, Zimmerman, and Johnson, "Consequences of Individuals' Fit at Work."
15. Patagonia's measures to realize Yvon Chouinard's dream of letting his people go surfing may not apply to other companies equally. Interestingly, however, such an approach can kick off developments that will ultimately result in policies that are relevant to other companies also. As Dean Carter states: "At first it was to help people who like the snow have more time to get to the mountains. We ultimately moved to a schedule where we close every other Friday, giving everyone in the corporate office 26 three-day weekends a year." Rock, "The NLI Interview."
16. "All Access Interview: Dean Carter | Talent Connect 2019 (CC)."
17. "Beyond Stoked: The power of living values wildly | Dean Carter | Talent Connect 2019 (CC)."
18. Debevoise, "Why Patagonia Gets 9,000 Applications for an Opportunity to Join Their Team."
19. When inspecting the empirical evidence, as in earlier chapters, some caution appears in order. This is because much of the research base we can draw on today has not been put together for the purposes of our analysis. Studies investigating the efficacy and efficiency gains of decentralization at the company or project level may not always provide information on their employees' personalities or cognitive abilities at the level of detail we'd like to have for the purpose of this book. The same disclaimer applies for information on autonomy support or other design measures these companies may have put into place. So our inference is often indirect and afflicted with some noise.
20. This assumption seems fair considering the context in which these studies were conducted—notably, the R&D and NPD context. See Patanakul, Chen,

and Lynn, "Autonomous Teams and New Product Development"; Aalbers, Dolfsma, and Leenders, "Vertical and Horizontal Cross-Ties."
21. Interestingly, related effects were reported in studies conducted in the public sector and in the healthcare services sector. See Kim, "The Contrary Effects of Intrinsic and Extrinsic Motivations on Burnout and Turnover Intention in the Public Sector"; Dysvik and Kuvaas, "Perceived Job Autonomy and Turnover Intention"; Iverson, "An Event History Analysis of Employee Turnover."
22. Pattnaik and Sahoo, "Employee Engagement, Creativity and Task Performance"; Aalbers, Dolfsma, and Leenders, "Vertical and Horizontal Cross-Ties"; Daugherty, Chen, and Ferrin, "Organizational Structure and Logistics Service Innovation."
23. Atuahene-Gima, "The Effects of Centrifugal and Centripetal Forces on Product Development Speed and Quality."
24. Aalbers, Dolfsma, and Leenders, "Vertical and Horizontal Cross-Ties."
25. Chen, Damanpour, and Reilly, "Understanding Antecedents of New Product Development Speed."
26. Damanpour, "Organizational Innovation."
27. Jansen, Van Den Bosch, and Volberda, "Exploratory Innovation, Exploitative Innovation, and Performance."

Bibliography

Aalbers, R., W. Dolfsma, and R. Leenders. "Vertical and Horizontal Cross-Ties: Benefits of Cross-Hierarchy and Cross-Unit Ties for Innovative Projects." *Journal of Product Innovation Management* 33, no. 2 (2016): 141–53.

"All Access Interview: Dean Carter | Talent Connect 2019 (CC)." *LinkedIn Talent Solutions,* October 2, 2019. https://www.youtube.com/watch?v=1-h9oXAqrJ0 (accessed April 15, 2021).

Atuahene-Gima, K. "The Effects of Centrifugal and Centripetal Forces on Product Development Speed and Quality: How Does Problem Solving Matter?" *Academy of Management Journal* 46, no. 3 (2003): 359–73.

"Beyond Stoked: The power of living values wildly | Dean Carter | Talent Connect 2019 (CC)." *LinkedIn Talent Solutions,* October 2, 2019. https://www.youtube.com/watch?v=9hqAr8fkZ_0 (accessed April 15, 2021).

Cardinal, L. B. "Technological Innovation in the Pharmaceutical Industry: The Use of Organizational Control in Managing Research and Development." *Organization Science* 12, no. 1 (2001): 19–36.

Chen, J., F. Damanpour, and R. R. Reilly. "Understanding Antecedents of New Product Development Speed: A Meta-analysis." *Journal of Operations Management* 28, no. 1 (2010): 17–33.

Damanpour, F. "Organizational Innovation: A Meta-analysis of Effects of Determinants and Moderators." *Academy of Management Journal* 34, no. 3 (1991): 555–90.

Daugherty, P. J., H. Chen, and B. G. Ferrin. "Organizational Structure and Logistics Service Innovation." *The International Journal of Logistics Management* 22, no. 1 (2011): 36–51.

Debevoise, Nell Derick. "Why Patagonia Gets 9000 Applications for an Opportunity to Join Their Team." *Forbes,* February 25, 2020. https://www.forbes.com/sites/nelldebevoise/2020/02/25/why-patagonia-gets-9000-applications-for-every-open-role/?sh=27b9751e612f (accessed August 2, 2021).

Dysvik, A., and B. Kuvaas. "Perceived Job Autonomy and Turnover Intention: The Moderating Role of Perceived Supervisor Support." *European Journal of Work and Organizational Psychology* 22, no. 5 (2013): 563–73.

Edwards, J. R. "Person-Environment Fit in Organizations: An Assessment of Theoretical Progress." *Academy of Management Annals* 2 (2008): 167–230.

Humphrey, S. E., J. D. Nahrgang, and F. P. Morgeson. "Integrating Motivational, Social and Contextual Work Design Features: A Meta-analytic Summary and Theoretical Extension of the Work Design Literature." *Journal of Applied Psychology* 92, no. 5 (2007): 1332–56.

"Innovation Almost Bankrupted LEGO—Until It Rebuilt with a Better Blueprint." *Knowledge at Wharton,* July 18, 2012. https://knowledge.wharton.upenn.edu/article/innovation-almost-bankrupted-lego-until-it-rebuilt-with-a-better-blueprint/ (accessed April 26, 2021).

Iverson, R. D. "An Event History Analysis of Employee Turnover: The Case of Hospital Employees in Australia." *Human Resource Management Review* 9, no. 4 (1999): 397–418.

Jansen, J. J., F. A. Van Den Bosch, and H. W. Volberda. "Exploratory Innovation, Exploitative Innovation, and Performance: Effects of Organizational Antecedents and Environmental Moderators." *Management Science* 52, no. 11 (2006): 1661–74.

Kearns, M., S. Suri, and N. Montfort. "An Experimental Study of the Coloring Problem on Human Subject Networks." *Science* 313, no. 5788 (2006): 824–27.

Kim, J. "The Contrary Effects of Intrinsic and Extrinsic Motivations on Burnout and Turnover Intention in the Public Sector." *International Journal of Manpower* 39, no. 3 (2018): 486–500.

Klapper, H., B. Maciejovsky, P. Puranam, and M. Reitzig. "Influence Structures and Information Aggregation in Groups." Working paper, Erasmus University Rotterdam / UC Riverside / INSEAD / University of Vienna, 2015.

Kristof-Brown, A., R. Zimmerman, and E. Johnson. "Consequences of Individuals' Fit at Work: A Meta-analysis of Person-Job, Person-Organization, Person-Group, Person-Supervisor Fit." *Personnel Psychology* 58, no. 2 (2005): 281–342.

McCubbins, M. D., R. Paturi, and N. Weller. "Connected Coordination Network Structure and Group Coordination." *American Politics Research* 37, no. 5 (2009): 899–920.

Patanakul, P., J. Chen, and G. S. Lynn. "Autonomous Teams and New Product Development." *Journal of Product Innovation Management* 29, no. 5 (2012): 734–50.

Pattnaik, S. C., and R. Sahoo. "Employee Engagement, Creativity and Task Performance: Role of Perceived Workplace Autonomy." *South Asian Journal of Business Studies* 10, no. 2 (2021): 227–41.

Puranam, P. *The Microstructure of Organizations.* Oxford: Oxford University Press, 2018.

Rock, David. "The NLI Interview: Patagonia's Dean Carter on How to Treat Employees Like People." *Forbes,* January 9, 2020, https://www.forbes.com/sites/davidrock/2020/01/09/the-nli-interview-patagonias-dean-carter-on-how-to-treat-employees-like-people/?sh=2272cdc5188c (accessed April 15, 2021).

Shore, J., E. Bernstein, and D. Lazer. "Facts and Figuring: An Experimental Investigation of Network Structure and Performance in Information and Solution Spaces." Organization Science 26, no. 5 (2015): 1432–46.

8

Where Does a Flat Structure Reach its Limits?

At this point, we know for which purpose (Chap. 7) we may consider implementing flat structures, how they should look like (Chaps. 5 and 6), and who should enjoy working within them and why (Chaps. 2, 3, and 4).

So, why this chapter still?

Clearly, we no longer need to devote too many pages to spelling out that you might not want to move toward a high-delegation environment in those situations where the three mismatches **between corporate goal and the flat structure, between the flat structure and the staff you took or take on board**, and **between the flat structure and how you treat your staff within it** prevail. So if your primary goal, say, is to deliver homogenous product and service quality across all geographies in which your international conglomerate operates, a quasi-decentralized structure may be of little help. Such a structure may also be incommensurate with the ambition to foster and nurture uniform personnel; it may not work when you lack sufficiently proactive yet humble employees; and it may not work if your remaining management still thinks in traditional categories. All this should be obvious by now.

More interestingly, perhaps, is the idea that even if none of the above mismatches prevail, there may be instances where you still want to think critically about implementing a flat structure.

In this chapter I'd briefly like to raise a couple of related ideas. They go back to the same fundamental insight that flat organizing faces one potential killer constraint: information costs.

Information Costs in (Quasi-)Decentralized and Centralized Structures

So far, throughout the book we've highlighted the *value of involving many employees* in the process of exchanging information. As we discussed, this may bring about many advantages: employees feel attached to environments where transparency in information flows exists (Chap. 3); sufficient decentral information exchange appears crucial to allow for high delegation in domains such as task division and task allocation (Chap. 5); and it plays a critical role in achieving the goals of creativity and speed (Chap. 7).

We must also face *another part of the truth*, however. And that is that *involving many employees in the information-exchange process comes at a cost*. These costs can take various forms, and we'll discuss them in more detail below. One of the most important and ubiquitous costs is the *time spent on exchanging information*, though. To illustrate my point, let's take a look at Fig. 8.1.

The figure shows two stylized information-exchange patterns. On the left side, nine employees bilaterally exchange information with one another. The dotted lines represent the talks taking place among them, and the number amounts to 36. If we had 10 employees, this number would increase to 45, for 11 employees it would be 55, and for 20 employees it would be 190.[1] This is

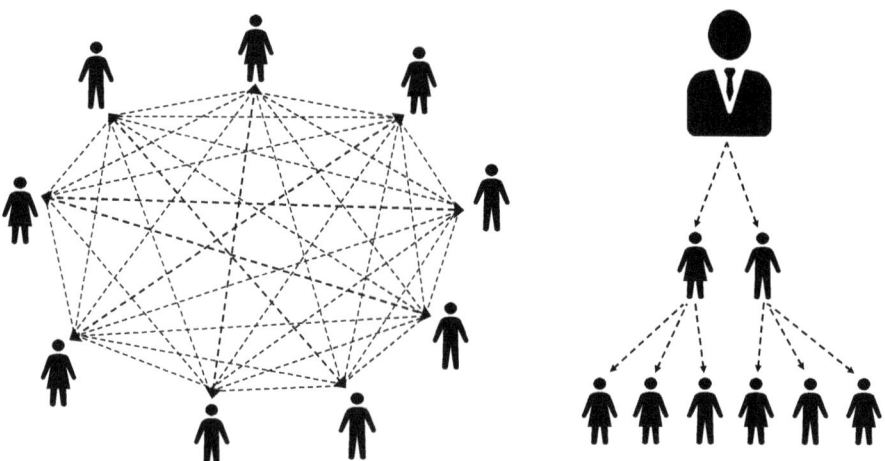

Fig. 8.1 Information exchange among nine members of an organization. Left: Decentralized setup. Right: Hierarchical setup. (© Markus Reitzig 2021)

the minimum number of exchanges it takes to aggregate all the information spread across the individuals so that each person of the group knows it all.

Now, to make matters worse, let's assume these employees need to talk more than once to update one another on novel information they've received from outside their circle. Or, very realistically, that employees, for practical reasons, must structure the sequence of their exchange so that it takes more than the theoretical minimum number of exchanges for each person to be aware of everything the others know. Then the ***increase in information costs*** may not be ***quadratic***, but potentially even higher.[2]

In contrast to that, compare a hierarchical information exchange as depicted on the right side. Here, the nine members of the organization are fully connected to one another, but only eight unidirectional information exchanges from top to bottom take place in the chosen example of a two-layered hierarchy. Clearly, in terms of basing a decision on the best possible information, such a hierarchy can only compete with the decentralized setup when the highest person in the hierarchy has all the information required to decide well, and when the transmission downwards works well. So when important information resides in the heads of the workforce, the hierarchy won't be able to extract it and thus will create a poorer informational basis for decision-making. That said, the hierarchy also clearly beats the decentralized structure in terms of avoiding costs in terms of time spent on information exchange.[3]

Considering these ***opportunity costs of time*** appears ***particularly important*** in the context of ***gathering information*** (Step 1 of the decision-making process) and ***analyzing it*** (Step 2 of the decision-making process), but less so when it comes to taking action (Step 3 of the decision-making process).

How these costs affect the choice of moving to a flatter structure or not is a question managers must ponder for themselves within their own organizations. What ***trade-offs*** they may want to consider in the process is what ***science can help with***. The rest of this chapter is devoted to elucidating these trade-offs.

First, in the following three sections, we'll revisit the trade-offs in the context of comparing traditional hierarchies and (informally) decentralized structures.

Second, in the last section of this chapter, I'd like to inspire you to think of additional structural options of organizing that lie beyond the black-and-white spectrum of complete centralization and decentralization.

Information-Gathering Performance as a Function of Group Size

In the previous chapter, when discussing how flat structures might help enhance corporate creativity and increase speed to market, we stressed the importance of recombining diverse pieces of information that needed to be gathered first. In this process of information gathering (Stage 1 of the decision-making process), so we said, peers should have the liberty to reach out to whomever whenever. As far as the gains from this process are concerned, this statement remains largely unchanged.[4] The more employees can exchange with one another, the better the aggregate information basis should become on which to found a decision. With an eye to the potential costs of such an exchange, additional considerations may come into play, however. In fact, it would appear that there's a ***trade-off between information completeness and information costs***. Critically, this trade-off is driven by two factors: (1) the ***returns to more information*** exchange ***decrease with group size***, and (2) the (opportunity) ***costs of time*** for such a decentral exchange ***rise quadratically*** or worse, as we discussed above.

So why does the marginal value of gathering information decrease the more people talk to one another?

There appear to be two mechanisms through which the benefits from additional information aggregation diminish with further interaction.

The first mechanism is rooted in the nature of interaction between individuals and has become well known in the literature as the "hidden profile" problem. This problem, originally reported by professors Stasser and Titus,[5] describes the (undesired) observation that groups of ***individuals***, when exchanging information with one another, tend to focus on what all parties know, as opposed to uncovering what each party could exclusively contribute in terms of insights. This ***focus on common knowledge*** obviously poses an impediment to maximizing the collective information base, and it gets worse with every talk between two members of an organization—because chances increase that they will hit on some common knowledge the more information that has been exchanged before.

The second mechanism is rooted in the nature of the distribution of information across members within a group, notably preselected groups such as companies in which employees were recruited for the specialist knowledge they hold. When ***specific levels of expertise*** are required, talking to ***select individuals may provide as much, if not more, information*** as contacting the entire rest of the company. No other stream of research has as neatly identified and quantified this effect than the one on "crowd wisdom." The term denotes the phenomenon that, for many settings, simply pooling (i.e., averaging) different assessments by various individuals may lead to a better answer to a given estimation problem than either asking select individuals or having the group interact in ineffective ways and come up with a joint answer. In fact, in wisdom-of-crowd (WOC) settings, individuals are not supposed to talk to one another at all; instead, their individual assessments get averaged, and the individually different mistakes they make cancel each other out. As an example, imagine you'd like to know how far Berlin is from Tokyo. Barring access to an encyclopedia, you'd have to go with answers from the people you're able to ask. The WOC paradigm states that, on average, the best answer will come from taking the averages of all the answers you can collect from as many different people as possible. Interestingly, however, recent research has shown that WOC assessments of select groups can be as good as those of large crowds. As my colleagues Albert Mannes, Jack Skoll, and Richard Larrick demonstrated, aggregating the information of only five experts could, under certain conditions, provide answers to a problem that would be no worse than those from a larger crowd of people.[6] Now, clearly these results have to be put into perspective: for most of the questions we cared about in Chap. 7, we'd need more information from different individuals than their mere assessment of a particular question to which there's a correct answer that can be determined at some point. However, what the results also clearly indicate is that there are diminishing returns to involving more people in the information exchange when the objectively needed information resides in the heads of only a few.

How much the above considerations matter in daily business is easily illustrated by examples from practice.

The hidden profile problem is known to affect the efficacy and efficiency of group discussions in firms. To that end, managers working for sophisticated HR departments at companies such as the Cheesecake Factory have put procedures in place by which they force themselves to assess job applications individually prior to entering structured discussion procedures that are designed to reveal as much information about a candidate as possible. Relatedly, Microsoft employees, during group discussions, toss around a rubber chicken called Ralph to pass on the speaker's baton. The idea here is to ensure that every voice gets heard, ideally in randomized order, to unearth as much information as is hidden in the heads of the different people.[7]

Similarly, companies have learned the hard way that relying on large crowds may not always improve performance. There may simply be settings where experts have more privileged knowledge. Consider the story of the Schaumburg

Flyers. In 2006 the US-based baseball team had decided to leave player setup to "diehard supporters, opposing fans, and Web surfers who know nothing about the team."[8] The eventual insight was that "some things are best left to the experts. Before this promotion started, the team was 31–17, leading their division. Since then? 15–33, and in last place."[9]

In seeking to optimize the trade-off between gathering as much useful information as possible and avoiding an explosion of the related costs, managers therefore need to ask themselves how attractive a quasi-decentralized structure appears to them eventually. To the extent that a flat structure still seems desirable, providing some guidance to employees on how to gather information most efficiently may help. Encouraging them to check on what their counterpart knows and to concentrate on centering talks on information that's exclusive to either party would be one piece of advice. Prespecifying expert groups to consult with on certain topics may be another to avoid an explosion of information exchanges that are of potentially little value.

Information Assessment Performance as a Function of Group Size

Gathering information was one issue; assessing it was another. Already in Chap. 7 we discussed the potential downside of involving too many individuals in the process of recombining different bits and pieces of information to arrive at creative solutions that might help the company speed up their market reactions eventually. The *censoring effect* in large groups—leading other peers to shut up when they feel they have nothing really new to contribute, *mental convergence, groupthink*[10]—these are effects that *create the diminishing returns to information assessment as group sizes grow*.

At the same time, the *nonlinear increase in information-exchange costs also prevails* in this part of the decision-making process—at least if team members are heavily discussing with one another, which appears to be an essential prerequisite for team performance, though. Probably the most illustrative data in this context stem from experiments that Professor Pentland and his team at MIT ran over many years. In these experiments, the researchers equipped real-world groups of employees across companies with so-called sociometric badges that would allow the scientists to record communication patterns between team members who wore the badges.[11] What Sandy Pentland and his co-workers found in analyzing the data from some of their studies was that "three simple patterns accounted for approximately 50 percent of the variation in performance across groups and tasks." High performance was associated with "many very short contributions rather than a few long ones," "dense interactions: a continuous, overlapping cycling between making contributions and very short (less than one second) responsive comments," and "diversity of ideas: everyone within a group contributing ideas and reactions, with similar levels of turn taking among the participants."[12]

In other words, for teams to succeed in recombining different pieces of knowledge, heavy information decentralization and repeated information exchange seem key—in turn stressing ***the need to limit these group sizes*** for two reasons: ***to avoid groupthink*** and to ***keep the costs of information exchange under control***. Where the exact optimum lies is a question managers will have to answer for their own companies. Most team structures that Pentland and his team examined had a group size of fewer than 30 people, however.

Taking Action on Information

Whereas conformity[13] and groupthink may decrease the creative potential of a group relative to its size, they may be the factors that can, at the same time, aid a group in speeding up action. To that end, picture two different scenarios: one in which top management has solicited suggestions from a number of different, smaller-sized autonomous teams of employees to propose novel business model ideas for implementation. And another, in which management themselves have undertaken a corporate-wide campaign to discuss the same challenge with all employees together. Taking eventual action will be faster in the second instance, as no further selection and debate about diverging ideas needs to take place, and since less communication to personnel will be required. Also, perceived shared idea ownership by the large group may facilitate solution implementation. Whether these advantages justify the expenses that come with increasing group size in the first two stages of the decision-making process is a managerial question to be posed and answered by each individual company, however.

Additional Thoughts—Rethinking Hierarchical Structures

Critically, so the above shows, there are limits to each structure—centralized or (quasi-)decentralized. We implicitly discussed the (motivational and informational) upside potential of flat structures in Chaps. 1, 2, 3, 4, 5, 6, and 7 of this book, but we've also had to admit that they may have their very own (informational) size constraints in this eighth chapter. Toward the end of the latter, I'd therefore like to introduce you to some very recent thinking of my colleagues Helge Klapper, Boris Maciejovsky, Phanish Puranam, and myself, in which **we try to theoretically nuance the debate** between the two canonical structures—traditional hierarchies, on the one hand, and (informally) decentralized structures, on the other.

Our point of departure is the following: if **traditional hierarchical structures do badly** in terms of allowing employees to share and debate information in ways that can lead to more creative output, faster speed to market, and higher employee attachment, but if **(quasi)-decentralized structures have clear limits when it comes to scaling**, is there perhaps a different type of structure that can help bring together the **best of both worlds**?

And by this different structure, we're not talking about a mix of traditionally hierarchical and flat elements of organizing under one corporate roof. Such compartmentalization can sometimes be observed across different areas within the same company and may well make sense, but it doesn't really represent what we'd call a coherent novel structure. No. Rather, we're thinking of a more homogenous structure that applies to the entire company.

This novel structure can probably best be described as an atypical, or partly symmetrical (learning), hierarchy. This is because the overall form—scientists would say topography—in which employees are connected to one another in this structure very much resembles a traditional hierarchy. But the nature of the connections differs substantially from a traditional command structure.

To that end, let's recall once more from Chap. 1 how we conceive of a traditional corporate command hierarchy. Generally speaking, these hierarchies simply denote systems (1) in which two members in adjacent layers of the hierarchy have asymmetric influence over one another—whatever the nature of that influence may be, and (2) in which these relations between such people are transitive so that if A has, say, more power than B, and B has more power than C, then A also has more power than C.

Let's now focus on **two different types of influence**.[14] The first one we'd call **normative influence**. By that we denote the influence that one person has to shape the behavior of another, irrespective of formal decision rights. The second one we'll refer to as **informational influence**, the possibility that one person has to shape the knowledge base and the beliefs of another person.

While there may be different sources for such influence that one person may have over another in a corporate hierarchy, **power and status** would appear to be the two overarching categories—where power denotes control over resources and status refers to the prestige or esteem that a person enjoys from her peers.[15] Arguably, the most important forms in which power

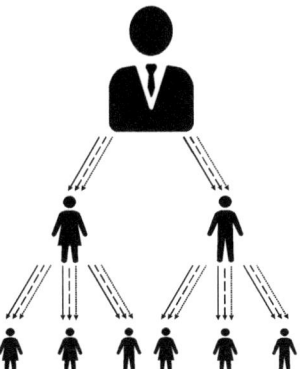

Fig. 8.2 Three sources of unidirectional influence in a traditional command hierarchy: Decision rights (straight line); status (long dashes); control over information (dotted line). (© Markus Reitzig 2021)

manifests itself in a corporate hierarchy are control over resource-related decisions, as captured by a person's ***decision-making rights***, and ***control over information***, a critical predecessor to making decisions. The latter source of power would allow its holder to influence the beliefs of others. The first source of power would allow her to influence the behavior of others, just as her status would.

Traditional hierarchies tend to bundle all three sources of influence—decision-making rights, status, and control over information. CEOs have the right to decide what they would like to decide, they often hold the highest status in the company, and they often possess superior information. As such, they can influence the behavior and beliefs of their subordinates. Senior-level managers can still influence mid-level managers drawing on the same three sources; mid-level managers, lower-level managers; and lower-level managers, the remaining employees (Fig. 8.2).

But there's ***no need to bundle all these sources of influence***, and in fact it may not be realistic to believe that it depicts reality well at all times. As Helge, Boris, Phanish, and I could show in a simulation experiment, interesting things happen in terms of the organization's ability to aggregate information and prepare the basis for good decisions (Stage 1 of the decision-making process) when we allow for bidirectional informations flows (Fig. 8.3). Here, we assume that employees also pass novel information on to lower-level management, lower-level management passes information on to mid-level management, and so forth. While the number of

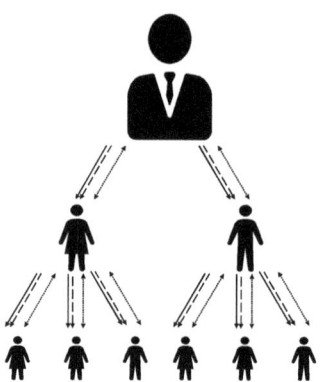

Fig. 8.3 Unidirectional normative influence and bidirectional information flow in a learning hierarchy. (© Markus Reitzig 2021)

information exchanges is far smaller than in a fully decentralized network structure, the actual amount of information the CEO may eventually base her decision on will allow her to take a potentially better decision than a flat structure with the same amount of information exchanges. This ***atypical learning hierarchy, in which the CEO integrates knowledge from all ranks of the organization but retains his normative influence and decision-making rights, can therefore outcompete a teams-based structure*** in terms of information gathering under certain conditions. At least in theory. Because of course the major challenge with such a structure in practice is to motivate folks to part with their private information, which is what they might not do if they feel they may be evaluated negatively by the person they reveal the information to (see Chap. 3).

One potential way to overcome the latter challenge is to do away with the part of the asymmetric normative influence that comes with the concentration of decision rights at the top and to delegate more decision-making power to the employees. The only traditional hierarchical element remaining would be that of normative influence arising from status (Fig. 8.4). As a result, subordinates would receive more degrees of freedom for taking action themselves, while still referring to their—former—superior for guidance of their behavior.

Interestingly, in this case, the nontraditional hierarchy does even better than before in terms of aggregating knowledge in our simulations for yet another reason. This is because the decentrally operating teams will benefit from pooling their information instead of merely exchanging it with their superiors, and crowd wisdom at the basic level of the pyramid will enhance

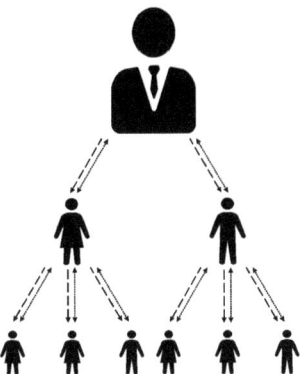

Fig. 8.4 Decentralized decision rights, unidirectional normative influence from status, and bidirectional information flow in a learning hierarchy. (© Markus Reitzig 2021)

the overall decision-making quality. Naturally, as we discussed in Chap. 5, the additional challenge in practice here would be to ensure, once again, that employees receive support to make decisions autonomously.

The above results should be treated with care. First, they're rooted in computer simulations only, and we have no empirical evidence as of yet for how much they matter in practice. I mentioned several potential pitfalls above. Second, for our simulations we assume that the gathering or aggregation of information (Step 1 of the decision-making process) is the key step in arriving at good decisions. This may be true in certain instances but perhaps less so in others, where the recombination and fast association with ideas of other people is key (Step 2 of the decision-making process). That said, there may be instances where the nontraditional or atypical or partly symmetrical learning hierarchy beats quasi-decentralized structures, notably when gathering information from many folks is key, when the organization is large, and when recombination doesn't require too much team interaction.

What to Take Away

Flat structures can be great when used for the right purpose, when staffed with the right people, and when these people are treated appropriately. But even then, sheer ***size considerations may impose limits*** on (informal) decentralization. These limits arise from the nonlinear increase in the ***time needed to gather and assess information*** in teams compared with other organizational structures, and from the decreasing benefits of doing so when team size grows.

What exactly determines the optimal size of a team in a teams-based structure is a decision that managers will have to make when considering the **trade-offs between decision quality and information-exchange costs**.

Occasionally will flat structures therefore take a shape where **teams are being formed at the employee level** that comprise **up to 20 odd members**, but not more. Often, the teams may actually be significantly smaller, however. These teams will then report to managers again, but to **managers** who have a **significantly wider span of control** than they'd have in a traditional hierarchy, as they **delegate a fair amount of decision rights** to their employees. Depending on the corporate size, these managers themselves will then again report to higher-level managers, but they will perhaps be only 1 of 10 or 12 direct reports to their superiors, not 1 of 4 or 5 as in a traditional setup. Because of the teams-based bottom, and because of an increased span of control across all layers in the residual hierarchy that sits atop the teams-based bottom layer, the overall structure eventually becomes flatter than the original hierarchy (Chap. 1). Most successful delayering projects in large corporations eventually yield such structures.

Only ***sometimes*** will ***flat structures*** in organizations with significantly more than 100 employees take the shape of an authoritative structure, in which **one top-level manager** together with his team supervise several teams simultaneously **without** drawing on **middle managers** at all. This only works when teams are given high degrees of autonomy along most of the 4+1 dimensions of organizing (Chaps. 2 and 3), when they need very little support (Chap. 5), and when they don't need to coordinate much with one another (Chap. 6). Valve is a case in point. This structure is often observed within smaller companies that seek to retain some of their startup culture, however. Just remember Reaktor.

Rarely will top management in companies of any size supervise one large crowd of employees. This is because the advantages of creating pockets of interaction—teams—are diluted when the group becomes too large.

One ***interesting alternative*** to the above structures, which build on teams and fewer layers of management, may be one that connects individuals like a traditional hierarchy but allows for and fosters bottom-up information flow in addition to the top-down flow, and that potentially delegates decision rights to employees, too. This ***atypical hierarchy*** may be especially attractive for corporations of a significant size. In fact, making a move from a centralized structure to such a learning hierarchy may, in many instances, represent not a halfhearted attempt at moving to a flatter structure but a bold move of trying to bring together the best of both worlds.

Notes

1. The number of these bilateral or dyadic exchanges is n(n - 1)/2, where n stands for the number of individuals. Each person can talk to everyone else but herself (n - 1), and talks are bidirectional, so we divide by two.
2. Note that there is also a quadratic increase in potential conflicts, which is not to be conflated with regular communication costs. The flat structure thus also faces constraints when it comes to exception management.
3. In essence, the latter argument would also hold for other topologies of network structures, such as hub-and-spoke networks.
4. I discuss the exception in the specific instance of crowd wisdom further below.
5. Stasser and Titus, "Pooling of Unshared Information in Group Decision-Making."
6. See Mannes, Soll, and Larrick, "The Wisdom of Select Crowds." In fact, for some settings, the authors report not only diminishing marginal returns to group size but even an inflection point in the data, meaning that fewer experts can provide a better assessment than a group that includes further less-qualified judges. These results were obtained under very specific boundary conditions, though. Thus, overall, it seems fair to say that "the more the merrier" prevails when it comes to information aggregation.
7. See Dunne, "3 Simple Principles to Run Productive Meetings."
8. See Gaither, "Baseball Gone Batty."
9. See *Fast Company* Staff, "Crowded Wisdom."
10. Gigone and Hastie, "The Impact of Information on Small Group Choice."
11. See, for example, Kim, McFee, Olguin, Waber, and Pentland, "Sociometric Badges."
12. Pentland, *Social Physics,* Chap. 5, page 2.
13. Asch, "Studies of Independence and Conformity."
14. This distinction is widely accepted in the psychological literature and goes back to a classic study by Morton Deutsch and Harold Gerard ("A Study of Normative and Informational Social Influences upon Individual Judgment").
15. Bunderson and Reagans, "Power, Status, and Learning in Organizations."

Bibliography

Asch, S. E. "Studies of Independence and Conformity: I. A Minority of One against a Unanimous Majority." *Psychological Monographs: General and Applied* 70, no. 9 (1956): 1–70.

Bunderson, J. S., and R. E. Reagans. "Power, Status, and Learning in Organizations." *Organization Science* 22, no. 5: (2010): 1182–94.

Fast Company Staff. "Crowded Wisdom." *Fast Company,* September 7, 2006. https://www.fastcompany.com/676461/crowded-wisdom (accessed May 18, 2021).

Deutsch, Morton, and Harold Gerard. "A Study of Normative and Informational Social Influences upon Individual Judgment." *Journal of Abnormal and Social Psychology* 51, no. 3 (1955): 629–36.

Dunne, C. "3 Simple Principles to Run Productive Meetings." *Tameday*, September 2, 2019. https://www.tameday.com/run-productive-meetings/ (accessed May 18, 2021).

Gaither, C. "Baseball Gone Batty." *LA Times*, September 1, 2006. https://www.latimes.com/archives/la-xpm-2006-sep-01-fi-baseball1-story.html (accessed May 18, 2021).

Gigone, D., and R. Hastie. "The Impact of Information on Small Group Choice." *Journal of Personality and Social Psychology* 72, no. 1 (1997): 132–40.

Kim, T., E. McFee, D. O. Olguin, B. Waber, and A. S. Pentland. "Sociometric Badges: Using Sensor Technology to Capture New Forms of Collaboration." *Journal of Organizational Behavior* 33, no. 3 (2012): 412–27.

Mannes, A. E., J. B. Soll, and R. P. Larrick. "The Wisdom of Select Crowds." *Journal of Personality and Social Psychology* 107, no. 2 (2014): 276–99.

Pentland, A. *Social Physics: How Good Ideas Spread–The Lessons from a New Science*. New York: Penguin, 2014.

Stasser, G. and W. Titus. "Pooling of Unshared Information in Group Decision-Making—Biased Information Sampling during Discussion." *Journal of Personality and Social Psychology* 48, no. 6 (1985): 1467–78.

9

The Guide(s) to Successful Decentralizing

Some of you may have jumped to this point directly upon finishing Chap. 2. That's fine—you chose the reading fast track that I offered you from the outset. To appreciate the guides in this chapter, you may have to make a leap of faith at times, as I'm building on insights developed in Chaps. 3, 4, 5, 6, 7 and 8 that may not always be intuitive at first sight. That said, you should still be able to apply the frameworks without problems. And if you have specific questions, you can always thumb through back—I provide pointers to the relevant sections.

Those of you who've followed me all the way to this point will see our thinking from Chaps. 1, 2, 3, 4, 5, 6, 7, and 8 condensed in a recipe-like fashion, molded into actionable guides for designing flat structures. Although embracing all necessary detail from earlier chapters, the key structure of these guides will reflect our understanding that flat structures can serve only certain corporate goals well, that specific organizational design decisions will have to map onto these goals, and that these designs can be maximally effective only when being staffed with critical numbers of employees who appreciate working in such environments. These guides also take into account that critical size constraints prevail when it comes to teams-based interactions.

Given these considerations, ***for all practical purposes*** it therefore appears useful to ***distinguish between different starting scenarios*** and the varying objectives associated with the implementation of a flat structure.

More specifically, let's discriminate between a scenario in which a ***large, traditionally managed organization seeks to delayer*** its hierarchy and a scenario in which a ***flat, teams-based startup seeks to retain its structure*** while growing. Figure 9.1 illustrates the structural transformation in the first

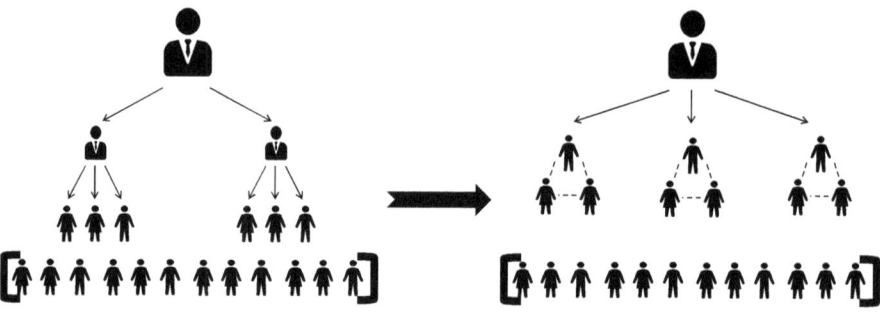

Fig. 9.1 Delayering of a traditional hierarchy to a teams-based structure. (© Markus Reitzig 2021)

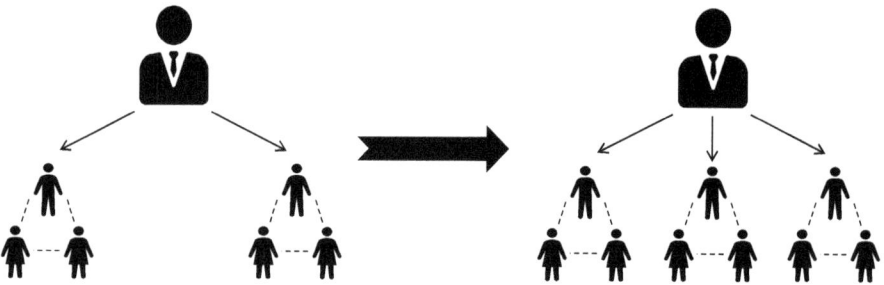

Fig. 9.2 Horizontal growth of a teams-based structure. (© Markus Reitzig 2021)

scenario. Note that (high) delegation may not necessarily trickle all the way down in the hierarchy but may instead stop at a level below which granting decision-making rights appears counterproductive.[1] Figure 9.2 depicts the design change in the second situation.

In the first scenario let's further distinguish between delayering attempts driven by different initial motivations: to make the company more creative, to make it faster, or to make it more attractive to current and future employees.

Over the following pages we'll therefore revisit four different templates that provide guidance for creating a custom-tailored flat(ter) structure depending on where your journey commences—that is, whether your company seeks to delayer or grow horizontally—and what the goal is you seek to achieve. Naturally, there'll be overlaps between the templates, and we'll highlight them when it seems efficient to do so. To familiarize ourselves with the use of the templates, and to cross-check on their actual explanatory power, we will, after their presentation, directly apply them to selected case companies described in Chap. 1. Using the information provided on T-Systems, Reaktor, Wistia, and Treehouse with the benefit of hindsight, we'll test whether the templates offered in this chapter would have predicted the outcomes of the delayering initiatives or attempts at flat growth observed across the different companies.

Delayering to Become More Creative—When You Seek Ideas to Roll Out across the Company

As we discussed in Chap. 7, a major motivation for large companies to reduce the steepness of their hierarchy is to foster an environment that nurtures the development of innovative solutions to corporate-wide business problems. Whether a flat structure seems suited in your context or not, and what to do in case it does, are questions the first decision tree is supposed to help you with (Fig. 9.3).

Delayering to Become Faster—When Speed Depends on Finding Local Solutions Fast

In Chap. 7 we also touched on one other major motive for large firms to delayer; notably, when speedier delivery of solutions would be required. Here, so we said, a flat structure could help if creativity was a means to the end of becoming faster. To the extent that a corporation's overall speed to react to market developments hinges on finding ideas that can be rolled out globally across the company, the rationale—and thus the recipe—for moving to a flat structure mirror images Fig. 9.1. However, speed may equally come from allowing for the roll-out of decentral creative solutions as we also discussed in Chap. 7. In this case, the decision-making rationale looks slightly different, and the ideal guide therefore needs a bit of adjustment (Fig. 9.4).

To cross-check the usefulness of the first two guides we developed, let's apply them to one of the case companies introduced to us in Chap. 1, T-Systems, and focus on their delayering of the global delivery unit Auto MI.[2]

To increase speed and deliver custom-tailored solutions to clients—the latter involving the need to devise novel solutions—both top management and the employees themselves had made advances to reorganize for a flatter setup prior to the actual reorganization. The alternative of pointing to just a few experts within the unit to achieve the same goals of enhancing creativity and speed didn't appear to be as feasible, as critical knowledge was distributed across the entire workforce.

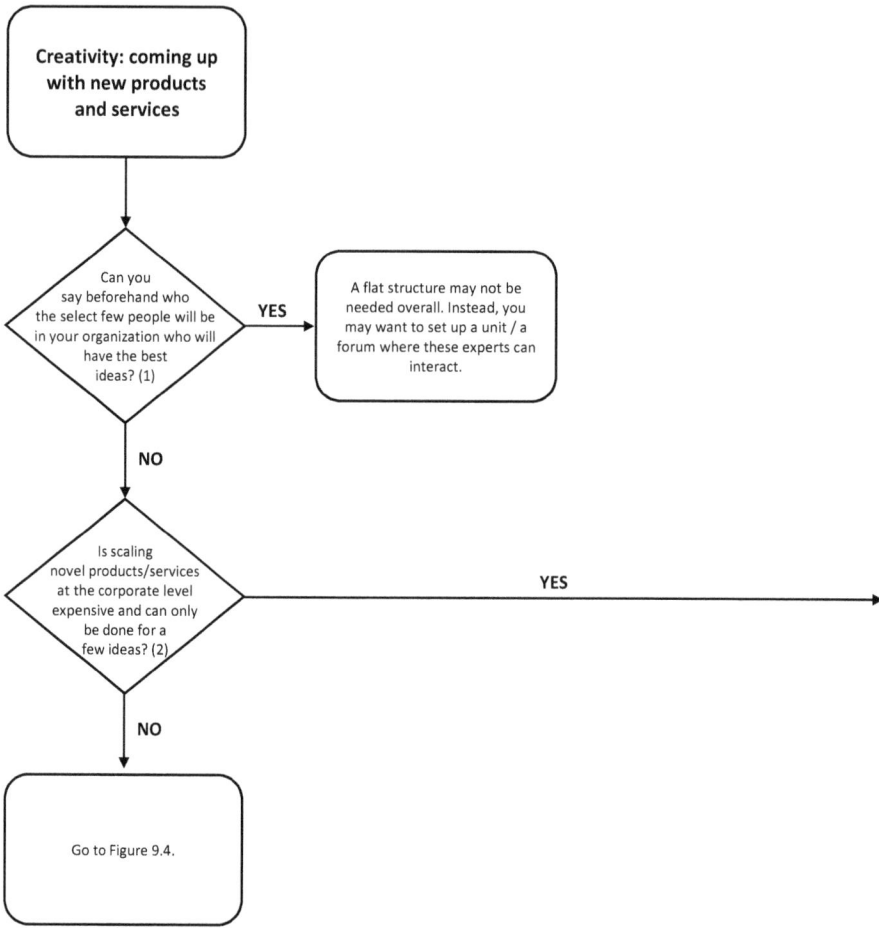

Fig. 9.3 Guide to delayering a hierarchy in order to make the company more creative. (© Markus Reitzig 2021)

Work in the unit had traditionally been structured in project-like fashion. Thus, there was reason to believe that some of the new ideas and decentral approaches developed on project teams would never have to be scaled across the entire unit, while other solutions might be of relevance to the entire company.

So when Georg Rätker took the helm of the unit in 2014, he commenced with the restructuring of the traditional hierarchy for the unit's 1000 employees and, compressing 4 layers of management between himself and the workforce into just 2 layers, with 2 different but equally suited goals in mind.

The delayering brought about the expected increase in Rätker's personal span of control—rising from four to about ten direct reports, and figures were similar for his subordinate managers. So the Vice President, who had always

> **Checklist for only executing prototype development in a decentral manner. Scaling will remain a central activity**
>
> **Design fits:**
> ☑ Determine the lowest level your hierarchy for interaction between reasonably sized and largely autonomously operating teams and bring in folks from this level and potentially from levels above, too (1). Orient yourself along the following questions:
> - ☑ Delegating task division for prototyping: how low can you go in your current hierarchy for employees to still be able to understand how to break the idea of a new product/service into work packages, and how these work packages then depend on one another (4)?
> - ☑ Allowing for self-selection: how low can you go in your hierarchy to assume employees can still reasonably effectively select themselves onto tasks that match their skills in this prototyping process (4)?
> - ☑ Allowing for decentral exception management: how low can you go to assume employees can reasonably effectively detect and resolve unforeseen problems and conflicts (4)?
>
> ☑ Provide these teams with the rights to take decisions with regard to task division, task allocation, information exchange, and exception management within the scope of their projects. Encourage them to extend information gathering to the wider corporation, but to limit information discussion to the actual team level (1).
>
> ☑ Provide guidance, support, and a playfield that facilitates their work (3).
> - ☑ Implement a sanctioning system that detects and sanctions freeriding or cherry-picking of tasks.
> - ☑ Offer autonomy support to the teams
>   - ☑ Share information teams require to do their jobs
>   - ☑ Information required to build architectural knowledge as needed
>   - ☑ Transparent task architecture
>   - ☑ Reduce your role to feedback partner
>   - ☑ Show humble leadership
> - ☑ Potentially offer structured procedures for effective and efficient conflict resolution within teams.
>
> **People fits:**
> ☑ Rely on existing and recruit new employees who rank high on personality traits that help with the high delegation (4). As far as possible, select
> - ☑ Agreeable, honest, and humble employees to foster collaboration, as well as
> - ☑ Conscientious and proactive people, the more so you rely on delegation in task division and task allocation, with a
> - ☑ High need for achievement, the more so you rely on delegation in task division and task allocation and potentially a
> - ☑ High locus of control, the more so you rely on delegation in managing conflicts.

(1) For questions pertaining to this part of the decision tree, see chapter 8 for details.
(2) For questions pertaining to this part of the decision tree, see chapter 7 for details.
(3) For questions pertaining to this part of the decision tree, see chapters 5 and 6 for details.
(4) For questions pertaining to this part of the decision tree, see chapters 3 and 4 for details.

Fig. 9.3 (continued)

operated a management style by which he would lead his employees on a long leash, began to delegate even more than he had done before—and his junior managers followed his example. Eventually, decision rights, albeit limited in scope, trickled down to the workforce, too. Rätker explained, "I think it's essential that—and I believe you have to slot that in ahead somehow—that you consider together what the goal is for the entire organization sector. That sector is then broken down into the necessary smaller parts. And together means: every one of the Directs carries the responsibility to partake in the

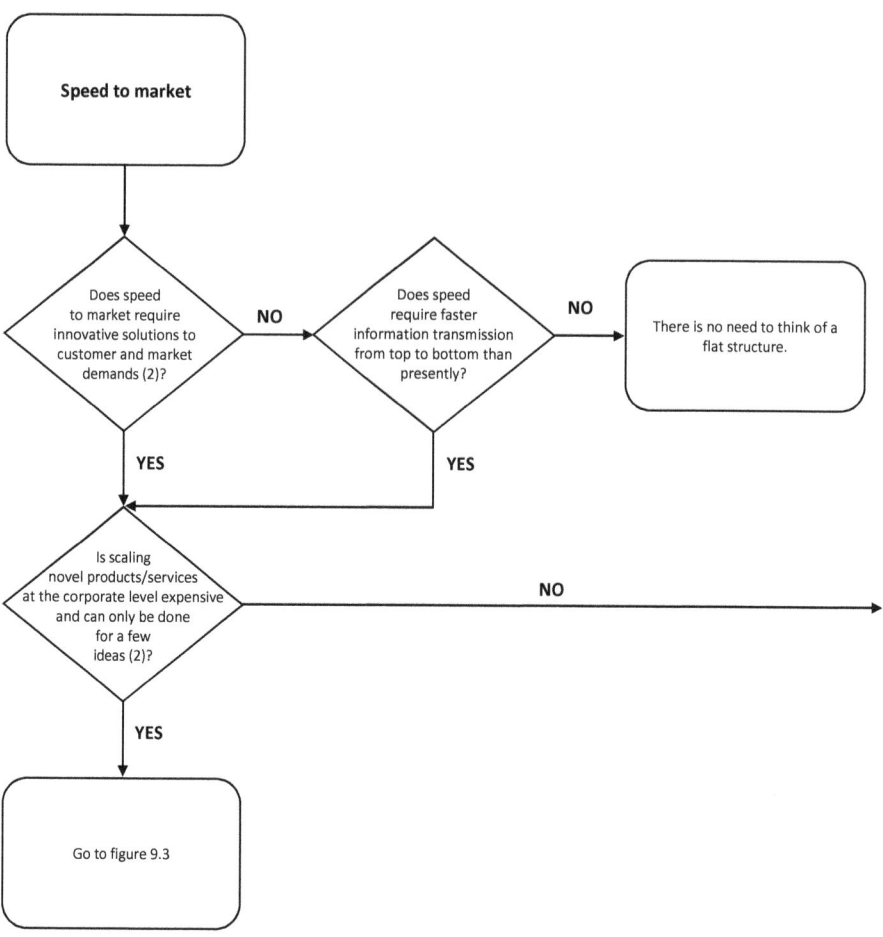

Fig. 9.4 Guide to delayering a hierarchy in order to make the company faster. (© Markus Reitzig 2021)

design process."[3] While overall project acquisition and coordination across projects remained a (senior) management responsibility, co-creation with clients now also meant that project members, particularly during the ideation phase, could make suggestions to their team leaders, who would take them seriously. But employees wouldn't be solely engaged in the process of task division; they could also express their preferences for working on particular projects, and the process of task allocation was moving further in the direction of self-selection. How to reward employees was still a formal management task, but instead of having to seek confirmation from senior leadership, middle managers and team leaders could now set individual remuneration for their subordinates directly. Information exchange happened decentrally, and corporate transparency was pushed by senior management.

Checklist for not only delegating prototyping but also executing a decentral product roll-out

Design fits:
☑ Determine the lowest level your hierarchy for such interaction between reasonably sized and largely autonomously operating teams and bring in folks from this level (1). Orient yourself along the following questions:
  ☑ Delegating task division: how low can you go in your current hierarchy for employees to still be able to understand how to break the idea of a new product/service into work packages, and how these work packages then depend on one another (4)?
  ☑ Allowing for self-selection: how low can you go to assume employees can still reasonably effectively select themselves onto tasks that match their skills (4)?
  ☑ Allowing for decentral rewards distribution: how low can you go to assume employees can reasonably effectively and efficiently determine how to split up the bonus of their joint work (4)?
  ☑ Allowing for decentral exception management: how low can you go to assume employees can reasonably effectively detect and resolve unforeseen problems and conflicts (4)?
☑ Provide these teams with the rights to take decisions with regards to task division, task allocation, rewards distribution, information exchange, and exception management within the scope of their projects. Encourage them to extend information gathering to the wider corporation, but to limit information discussion to the actual team level (1).
☑ Provide guidance, support, and a playfield that facilitates their work. (3)
  ☑ Implement a sanctioning system that detects and sanctions freeriding or cherry-picking of tasks
  ☑ Offer autonomy support to the teams
    ☑ Share information teams require to do their jobs
      ☑ Information required to build architectural knowledge as needed
      ☑ Transparent task architecture
    ☑ Reduce your role to feedback partner
    ☑ Show humble leadership
  ☑ Provide a modular structure that reduces duplication of effort across teams and reduces undesired interdependencies between teams' autonomous actions
  ☑ Potentially offer structured procedures for effective and efficient conflict resolution within teams

People fits:
☑ Rely on existing and recruit new employees who rank high on personality traits that help with the high delegation (4). As far as possible, select
  ☑ Agreeable, honest, and humble employees to foster collaboration, as well as
  ☑ Conscientious and proactive people, the more so you rely on delegation in task division, task allocation, and rewards distribution with a
  ☑ High need for achievement, the more so you rely on delegation in task division and task allocation and potentially a
  ☑ High locus of control, the more so you rely on delegation in managing conflicts.

(1) For questions pertaining to this part of the decision tree, see chapter 8 for details.
(2) For questions pertaining to this part of the decision tree, see chapter 7 for details.
(3) For questions pertaining to this part of the decision tree, see chapters 5 and 6 for details.
(4) For questions pertaining to this part of the decision tree, see chapters 3 and 4 for details.

Fig. 9.4 (continued)

The unit never installed a formal watchdog or sanctioning system that would go after freeriders or shirkers. However, Rätker recalled, "I'll just say that, if you consider the core group, and an employee did not conform at all, or behaved in a super egoistic way or something, then this got reflected or reported back to them somehow, even before our agile transformation."[4] Perhaps, so the VP reflected later, more formalization was not really that necessary in this regard, as the unit had had a fair amount of experience with project-based work before, and peers had already found ways to discipline those members who wouldn't play for the team.

Clearly, so Rätker recalls, the management style in the unit changed over time. While he himself had never followed a command-and-control orientation but had instead seen himself as a feedback partner, this behavior was also adopted by his junior management colleagues. So, overall, management did what they could to make the move to a flatter structure a success—in terms of putting a suitable design in place and defining their roles accordingly.

But naturally, to push the reorganization through, management was also critically dependent on the workforce. Here, the team around Rätker, as is so often the case, operated with very heterogenous personnel. Departing from the old wisdom that a third of the workforce embraces change, a third sits on the fence, and a third is against it, the management team worked on two fronts. First, they enabled those peers who'd welcomed the flatter structure to infect their peers with their enthusiasm. Visible measures were important in that regard: "One has to change things that are visible quickly. That starts with modifying and renovating some things, making them a bit more colorful. That you offer workshops, yes? That you set up an ideas competition somehow … but if you have three people, who are really into this, then that serves you better than having 20, 30 people and they're all … they know the necessity, but … I mean they'll really have to put in the effort after all,"[5] so the VP says. At some point, so Rätker recalls, he felt that a nucleus of a handful of people really initiated the transition on a site of several hundred employees. Second, the management team went to great lengths to not intimidate those who'd be critical. Subject matter experts who'd deliver great value to their clients were not pushed beyond reason to engage in picking up other tasks that would result from the high-delegation environment in which they operated. As Rätker put it, he was not expecting each and every one of his employees to be "painted agile."[6] That said, management was aware that the entire reorganization's success would hinge on the proactive behavior of high achievers just as much as it would depend on their ability to be team players—and these characteristics became priorities in the hiring process.

Having analyzed the reorganization through the lens of our guides Figs. 9.3 and 9.4, as we just did, it should come as no surprise that T-Systems Auto MI GDU can, a few years later, look back happily on their restructuring: not only does the company deliver solutions faster to their clients than before; the cocreation has also led to quality improvements in devising these novel solutions. Naturally, the transition had its own hiccups, too: dealing with overly career-oriented employees who would want to use the reorganization to shine, and motivating the deeply critical peers were just two issues the VP recalls as challenges.

Delayering to Retain and Attract Talent

Retaining and attracting talent, as we discussed in Chap. 7, can come about in a variety of ways. The decision tree in Fig. 9.5 distills our thinking and guides you through the different stages of delegating decision rights to make your workplace more attractive to current and future employees.

How well does our template explain what eventually happened at Treehouse?[7]

When in 2013 the company decided to remove their seven mid-layer management positions to return from a three- to a two-layered structure, the main goal was to retain employees who'd expressed severe unhappiness at their voices no longer being heard by senior management. Moving to a flatter structure for this purpose seemed potentially reasonable. Also, given the nature of Treehouse's business and the need to tailor solutions to different clients, speed and creativity mattered. As it might have seemed difficult to point to just a small group of experts who'd have the knowledge needed for that, going flat was no implausible move at all.

When Ryan Carson and Allan Johnson embarked on the restructuring, they delegated task division—to a large degree—down to the level of the employee. People could now propose to initiate projects. Decision rights for the "go" were still held centrally, but the actual tasks were largely devised by the employees themselves. Also, employees could select themselves onto projects that would suit their preferences, and a decentral information exchange within the teams was fostered.

The rather modular project architecture would have allowed for relatively independent work across teams, which would have seemed helpful with the restructuring, whereas the lack of a visible system to incentivize and sanction employees who weren't willing to carry the burden of maintaining the decentral workplace was potentially problematic when implementing a flatter structure.

Helpfully for the quasi-decentral restructuring, information transparency was emphasized throughout the company. Most importantly, it related to the task architecture: an internal website allowed people to effectively self-select.

While it seems difficult to tell exactly why some folks still felt like they'd become "lonely islands" a while after the reorganization, one possibility is that the executive team faced a dramatic increase in requests for communication by employees, inevitably leading to the impression that employees received less managerial attention than they would in a structure boasting of another layer of mid-level managers.

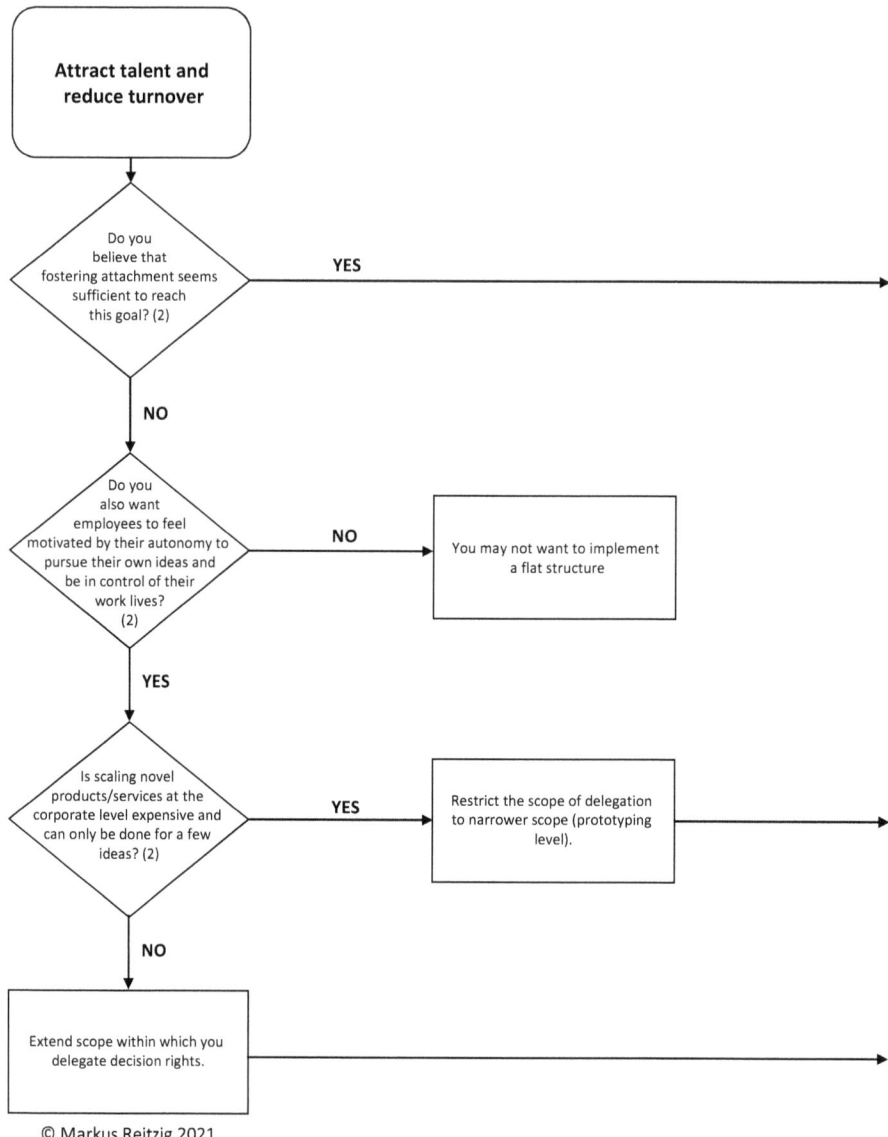

Fig. 9.5 Guide to delayering a hierarchy in order to attract and retain talent. (© Markus Reitzig 2021)

9 The Guide(s) to Successful Decentralizing   145

Checklist for fostering attachment in your organization

☑ Allow for decentral information exchange on as many issues as appear relevant to employees to foster sense of attachment. Allow for corporate-wide information gathering, seek to limit debate to focal groups (1).
☑ Potentially allow for decentral autonomous reward choice by individuals.
  ☑ Determine the lowest level of your hierarchy at which individuals will still be able to assume related accountability and appreciate the autonomy that comes with the delegation (4).
  ☑ Provide human resource slack that helps with frictionless company operations even when giving employees more autonomy to decide when and how they want to work (3).

Checklist for designing your organization toward employees feeling motivated by their autonomy to pursue their own ideas and be in control of their work lives

Design fits:
☑ In addition to the above, allow for decentral task division within scope that seems reasonable to those individuals within the hierarchy that have the cognitive skills to engage in it. Determine the lowest level of your hierarchy at which an interaction between them within largely autonomous and reasonably sized teams may still be the case (4).
  ☑ Share information required for these employees to build architectural knowledge as needed
  ☑ Provide a modular structure that reduces duplication of effort across individuals and teams and reduces undesired interdependencies between teams' autonomous actions
☑ And/or Allow for self-selection onto tasks to those individuals who have the cognitive skills. Determine the lowest level of your hierarchy at which this may still be the case (4).
  ☑ Provide information on nature of individual task (task architecture transparency) to affected individuals
☑ Provide guidance, support, and a playfield that facilitates employees' work (3).
  ☑ Implement a sanctioning system that detects and sanctions freeriding or cherry-picking of tasks
  ☑ Offer autonomy support to the teams
    ☑ Reduce your role to feedback partner
    ☑ Show humble leadership
  ☑ Potentially offer structured procedures for effective and efficient conflict resolution among individual employees

People fits:
☑ Rely on existing and recruit new employees who rank high on personality traits that help with the high delegation (4). As far as possible, select
  ☑ Agreeable, honest, and humble employees to foster collaboration, as well as
  ☑ Conscientious and proactive people, the more so you rely on delegation in task division and task allocation, with a
  ☑ High need for achievement, the more so you rely on delegation in task division and task allocation and potentially a
  ☑ High locus of control, the more so you rely on delegation in managing conflicts.

(1) For questions pertaining to this part of the decision tree, see chapter 8 for details.
(2) For questions pertaining to this part of the decision tree, see chapter 7 for details.
(3) For questions pertaining to this part of the decision tree, see chapters 5 and 6 for details.
(4) For questions pertaining to this part of the decision tree, see chapters 3 and 4 for details.

© Markus Reitzig 2021

Fig. 9.5 (continued)

Reflecting on their workforce at the time, Treehouse founders reported that there were several who really were keen on working in a flat structure—notably those who'd raised the issue with top management in the first place. But, so Carson recalls, there were others, too. Overall, there appeared to be a mix of those colleagues who had the preferences, personalities, and abilities to work in a quasi-decentralized structure and those who wanted to be managed.

Based on the above analysis of the Treehouse history through the lens of Fig. 9.5, it would appear that, back in 2013 and shortly thereafter, some parameters would have spoken in favor of the implementation of a flat structure whereas others would not have. Based on our guide, we'd likely have predicted that the flat structure might work for Treehouse, but we might also have retained some doubts about whether a more traditional hierarchy wouldn't be more appropriate in the company's context. Interestingly, this prediction that we might have made back in those days neatly maps onto what happened: Treehouse did work with the flat structure for some time, and considered it helpful up until a point, but eventually abandoned it when mismatches between the design and people's preferences became visible—which, with the benefit of hindsight, was perhaps not entirely unexpected.

Growing in a Flat Way

Finally, teams-based organizations, when seeking to grow, face a challenge when they seek to retain their flat DNA. When does it make sense for them to forgo the traditional growth path of becoming more hierarchical, and what is it they need to pay attention to? The guide in Fig. 9.6 seeks to help you maneuver the challenge in a structured way.

Reaktor and Wistia provide excellent examples to validate the usefulness of our fourth and last template. Both companies were founded as startups in the early 2000s, operated in similar industries, and grew to three-digit employee figures as of the writing of this book. However, whereas Reaktor has retained its original flat structure until today, Wistia eventually opted for a more traditional hierarchical structure. Why?

Our guide to flat growth provides some explanation for the different directions which the two companies took.

Let's take a look at Wistia first.[8] The company founders, Chris Savage and Brendan Schwartz, had created the company with the vision that employees would thrive on project ownership, being entrusted with responsibility and able to create opportunities for themselves. So, growth for the company meant not replicating existing projects but creating new ones, the interdependence across which would be limited. Flat growth thus seemed like a good option in the first place.

But somehow the design did not fit with the growth plan. Work was being chopped into smaller and smaller pieces, and this task division made it difficult for senior management to still recognize individual accountabilities and responsibilities. Most importantly, so the founders realized, mundane tasks were increasingly left over, as people wanted to be engaged in the most important projects; yet there was no sanctioning system in place to ensure that employees played as a team (or as teams). At the same time, instead of being able to focus on their new roles as feedback partners and information providers, the two founders were being dragged back into traditional top-down decision-making when their people kept coming back to them to draw on the help of the shadow hierarchy that still existed.

Notably, so it appeared, this was because several employees preferred a classical way of being managed. Although some enjoyed the autonomy that came with a quasi-decentralized structure, a significant proportion did not.[9]

The outcome, Wistia abandoning their flat structure and moving to a more traditional structure, therefore maps onto what our guide to flat growth would have predicted, too. While the horizontal growth goal seemed plausible initially, the design was not the one that worked best for Wistia, in large part because of the people working for the company. Instead, the company successfully implemented mid-level management layers and continued its growth plan in a different manner.

Reaktor, by contrast, has grown to over 500 employees without relying on mid-level-management layers to this day.[10] Because of Reaktor's business model and their delivering custom-tailored solutions to their clients, growth cannot come from mere repetition of prior work. Also, project work, as always, allows for a rather independent work across teams—factors that speak for and facilitate flat growth.

The design the company has adopted is one that shows a high level of delegation down to the actual employee level. Whereas the project architecture is still shaped centrally in the sense that project acquisition remains a management task, employee selection into projects and information exchange across projects is handled in a highly decentralized manner. Within projects, so it would appear, all 4+1 fundamental problems of organizing are approached without management intervention. To cope with the need to maintain the decentral workplace, Reaktor has introduced a model that demands that employees contribute 20 percent of their time to tasks that eventually benefit everyone, such as recruiting. Information required to operate in a high-delegation environment is being made transparent throughout the company,

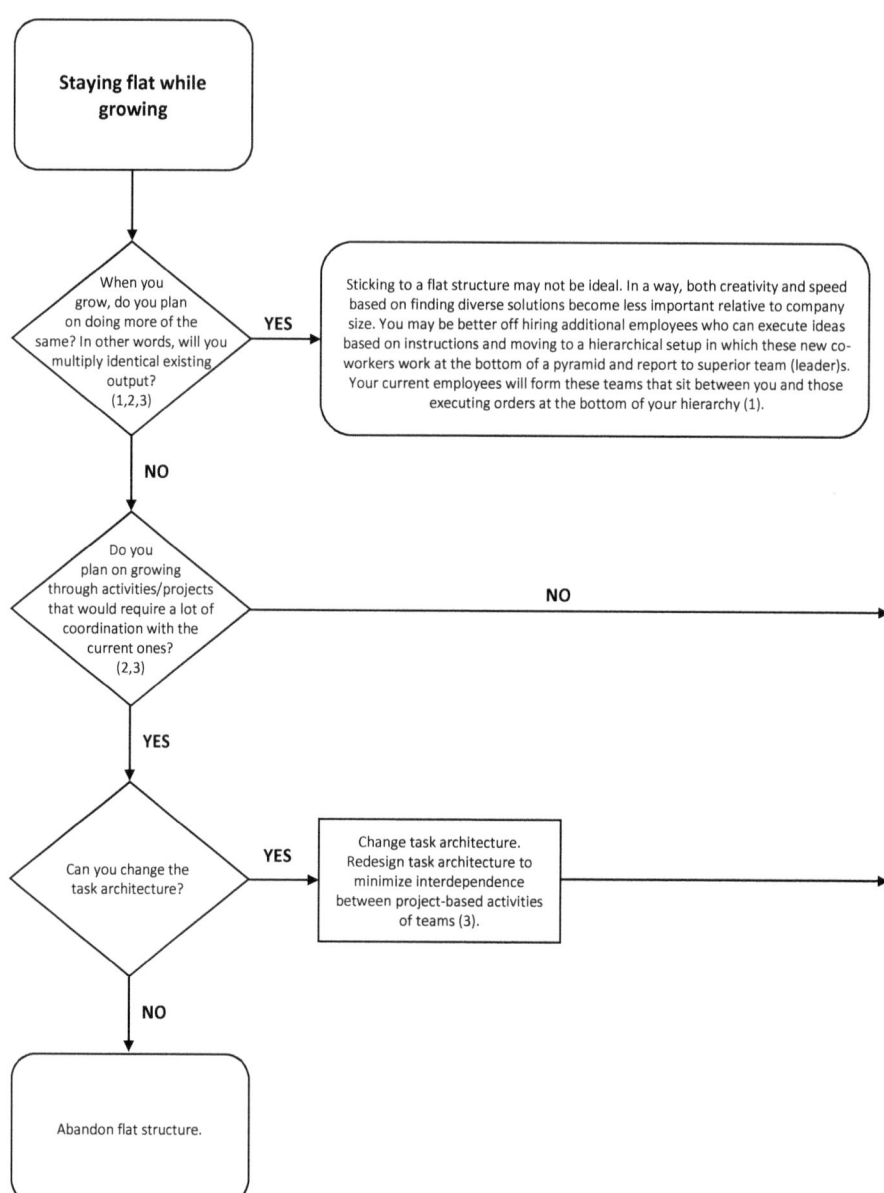

Fig. 9.6 Guide to growing a company in a flat manner. (© Markus Reitzig 2021)

Checklist for designing your organization

Design fits:
☑ Provide existing employees with the rights to take design decisions (task division, task allocation, (potentially) rewards distribution, information exchange, and exception management) within the scope of their projects. Ensure that these project teams will not grow beyond a critical size (1).
☑ Provide guidance, support, and a playfield that facilitates their work (3).
  ☑ Implement a sanctioning system that detects and sanctions freeriding or cherry-picking of tasks
  ☑ Ensure that you can spend enough time offering autonomy support to the teams
    ☑ Share information required to build architectural knowledge as needed
    ☑ Reduce your role to feedback partner
    ☑ Manage expectations as your span of control may become very wide. Direct reports will not receive as much time from you as they did before
    ☑ Show humble leadership
  ☑ Potentially offer structured procedures for effective and efficient conflict resolution within teams

People fits:
☑ Rely on existing and recruit new employees who rank high on personality traits that help with the high delegation (4). As far as possible, select
  ☑ Agreeable, honest, and humble employees to foster collaboration, as well as
  ☑ Conscientious and proactive people, the more so you rely on delegation in task division, task allocation, and rewards distribution, with a
  ☑ High need for achievement, the more so you rely on delegation in task division and task allocation and potentially a
  ☑ High locus of control, the more so you rely on delegation in managing conflicts.

(1) For questions pertaining to this part of the decision tree, see chapter 8 for details.
(2) For questions pertaining to this part of the decision tree, see chapter 7 for details.
(3) For questions pertaining to this part of the decision tree, see chapters 5 and 6 for details.
(4) For questions pertaining to this part of the decision tree, see chapters 3 and 4 for details.

Fig. 9.6 (continued)

facilitating team-building and self-selection into projects. Top management, given their relatively wide span of control, have communicated that their role is being reduced to that of facilitators more than anything else, making it clear to whoever wants to work for the company that individual responsibility is key for each employee, and that autonomous work is a given.

This design not only appears suited to facilitate self-organization. It also appears to resonate with the people the company has hired and continues to hire.

Taking a closer look at Reaktor's workforce, the company appears to employ people who tend to be more ambitious and who are willing to take on more challenging projects,[11] as well as those who feel attached to and convinced of the company, as manifested in their enthusiasm for buying shares.[12]

Typical problems such as the emergence of shadow hierarchies, employees free-riding on their peers' efforts, their cherry-picking of important work, and leaving unattended less glamorous tasks are nothing Reaktor's management would seem to complain about. Nor does the company seem to suffer from excessive personnel turnover rates. These are observations that neatly map onto what we would have expected when revisiting Reaktor's growth story through the lens of our guide to flat growth.

Takeaways and Outlook

This chapter served ***three purposes***. First, to ***crystalize knowledge*** gained through Chaps. 1, 2, 3, 4, 5, 6, 7, and 8 ***into actionable decision-making diagrams*** that would help executives systematically approach the organizational challenge of moving toward a flatter structure, or maintaining one while growing. Second, to ***validate these guides*** by applying them to our case companies from Chap. 1—notably T-Systems, Treehouse, Wistia, and Reaktor. And thereby, third, to ***help readers see how to apply the decision trees*** when moving to the next two chapters of this book.

You're now in a position to tackle the challenges presented in Chaps. 10 and 11—real-world cases of delayering and horizontal growth that I've put together specifically for the purpose of this book with senior executives of two German companies: Borek and wirDesign.

In moving forward, ***I encourage you to retain our approach of staying undogmatic and sober*** when it comes to judging the appropriateness of moving to a flat structure. In particular, let me reiterate that ***no company is better or worse merely because it operates one structure or another***. Wistia and Treehouse, just because they returned to traditional forms of organizing, are no worse than T-Systems or Reaktor, who felt that the move toward a flatter structure works for them. The complex interplay between the goal, the design, and the people determines what seems like a smart organizational solution and what does not. Finally, please view the checklists in Figs. 9.3, 9.4, 9.5, and 9.6 as what they are: comprehensive summaries of most of the issues one might like to consider in an ideal world but not all of which may be addressable in real-world setups. You'll be best positioned to attribute weights to the different items when it comes to applying them in your corporate context. You'll also be best positioned to judge whether additional issues may require addressing in the specific context of your firm. Here, a recurring theme that appears relevant across many, albeit not all companies, is how to reward those mid-level managers who, over the course of a delayering initiative, lose decision-making power. To get you started in this process, let's recall two insights from earlier chapters: that with increasing age, the motivation shifts from extrinsic to intrinsic for many employees (Chap. 4); and that normative influence is engendered by both decision rights and status (Chap. 8). If you put the two together, it may seem like a reasonable idea to create smaller corporate playgrounds for these former executives where they can pursue their own interests more so than they could before, albeit with fewer employees under them. This way, they can follow their own callings and, by retaining some form of expert status, still feel that they retain some influence over others, albeit in a narrower domain. Rather than a blunt degradation, this would be perceived as a ***lateral career move*** by these former mid-level executives.

Notes

1. Essentially, this is the lowest level at which, according to senior leaders, employees would still have the skills to take on managerial tasks along the 4+1 dimensions.
2. All descriptions pertaining to the delayering of the T-Systems Auto MI GDU in this chapter are based on an interview with Georg Rätker, April 29, 2021, via videocall.
3. Ibid.
4. Ibid.
5. Ibid.
6. Ibid.
7. The following account of what happened at Treehouse draws, in large part, on the material presented in Chap. 1 of this book. Additional material is referenced separately.

8. The following account of what happened at Wistia draws, in large part, on the material presented in Chap. 1 of this book. Additional material is referenced separately.
9. Savage, "Flat Is not a Value."
10. The following account of what happened at Reaktor draws, in large part, on the material presented in Chap. 1 of this book. Additional material is referenced separately.
11. Terävä, "How Reaktor Grew without Hierarchy."
12. Ibid.

Bibliography

Savage, Chris. "Flat Is not a Value: How a Clear Org Structure Unlocked Growth at Wistia." *ChartHop*, September 24, 2020. https://www.charthop.com/blog/org-chart/flat-is-not-a-value-org-structure-growth-wistia/ (accessed February 6, 2021).

Terävä, Hannu. "How Reaktor Grew without Hierarchy." *Reaktor*, September 3, 2015. https://www.reaktor.com/blog/how-reaktor-grew-without-hierarchy/ (accessed February 4, 2021).

Part IV

Test Your Understanding

10

Delayering the Hierarchical Firm: The Case of Borek

The following case study, consisting of parts A and B, draws on both publicly available data and in-depth interviews with Richard Borek, owner and Chief Executive Officer of the eponymous corporation.

Part A: 1893 Until 2018 in Fast Motion

The Richard Borek group is a family business in Braunschweig, Germany. The company, currently run by the fourth generation, was founded in 1893 as a purveyor of postage stamps. Over the decades, the group has grown to be a world leader in collectors' items (e.g. stamps, coins, historical securities), serving as of this writing over a million active customers worldwide. The current main business drivers are precious metal products that are sold to collectors or investors. Over the past three years, much of the trade has moved to online sales, and e-commerce has thus become a key activity within the group.[1]

Like many family-owned companies founded around the late 1890s, the corporation has grown in traditional fashion over the years. So, when in 2018 the company counted about 650 employees, a seven-, sometimes even eight-layered management hierarchy characterized the formal organizational structure within the group. However, since then the CEO has, over the past three years, led a major reorganization that ultimately left him with just four management layers in the conglomerate. This move to what Richard Borek would call a more "process-driven" approach was all but a small one for the company. On the contrary, "for us as a medium-sized company it was a major step and an incredible accelerator."

Why Reorganize in the First Place?

When, back in 2018, the CEO concluded that the group would benefit from a reorganization, flattening the structure was not a goal in itself. Instead, management had realized that information traveled too slowly from top to bottom in the hierarchy. Perhaps even more critically, information was unintentionally altered and reinterpreted along the way, and by the time it reached the workforce it would differ substantially from its original content. We simply had "the revelation that information flows too slowly from the top to the bottom. Changes and strategies, defined at the top levels, were not executed at the bottom," as Borek recalls. Speedy decision-making, however, had become a high priority in the company. Borek was aware that the industry overall, and especially the e-commerce sector, demanded fast and autonomous decision-making. This clearly marked a change in the business environment. The organizational structure, devised in the late 1980s, had served the company well in detecting commission errors and delivering flawless quality since then. However, it had become ill equipped to deal with the contemporary challenges management faced going forward.

It wasn't until Borek had participated in a series of workshops with his senior executives that it eventually became apparent that delayering the traditional hierarchy would be inevitable if the company was to become faster and return to the growth track. One of the insights, perhaps trivial in hindsight but not obvious to the executive team before reflection, was that mid-level managers were "the linchpin of success and failure, and the dependency on these was great." Delayering would reduce this dependency.

Today, Borek looks back on the journey with a smile. Transitioning to and working within a far more decentralized environment "has been fun"—and part of this fun comes from seeing it bear the fruits he was hoping for. Needless to say, there were many decisions to be made along the way and several challenges to be mastered.

* * *

What, in your view, were the critical decisions the CEO had to make? What challenges along the way could he have encountered? Use our guide in Fig. 9.4 for inspiration.

Part B: from 2018 Until Today

As Borek mentioned, overhauling the structure was no small affair for the company, which, itself once a startup, had become an organization exuding an air of tradition more than 125 years later. And so he faced a series of questions and decisions.

How Far Down Can We Go in Delegating Decision-Making Power?

While he was convinced that having too many layers of mid-level management had become a roadblock to speed and communication, it was equally apparent that delegation would become paramount in dealing with increases in his span of control. Borek chose to tackle the problem by forming a committee of 22 people in the company. This group included not only the three executive board members but also managers from the three remaining management levels down to the level of team leader. This committee became central in discussing and preparing major strategic decisions within the company going forward. The decisions it made related to the definition of overarching goals and the highest level of task division within the company structure. Thus, by including lower ranks in these deliberations, the management board de-facto delegated parts of their decision-making rights on task division to their subordinates. And this had implications even for the actual teams-based work at the bottom of the pyramid.

How to Give Teams the Rights to Make Design Decisions Within the Scope of Their Projects?

Eventually, greater autonomy would also trickle down to the level of the operating teams. But, as Borek recalls, "This is a very difficult process, it is actually a marathon. That must not be underestimated." Executives had been used to command-and-control structures, and sought to ensure that greater delegation would not be confused with a lack of expectations for outcomes. Introducing custom-tailored KPIs for each department in addition to working with quarterly "objectives and key results (OKRs)," to be met at both company and department levels, and continuously reflecting within the team as to what could be optimized, tremendously helped with the process. As did a business partner concept in which Borek's executives learned from initially external, now internal human resource specialists how "to withdraw even more from operational issues, approach meetings more selectively, and look for talents within the team—in short, mastering the new leadership style." A lot has happened since; notably, as of this writing, the department heads autonomously define their quarterly goals themselves, within the broader strategic frame provided by senior management.

On the Scope of Delegation to Operating Teams

While overall task division, as discussed above, had become a joint effort between senior management and lower-level decision-makers, the CEO also delegated more rights along other dimensions of organizing.

Outside the daily business, accounting for about 80 percent of a co-worker's time, employees now had opportunities to apply to participate in or even run new projects that were being communicated.

In a way, as Borek argues, this was the real reward for his people, who could now attract senior management's attention by taking on projects that allowed them to show their full potential.

Decentralized and transparent information exchange became the norm, both across and within teams.

Finally, without any formal delegation, tendencies emerged for more dialogue-based conflict resolution between superiors, for example, team leaders, and other employees.

Provide Managerial Guidance, Autonomy Support, and a Suitable Playing Field for Self-organized Work

Preventing the cherry-picking of projects by employees and ensuring that important initiatives would not remain unstaffed became a new executive task. Although self-organization was nurtured and fostered, reminding employees of their responsibilities to get the work done and challenging them when necessary remained a managerial activity. Balancing such residual control with implementing a different leadership style was not always easy for all remaining managers. With regard to the latter, Borek was well aware that "this change necessitates giving up more responsibility, and in parts also giving more trust. […] One has to understand that it is necessary to build a new form of collaboration. […] This, too, was a task for management, to be very committed to working on these issues together with their respective employees."

In that vein, management transparently providing information became key. But, as Borek insists, this information exchange did not have to become a one-way street in which management made available information for employees to pick and choose what they fancied. Information would also have to travel in the other direction. "We need data transparency on all levels," says the CEO, and he adds, "we have to make sure that information circulates during this process of change. That we have an intense data exchange. At the same time, we may want to think of deriving additional key performance indicators to help with "health checks." In addition to monthly performance reviews that may serve other purposes."

In terms of the playing field, the Richard Borek Group had traditionally been operating a structure in which there were relatively few overlaps between different divisions. Outside this divisional work, for most novel projects that were initiated, there were, at least initially, few interdependencies. So the e-commerce section of the company initially, for example, had a chance to grow out of an autonomous project—at least, up until a point when this setup would no longer be scalable.

Signs of Increased Motivations Through Autonomy: Self-determination, Control, Engagement, and Attachment

An early indicator of his reorganization becoming a potential success can be traced back to visible increases in employee motivation that accompanied higher delegation. Reflecting on why his people appreciated the new regime—increased self-determination, perceptions of control, engagement, or a sense of attachment—Borek felt that "all of those mattered." With regard to engagement and attachment, Borek felt that "one of the main topics is simply contributing something, where you feel very connected to a project or to a situation and you want to make an impact." The possibility of escaping from the routine of daily work and explore other activities within the company also plays a major role. "There are no monetary incentives. It is then simply about the fun factor, experiencing something new in a team that goes beyond the department. In contrast to the 'monotonous' everyday life, driven by day-to-day business." And, finally, so the CEO is convinced, there were those who very much appreciated the possibility of rendering themselves more visible throughout the company "with respect to career opportunities."

Changes in Behavior and Personality Traits Shining Through

Interestingly, the CEO made the above observations among his extant workforce, which has seen less (forced) personnel turnover over the past three years than one might think. Part of this has to do with Borek's general attitude of getting things done. Notably, once it was decided that the organization should move to a flatter structure, the CEO's first thoughts would not center on whom to hire and whom to let go in order to create a perfect "HR fit" for the new structure. "I thought to myself: 'The best people I have are those right here in this room.' And then I got started," says the CEO. He was convinced that changing the processes and restructuring work could bring the desired changes in the current workforce, too, even if they'd been operating in a different regime before. "The first step toward change is a step in the right direction, no matter which people I have, as long as we systematically reflect on that first step in retrospect. Then we can agree on new actions," Borek was convinced. At the beginning of the transformation, he thus emphasized treatment rather than the selection of new people. In a large heterogeneous workforce, there will always be those who like the change. And his observations appear to confirm his initial views. While the company has not submitted their employees to actual personality tests, the CEO is convinced that the reorganization has fostered certain types of behaviors, which are particularly visible with employees who have certain personality traits. And identifying such employees has become much easier for the CEO. Notably, proactive people. "I do see that people apply for 'Project-Owner' positions and be accountable for a quarterly key result, people I would have never had on my radar otherwise," says Borek. Equally interestingly, so he recalls, is that there were some he would never have expected among that subgroup. In fact, there were some who were close to retirement, who had been suffering from low performance for a while, when the high-delegation environment really revived their motivation: "In this process of change I have seen a lot of people who suddenly woke up. Who, in the home stretch—people who just had a little longer until retirement—pulled off projects, showcased a firework of motivation, because they enjoyed the new transparency and appreciation in a much bigger group and because it was fun."

Overall, so the CEO estimates, 70 percent of the workforce reacted positively to the new autonomy they'd been granted. "For the remaining 30 percent it was part of leadership's responsibility to see it done," notably as motivators and ambassadors for change. Naturally, as the CEO admits, this transition did not come easily for all employees—managers and operating team members alike. Some simply did not fit into the new system and left or had to leave the company.

Challenges Along the Way

People leaving the company was not the main challenge, as Borek recalls. Rather, he admits that, at least initially, he'd dramatically underestimated how time-consuming the process of moving toward a flatter structure would be, and how demanding it would be in terms of time and communication to keep it alive. "In the beginning I didn't realize that this transformation, this process, this impulse, how much time it would command. […] I mean, also in terms of time that had to be invested. We did this together with an external team, and had tight exchange rounds to coordinate again and again." In hindsight, Borek feels that the dual challenge of running the daily business and the organizational transformation was, at times, too demanding, and if he had to do it over again, he'd delegate the daily business earlier in order to be able to devote more attention to the transformation process.

Another challenge was establishing the new leadership style. Becoming more of a feedback partner and working collaboratively was important, but it was "not to be confused with a laissez-faire" attitude. "No matter the organisational system, people either feel, or must be held, accountable for what they do." Borek lived this insight by example, as he was hoping that lower-level management would eventually understand and adopt his style.

And it was for the same reason that the CEO, from the very beginning, sought to retain some focus on measuring progress, irrespective of knowing how difficult it would be. While standard KPIs would not be suited to capturing the progress of the reorganization, custom-tailoring new ones would not be a straightforward issue either.

Outcomes So Far and Opportunities Ahead

Three years after the CEO and his senior team kicked off the delayering process and the move to a more process-oriented organization, they're convinced that they've reached their goal of becoming faster at making and implementing decisions. Also, as Borek feels, people throughout the organization are more empowered, and particularly those who performed suboptimally prior to the transition. The new organizational structure challenged management and employees to reflect more on key questions such as "who does what, when, and how?" And as for the CEO himself: "It's a lot of fun with the team we have now."

The potential of the flat structure hasn't yet been fully exploited, and there are more opportunities to reap in the future. Clearly, it became easier to spot new talent among the company's own ranks: not only do employees have the chance to increase their visibility by participating in different projects; executives have also become better at spotting high performers in their teams.

Enhancing creative business development, by pooling the knowledge of more than 650 people from different backgrounds, is another chance for the future. The CEO views it as an advantage: "this is a more heterogeneous structure, in which an organisation, such as we are, can better play on its strengths."

Note

1. All quotations are from the author's interview with Richard Borek, June 15, 2021, via video call.

11

Flat Growth: The Case of wirDesign

The following case study, consisting of parts A and B, draws on both publicly available data and in-depth interviews with Andreas Schuster, founding member of wirDesign, and currently consulting executive board member.

Part A: 1982 Through 2021—Flat Back Then, and Flat Today

When Andreas Schuster, together with seven of his peers from the College of Arts in Braunschweig, Germany, founded wirDesign, the group of eight were still students of graphic design. They'd been taking classes together, they'd had befriended one another, and it just seemed like a good idea to set up what Schuster would describe as a collective of distinct studios working on graphic design and advertisement. The goal was to create a platform for joint work on projects and to signal some critical mass to the outside world of potential clients, most of them in the region around Braunschweig. At that time, wirDesign's service portfolio included "individual needs assessment, consulting, order clarification, creation, presentation, implementation, production," as the former board member recalls, and, with his typical humble smile, he adds: "We were a 'general store' in the regional league."[1]

Legally speaking, the company was structured as a very simple partnership under the Civil Code of Germany. There was no common capital stock, no shareholder contract, and so forth.

wirDesign's Organizational Design During the Early Days

The company, not surprisingly given the circumstances under which it was founded, operated with a very flat structure in which the eight members essentially had an equal say in all critical decisions.

The overall task architecture was project-based. The acquisition of individual projects was open to everyone.

The person who attracted a project from a client would usually not work on it just by herself but would ask her peers for help on specific issues, leading to a kind of restricted self-selection onto projects. Those who were asked to help could decide whether they were interested and had the time.

Compensation was really meant to be proportionate to what individuals brought to the table while working on a project. Often, these splits were discussed among and eventually determined by all participating parties. "Those who had worked on a specific job sat down together and basically negotiated freely, and not based on some working hours or something like that […] but more like 'Look here, I think you did most of the work. Why don't you take 60%?'"—so Schuster recalls. However, there were also other instances when project owners—that is, those who acquired the project—would effectively subcontract part of the work to their peers against a predetermined fee. "Sometimes I worked on a job on my own, and then asked a colleague: 'Would you like to come up with a headline for 100 Deutsche Mark?,'" says Schuster.

Everybody participated in the exchange of information that appeared at least remotely relevant for the organization overall. To that end, wirDesign relied on regular weekly meetings during which they discussed important issues of company-wide relevance. In addition, the founders held an annual strategy meeting aimed at developing wirDesign in the future. Most important, however, was the informal information exchange that happened on a daily basis.

And, not surprisingly, things did not always go according to plan, and the team had to deal with exceptions. This included sorting out unforeseen clashes between the different founders. As Andreas Schuster remembers, such "conflicts would either be addressed directly with those involved or in general meetings, discussed extensively, postponed or decided. In principle, anyone could solve a conflict, but some were more talented in this regard than others."

Here, both the equal decision-making power and veto rights posed challenges: conflict resolution could end up consuming serious amounts of time and would sometimes lead to bagatelles being discussed for too long. Overall, however, the former founder feels that these debates brought the friends closer together again and helped avoid separation.

The People Behind the Early wirDesign

Being able to realize one's own ideas, being able to control one's own destiny more so than if working for a larger traditional company, and seeing things move forward—these to Schuster were the driving forces for his peers and himself to set up the company in the first place. Probably, as Schuster recalls, the founding members traded workplace security for these other workplace characteristics, for there was, not seldomly, a fear of failing and not earning sufficient money.

Not surprisingly, the former founder would rate himself and his colleagues of long standing as honest and conscientious but not necessarily humble or agreeable. And tellingly, when the founding members, decades later, took their first personality test together, they interestingly all scored similar on the different dimensions of the questionnaire, which, according to Schuster, "was the biggest strength and weakness of wirDesign."

Success and Growth

Perhaps because the founders had paid the price of waiving corporate job security, they were also wary of risking their beloved autonomy and independence by behaving in a hazardous way. So the company focused on delivering approaches that were "individually developed, […] well-founded […], and not somehow super crazy, wacky." And these, as Schuster is convinced, eventually earned them respect with their clients.

"Especially those, let's call them overly creative types, they often push their amazing ideas onto the customers, irrespective of what that customer actually needs. However, for us the needs assessment has always been one of our strengths. So, for example, sometimes we've told a customer: 'Thank you for the briefing, but we see your problems in a completely different area. That's why we would recommend you do something else first.' Some customers were put off by that: 'What are they telling us that for, we know best what we need.' And others we've won because of that. And basically that's our approach even today, this well-founded-ness."

Success led to more success and eventually to growth. From where Andreas Schuster sits today, he overlooks the offices of the designers working in the

Braunschweig headquarters of the company he once brought to life. Together with the designers working in the Berlin offices, the company today counts over 70 employees, creating an annual turnover of 7.5 million Euros. The key areas of business are still graphic design, brand strategy, and corporate communication. wirDesign still serves clients similar to those they worked with in the early days, and the company still offers a similar product portfolio. Many of the designers working with wirDesign, as Schuster is convinced, also still work for the same motives. And most importantly, the organizational structure today does not differ too dramatically from the one of the eight-person startup back in 1982 if one considers the actual increase in personnel. There are just two layers within the company, the executive board and the employees. wirDesign has no interim mid-level manager positions. In fact, the company doesn't even operate an organizational hierarchy, just a structure in which some people hold some authority.

* * *

Having heard the story thus far, what are your thoughts on why the company retained its flat structure after growth? Which hiccups might there have been along the way? Use our guide from Fig. 9.6 for inspiration.

Part B: What Happened in Between…

Just comparing the two structures—1982 and 2021—and reflecting on wirDesign's business model makes the company look like a textbook case of horizontal growth. Clearly, the project-based business would enable the company to design a teams-based architecture that would not require excessive inter-team coordination while growing; and clearly, given the nature of the creative industry they operated in, no project would be identical to the next. So, the conditions for flat growth were there (see Fig. 9.6).

And yet, the true journey was a very different one—one that reveals much about the actual challenges that may arise when a company seeks to grow and retain its organizational DNA at the same time.

From 1982 to 1987

The company was in its early years when the first founding member left wirDesign for a permanent job in the industry. As Schuster recalls, she could not handle the financial uncertainty that came with life as an entrepreneur. The initial team also lost another member to a different employer. That said, during this period, five new employees—mainly designers but also others—joined wirDesign, and the organization began to flourish.

It was in this environment that the founders discussed how they could grow the company further and what this growth should look like. "Should we take on more designers with equal rights, meaning we would enlarge our community of design studios […] or should we do it differently and actually employ the new designers"—those were the different options being contemplated, as Schuster recalls. Eventually, the company decided to hire new designers, founded a limited corporation, and three of the founding members served as (initially honorary) managing directors.

Its reputation grew, and although customers became more demanding, business was sound. Occasional interpersonal issues weren't fundamental to the operations of the firm; they simply required more communication and brought about the occasional normal frustrations. Mutual respect and tolerance still characterized the dealings between the different organizational members, both founders and employees.

From 1987 to 1992

Around five years into its existence, problems began to manifest that Schuster recalls as being more fundamental. In hindsight, it seems that high demand on everybody's time laid open the issues of an imperfect division of labor and integration of effort. Founding members, too often for his taste, began to find themselves in situations where they simply had too much on their hands. Problematically, much of this work was nondesign-specific work, which the creative people found particularly tiring. In total, there were now ten new people—freelancers and permanent employees alike—who did not belong to the founding team of the eight fellow students from 1982. And questions began to arise: "How do you deal with employees, what kind of expectations are there, and how are things calculated?" and so on.

At the time, the organizational structure still resembled the original "Ateliergemeinschaft" ("design studio community"), but now the three leading board members had also officially been elevated to management level. This was not without problems. Nonfounders, as Schuster put it, suddenly felt like "second-class wirDesigners." Yet, in the end, deference to the founding members prevailed, and they were accepted as authorities by the others.

The fact that the new structure allowed wirDesign to take on more projects and make more money overall clearly helped with establishing the authority structure the company had not seen before. "Everyone was the master of their own fortune; there was no fixed salary structure."

At the same time, "a certain specialization emerged slowly among us. At some point I felt responsible for personnel and organization."

From 1991 to 1992 in Detail

It was toward the end of 1991 when cracks began to show in the wirDesign system. Ten employees were governed by six bosses who had no clear responsibilities but drew on the help of different people as they saw fit. This situation led to a first conscious reflection of how the company should be organized going forward. External consultants the founders brought in felt that "we were not a unit, but 6 individual design studios in a state of competition," as Schuster recalls. And in the spirit of classic management consulting of the early 1990s, the standard repertoire of solutions was being unleashed on the company to bring about the "process of distinction, restructuring and growth of the next phase."

Not too surprisingly, and not too creatively either, the setup of the "Ateliergemeinschaft" had to give way to a matrix structure in which the founding members acted as team leaders and project acquirers who could draw on a pool of designers. Comprising about 20 to 25 people overall, the company still felt like "a big family" then.

From 1999 Through 2001/2002

The company continued to grow, however. wirDesign moved into a new office and strived to become a design agency of national recognition instead of a regional "Gemischtwarenladen" ("general store"). And, in the beginning, their business success was considerable.

In 1999 wirDesign grew very rapidly over the course of just half a year and suddenly counted over 70 employees. With the latter success, however, and the constant quest to serve more clients, the matrix structure of the past decade had begun to feel too complicated. Coordinating the different employees and distributing information properly became cumbersome. So, between 2000 and 2001, wirDesign introduced a different organizational structure in collaboration with a consulting branch from Volkswagen. Again, the standard organization designer's toolkit was being applied to the design agency. And as expected, what resulted from this process was the introduction of a hierarchical structure that should help define responsibilities more clearly and reduce communication costs throughout the system. Within that hierarchy, founding members acted as board members and would represent the highest management level. They would instruct the team leaders, who now embodied mid-level manager positions within the company. At the bottom of the pyramid was the workforce of designers. Schuster himself took on the role of a classic CEO, coordinating team leaders and other board members.

Yet the change "led to a lot of confusion," as Schuster remembers. One noteworthy observation was that board members actually had a span of control of around one. In essence, most board members kept repeatedly working with the same team leader, calling into question the usefulness of the mid-level manager position. Admittedly, when projects grew bigger, the founding members had to invest more time in key account management, finance, accounting, or marketing. So when the team leaders took over some of the heavy operational lifting, the division of labor that accompanied hierarchical separation appeared useful. Also, giving designers a chance to be promoted within the company by making them team leaders helped continue to prevent turnover, which at wirDesign had traditionally been lower than the industry average during the first 15 years of the company's existence—an advantage wirDesign sought to retain. Still, the hierarchical setup felt alien to the company, given the business it was working in, and given where it had come from. In Schuster's view, the reasons why the hierarchy did not experience greater attrition in the first place were the following. First, owners still kept the designers on a long leash; the designers still enjoyed much freedom in their work, a key reason why they stuck with wirDesign. Second, in parallel with the restructuring, the board began bringing in people from other professions, such as accounting, controlling, and project management. This in turn freed up time for the designers, who, prior to this, had felt that "everybody was doing everything" and that this was inefficient: "With this we relieved the designers of a lot of stuff they didn't want anyway, because that was not what they had studied for, after all." And third, there were simply few other employers in the region for designers at the time.

From 2002 to 2010

These years in the company's history, in retrospect, are probably best characterized by one word: turmoil. In 2001 the company had become a stock corporation (Aktiengesellschaft) for two daughter companies—a limited company headquartered in Braunschweig and another one headquartered in Berlin. The change in governance appeared to make sense given the continued expansion. But when the company, which had grown to 70 employees, in 2002 suddenly lost several of their big clients and nearly went bankrupt, it had to let go of many employees. The hierarchy was no longer needed, and the matrix structure returned. Only when, around 2006, business picked up again and the company began to grow once more, management introduced the two-layered hierarchy, but with now employing several experts and functional specialists, the new structure was more complicated than the one from 2000/2001.

From 2010 Through 2015

There is no particular event that Schuster could recall as being a trigger. Rather, so he recalls, from 2010 onward problems began to emerge. "We had reached some limits, there were considerations as to how we would have to reorganize, because people were not content with the status quo." At the same time, the founding generation had begun to toy with the idea of retiring from operational business and to reflect on which firm they wanted to leave behind. In any case, they wanted to ensure that they'd be less in demand than they'd been so far. It was at this point that thoughts about moving back to a flatter setup began to creep in—to reduce the role of senior management. These ideas also seemed plausible given other trends observable in the industry: speed requirements increased, technology gained more importance—and core competencies were often held by the younger generation of employees.

From 2015 to Today

It was for the above reasons that a process was set in motion that ultimately yielded the organizational structure that wirDesign has been operating with over the past six years now. Labeled "Pancake" for no particular reason other than pancakes being flat by definition, the company, now sold to a different owner, has just one management layer: the board. The board retains some decision-making power on distinct questions, notably compensation and recruiting. But it retains a low power profile. "Actually we are all equal. Everyone can get involved in any way they like. But of course, there is being an owner and a board of directors, who are responsible for certain matters in front of the local court and [etc.] […]. But that is the only elevated hierarchical layer."

The employees themselves are organized in teams.

Teams may vary in composition, depending on what the customer wants and a project requires. "People who work together for a customer are a team." The teams choose a "Teamsprecher" ("team speaker"), who represents them in the "Teamsprechermeetings" ("team speaker meetings"), a council that decides important issues. This "Teamsprecher" role is not a permanent one, but the members of a team decide whoever goes to those meetings on their own.

Teams enjoy much freedom in terms of task division and self-allocation to work. How a team wants to approach a customer, what they want to offer to them—that's entirely up to them. Self-selection is the default mechanism of task allocation, although Schuster admits that there is some helpful informal pressure for everybody to bring their own skills and abilities to projects where these are needed. Information sharing, like in the olden days, again happens spontaneously. With team compositions changing, people share information naturally again. And the exchange between employees and founding members has also increased again.

Flat Growth?

So, would the wirDesign story fit our understanding of flat growth, as depicted in Fig. 9.6? Having read part B, our immediate inclination would be to say no. And admittedly, the company's growth story was a more complex one. It moved from a teams-based structure to a matrix organization, implemented a hierarchy, had to delayer it, just to reintroduce it again before finding out that a traditional stacked system of authority would not suit the company's employees in the long run.

And yet, so I would argue, wirDesign is eventually a beautiful example of a flat-growth case; notably, today's flat structure is not an artifact of the company not having experimented with alternative organizational designs. On the contrary: it was the experimentation that led the founders' return to their roots after decades of being in the business because they felt that this was the most appropriate design for their firm. The company's organizational design today is the result of a conscious choice. It's flat for a reason.

As Schuster summarizes his experiences from 2000 until today: "We've looked a lot, with little self-confidence, to business economists […] and managers from other companies, with regard to how things are done and so on. Listened less to ourselves. […] And ultimately referred to our own DNA again."

Could they have gotten there faster? Perhaps. It would be presumptuous to say that if they'd seen Fig. 9.6 before. But all's well that ends well.

Note

1. All quotations are from the author's interview with Andreas Schuster, May 5, 2021, via video call.

12

Flat Fads or More? From *a* as in "agile" to *z* as in "zi zhu jing ying ti" …

In this last chapter, let's try to round off our understanding of flat structures. And to do so, let's pick up on the key question from the introduction: why would it take yet another book on nonhierarchical organizations like this one?

While my hope is that you've enjoyed the process thus far and found it worthwhile, a few questions may remain. Those of you who hadn't already read about nontraditional organizations may **wonder whether everything we've discussed is identical to other approaches** you've heard mentioned in the context of making organizations more creative, speedier, and more attractive to employees: approaches **such as agility, blockchain-based decentralized autonomous organizing (DAOs), holacracy, RenDanHeYi, or Scrum**. Those of you who *have* been hearing or reading about these approaches should immediately see that there are both distinct differences and overlaps between these concepts and ideas and the teachings of this book. For all of you, it would appear desirable to have a **clear understanding of how the above contemporary approaches compare with one another, what insights and solutions they offer**, and, most importantly, **whether or where they challenge** the insights from organizational research that we drew on for **this book about designing decentralized structures**, and, thereby, our own thinking developed on flat organizations. In this chapter, we'll attempt to develop this understanding together.

To that end, we'll scrutinize the above approaches to nontraditional organizing by posing three questions: (1) why these approaches were created in the first place, (2) what they actually provide to users, and (3) how they map onto the understanding of designing flat organizations developed in this book. To answer question 3 we will, for one thing, be drawing again on the 4+1 dimensions of organizing framework that you're by now familiar with. In addition, to answer questions 2 and 3, we'll need to *introduce one final set of ideas from organizational science on the differences between logics of organizing (LoO), design principles,* and *design solutions*. Jointly, the 4+1 framework and the distinction between LoOs, design principles, and design solutions will enable you to put everything into perspective and apply as you see fit (or not). It will also make you feel confident that your learnings from this book are rather timeless and will likely help you easily categorize and analyze many of the organizational design trends that may pop up in the future.

A Potpourri of Applied Approaches to Nontraditional Organizing—Why Did They Come About at All?

As in every walk of life, solutions emerge as answers to perceived problems. Novel solutions feature novel answers to old or new problems. Inventors always believe in the novelty of their answer, and sometimes also in the novelty of the problem they've stumbled upon. The domain of designing organizations is no different from engineering or medicine in that regard. However, whereas in the sciences, inventions often get scrutinized by patent offices, that rarely happens in the field of organizations. So, whether an approach to nonhierarchical organizing qualifies as novel often lies in the eyes of the beholder. Not surprisingly, this may lead to various assessments of the same idea or concept, depending on who scrutinizes it.

What may seem like a great and original solution to an executive facing the issue of designing a company for the first time may be reminiscent of earlier ideas and approaches to scientists who have studied organizations for a living. The fact that such "fads," as scholars may call them, keep resurfacing is due to a variety of factors. In part, as my colleagues Phanish Puranam, Oliver Alexy, and I argued many years back,[1] the field of organizational theory, for quite some time, had failed to uphold and renew its claim that it can explain and help with understanding nontraditional forms of organizing in modern contexts. So, the chances of practitioners reinventing ideas or concepts known from science had to increase.

Inasmuch as these developments therefore seemed inevitable, their unreflected-upon adoption may come at a high price. Chances are that executives will wind up with a patchwork understanding of how organizations shall be designed. At best, the new patches provide truly new value by extending prior theory without contradicting the latter. At worst, they seem inconsistent, leaving managers with the question of when to draw on which kind of thinking—a notoriously unsatisfactory state of affairs. In between the best- and worst-case scenarios, leaders may simply create duplicate knowledge by relabeling old wine bottles.

To avoid ending up in any of the above scenarios, let's take a different approach and see how any of the novel approaches either replicates or extends our extant understanding of creating flat organizations.

To that end, let's move slowly and take one step at a time. In a first step, let's critically review the nature of the perceived problem that each of the approaches seeks to address. In other words, let's recall why they were created in the first place, so that we can later wonder whether that problem was a truly new one in the grand scheme of things.

Why They Were Created in the First Place

Agile

As far as its meaning relates to management, the term—ubiquitously applied across corporations and sectors nowadays—was originally introduced in the field of software development.

Toward the end of the twentieth century, an increasing number of entrepreneurs and companies felt that too many traditional software projects were failing because of the slowness and rigidity that accompanied the traditional waterfall approaches in the sector. When a group of prolific software engineers met in 2001 in Snowbird, Utah, to draft the "Agile Manifesto," they were keen on defining an approach that would *"answer a need to develop software quickly, in an environment of rapidly changing requirements."*[2] The first lines of their manifesto summarize their intention: "We are uncovering better ways of developing software by doing it and helping others do it."[3]

Scrum

Scrum's official origins date back to 1993. This was when Jeff Sutherland, John Scumniotales, and Jeff McKenna worked for the Easel Corporation and implemented a solution to designing software that would be *more flexible than the hitherto adopted waterfall techniques.*[4] Scrum and agile are intricately connected. In fact, Sutherland, together with Ken Schwaber, belonged to the founding team of the agile manifesto, and their ideas for why the software sector would need agile are comparable to why the software sector needed Scrum.

DAOs

It seems fair to say that most sizeable DAOs that exist today were created because the technology became available. Critically, DAOs draw on the blockchain technology, which facilitates the forgery-free, decentral exchange of information. Originally designed by Leslie Lamport, Robert Shoshtak, and Marshall Pease to ascertain that malfunctioning components within an interconnected computer system would not pass on conflicting information,[5] this technology soon caught the attention of **organizational designers who spotted an opportunity to replace trusted middlemen with computer technology for sensitive information transfer.** Needs for implementing the technology were predominantly felt by startups in the financial sector seeking to provide alternatives to extant ways of carrying out transactions. To this day, Bitcoin serves as the most prolific case in point.

Holacracy

Holacracy was created as a response to a problem that its founder, Brian Robertson, perceived as what he observed in terms of how companies would organize at the time. As Robertson put it in 2015, "Today, something about the fundamental structure and system of how we organize and how we scale and how we build companies is stopping everyone from bringing all of their insights and all their talent."[6] Holacracy was intended to resolve these issues. *"I was looking for a new social technology to use in a company,"* Robertson stated.

RenDanHeYi

The RenDanHeYi organizational model grew out of two business needs perceived by Zhang Ruimin, chairman of the Chinese corporation Haier. These needs, as my colleague Bill Fisher from IMD and an intimate expert on Haier would put it, are *"[first] to provide a better customer experience and the second … a faith that his employees know a lot,"* which is why he considers it necessary to *"release that knowledge and their innate entrepreneurial energies."*[7]

What They Actually Provide to Users

Before we take a closer look at how novel the articulated needs appear against the backdrop of what is known from organizational science, let's first ask the second important question we raised in the introduction to this chapter. What is it that these different approaches actually do for us as users?

Agile

Even for someone who has worked on the topic of new organizational forms for decades, it has become difficult to keep track of what's been summarized under the term *agile* over the past 18 years or so. An entire universe of methods, practices, and procedures has developed around the term, and it would blow the scope of the book to even attempt at providing a comprehensive overview.[8] Luckily, such a summary not only may appear unnecessary but may in fact be obstructive to this book's purpose. Eventually, our goal in this book has always been to master the basic mechanics of designing flat organizations to then think through their consequences ourselves. In the same spirit, let's also focus on the original idea behind agility rather than reviewing all its spin-offs.

In doing so, we can't but acknowledge that the agile ***manifesto essentially just lists a set of***—what organizational scientists would call—***principles***. These four core principles are:

Individuals and interactions over processes and tools
Working software over comprehensive documentation
Customer collaboration over contract negotiation
Responding to change over following a plan.[9]

But what are principles at all in the context of organization design? Are they are the same as actual design solutions that tell me where to centralize and where to decentralize along any of the 4+1 dimensions? As my colleagues Oliver Alexy, Phanish Puranam, former postdoctoral candidate Katharina Pötz, and I could show in a recent article, distinguishing between these terms—design principle and design solution—is critical to avoid confusion in understanding organizations.

A design principle refers to a manager's "proposition about which organization design solutions are appropriate to divide labor and integrate effort."[10] So, in the case of agile, one proposition would be, for example, that customer

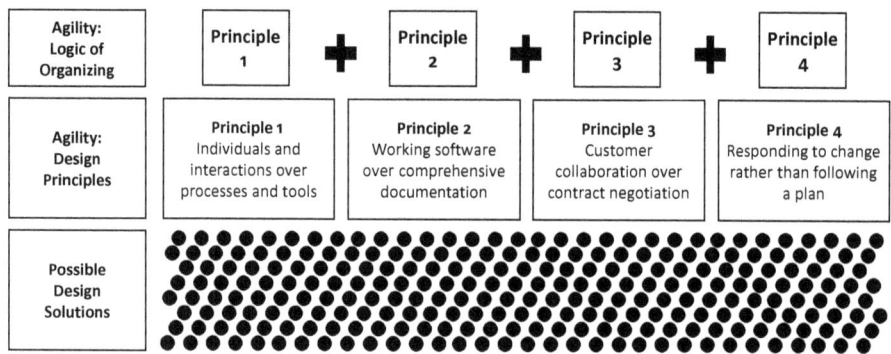

Fig. 12.1 On the relationship between design solutions, design principles, and Logics of Organizing (LoO): The example of agility. (© Markus Reitzig 2021)

collaboration will always yield better results than contract negotiation and should thus be pursued (principle 3). How exactly that principle translates into a tangible design solution—what managers "actually do to address the universal problems organizations face in terms of division of labor and integration of effort"[11]—is a different question; in the concrete case above, the superiority of collaboration over contract negotiation can be implemented in many different ways. What's clear, however, is that a set of principles jointly forms what professors James Baron, Diane Burton, and Michael Hannan would refer to as a "logic of organizing."[12] The agile manifesto, in its original form, thus provides its users a logic of organizing that consists of different propositions. It does not, at least in its original form, suggest a concrete set of solutions. These one has to devise oneself or, more likely, take from the shelf of methods that follow the agile logic (see below, e.g., Scrum).

Figure 12.1 illustrates the relationship between design solutions, design principles, and LoO for the agile case.

Scrum

"Scrum is not a *methodology*. Scrum implements the scientific *method* of empiricism."[13] So it says at http://www.scrum.org, the self-stated "Home of Scrum." What, in the context of this book, appears key in that statement is the term *implement*. In fact, taking a closer look at **Scrum**, it **suggests a clear path to implementing a design solution**. This design solution proposes teams-based work with clearly defined roles and equal authority levels of members within these teams (we'll elaborate on this in the next section). Many of the activities these team members are then supposed to engage in are commensurate with the LoO of agile. The so-called sprint may serve as a case in point.[14] In essence, sprints represent rather short-term project periods that aid in gathering new information about the chosen plan of action, to revise the latter at fixed points in time—the so-called sprint reviews.[15]

DAOs

Not too long ago, I had the pleasure of being asked to comment on an article by Ying-Ying Hsieh and Jean-Philippe Vergne in the *Journal of Organization Design* that was devoted to the rise of decentralized autonomous organizations. In their article, Ying-Ying and Jean-Philippe define DAOs as "non-hierarchical organizations that perform and record routine tasks on a peer-to-peer, cryptographically secure, public network, and rely on the voluntary contributions of their internal stakeholders to operate, manage, and evolve the organization through a democratic consultation process."[16] Here, the "machine consensus" arises through forgery-free timestamping using the Blockchain ledger, while the establishment of "social consensus" is reminiscent of the way that open source software (OSS) communities achieve collaboration.[17] So, **DAOs provide their users or adopters an actual design solution that blends the decentralized structure of OSS with the use of a supporting blockchain technology**. Thus, DAOs would appear to be solutions that are commensurate with the LoOs of OSS development. Whether DAO provide solutions that are also commensurate with other LoOs is an open question.

Holacracy

Adopting holacracy, so it appears, means adopting ***a total packaging approach to organizing that has elements of both principles and solutions*** but which—at the same time—allows for customizing both the LoO and the design solution space. To appreciate that holacracy has distinct principles, let's look at one of its key claims of differentiation, notably how authority should be distributed compared with a traditional organization. Rather than bundling decision rights at one hierarchical node, the system proposes to endow different people with contextual authority over subsets of tasks. To appreciate that holacracy offers parts of a design solution, let's briefly review its most basic suggestions: work should be distributed across roles. Groups of roles form circles. And circles can be nested in hierarchical fashion, according to which supercircles include lower-level circles. Key roles within (and across) circles are lead links, which serve as top-down connections within a circle, and so-called rep links, which represent the peers bottom up to their lead link. Lead links have the authority to assign peers to all roles, except for the rep link, facilitator, and secretary role, to which peers must be democratically elected.[18] At the same time, there appears to be no single comprehensive LoO in holacracy, as users are free to customize holacracy to their contexts as they see fit. Such customizations may include different additional design principles and thereby change the LoO. For the same reason, the spectrum of design solutions that can be attained seems wide depending on how the system is being implemented.

RenDanHeYi

Like holacracy, **RenDanHeYi provides users both design principles and a design solution**. However, whereas holacracy can mean very different things in different contexts, RenDanHeYi can be rather clearly defined. While it is difficult to point to one comprehensive summary of the defining principles, a recurring element in Zhang Ruimin's thinking appears to be that "nothing is allowed to get in the way of Haier accessing fresh insights and then testing them, putting them to work right away."[19] Maintaining this zero distance to customers means that employees must be placed in a way to actually articulate customers' wishes before they express them themselves. The structural solution that Haier's founder proposed and implemented "pivots around ZZJYTs (zi zhu jing ying ti, which means independent operation units)."[20] At Haier, 80,000 employees are organized across 2000 teams consisting of a manager and other peers.[21] There is no mid-level management that could delay the decision-making process. While these teams were organized as microdivisions or ZZJYTs in an organizational hierarchy until 2014,[22] as of 2015 they have become microenterprises that are coordinated by node enterprises and an overarching headquarters using a platform model.[23]

Mapping the Approaches onto the Thinking Underlying and Developed in this Book

Two key questions remain toward the end of this chapter, and the book for that matter.

First, to what extent do the above approaches challenge the knowledge base we drew on for this book and, in turn, question our own thinking on how to design flat structures?

Second, to what extent and how exactly can we categorize the above approaches using the terminology developed in this book, to shelve the contemporaneous ideas in our timeless library of thoughts?

The two following subsections will address the above questions in turn.

So What's Really New?

You may recall the beginning of this chapter. Novelty may not only lie in the eyes of the beholder. It can also be constituted in different ways.

First, a problem itself may be new. More often than not, it will require a novel solution, too. So: from agile to zi zhu jing ying ti, how new would the problem appear to someone with access to the research done in the field of organizations? Has the perceived need (see above) been acknowledged before?

In the case of agile and Scrum, I believe it's fair to say that it has been. In their seminal paper, David Teece, Gary Pisano, and Amy Shuen, as early as 1997, asserted that "change is costly and so firms must develop processes to minimize low pay-off change."[24] Sprints in Scrum, following the agile logic, are a response to the need to keep costly change under control. In the same paper, the authors expressed the need for firms to "quickly accomplish reconfiguration and transformation ahead of competition," and they acknowledged that "decentralization and local autonomy assist these processes"[25]—a need that resonates with what Haier's CEO had expressed when implementing RenDanHeYi. If you now consider that Teece, Pisano, and Shuen, for their paper, draw on even older root insights by scholars such as Richard Nelson and Sidney Winter, not to invoke Joseph Schumpeter himself, it becomes obvious that the problems articulated by the above approaches were already well known to the world of organizational science more broadly.

Similarly, when stripping off the Blockchain ledger from a DAO, we are left with the perceived need for collectives of individuals to find a way to virtually collaborate so that different contributors can partake in a decentralized manner. In their paper, Georg von Krogh and Eric von Hippel, as early as 2003,[26] explained not only how OSS collectives operate but also why they arose.

And, finally, the perceived need to leverage the knowledge of as many employees as possible, as articulated by Holacracy founder Robertson, is as old as the field of modern organizational science itself. In fact, one might argue that the entire Carnegie School of Management, named after a group of prolific scientists working at Carnegie Mellon University from the 1950s onward, and spearheaded by no less than the polymath and Nobel laureate

Herbert Simon, had devoted the better part of their careers to understanding how to optimally aggregate information across individuals working within organizations. Their many descendants, working as professors at leading business schools and universities across the globe, have advanced their thinking through uncounted articles to this day. All of them would take for granted that it is imperative, if an organization is to do well, that every individual contributes their knowledge. That premise is shared by scholars working within a second stream of literature, organizational psychology. Here, colleagues such as Elisabeth Morrison and Frances Milliken observed early on that aggregating information within organizations, irrespective of their structure, can be hampered by employees' silence.[27]

Thus, in sum, at least from a scientific angle, the value of the above approaches may not lie so much in the articulation of hitherto unknown problems of organizing.

So what about the solutions they offer to the problems they seek to address? Remember that even if the problem may be known, the solution itself may be novel and, to the extent that it appears superior to extant solutions, still add to our understanding of how we should design organizations.

Here the picture becomes somewhat more blurred. While, as of today, there is no serious large-scale empirical evidence that implementing either DAOs, holacracy, or RenDanHeYi helps increase corporate performance compared with suitable benchmark organizations that operate differently, in the case of agility preliminary, data do exist. Recent studies seem to indicate that organizational designs that follow the agile LoO are associated with higher (financial) performance of companies operating not only in the IT sector[28] but also in manufacturing.[29] Similar results are observable for Scrum in particular, although the measures of performance are softer for these studies.[30]

When we take a closer look at some of the above results, however, an interesting observation emerges. Notably, how scholars measure agility at the corporate level may be regarded as tautological by some. Measuring organizational agility as the "amount of time required to introduce new products or services" or as the "speed of delivery for products or services"[31] means equating the desired outcome of the agile LoO with the LoO itself. In which case, finding a positive performance effect overall is hardly surprising.

Most importantly for us, we can summarize our answer to the first question we posed above. Which is: *none of the contemporary approaches—from agile to zi zhu jing ying ti—provide an indication that we need to question the knowledge base we drew on for this book.* In turn, there's no need for us to question our own thinking on how to design flat structures at this point.

How Would We Classify the Above Approaches?

Irrespective of whether agility, Scrum, DAOs, holacracy, or RenDanHeYi provide novel solutions to old or new problems from the perspective of an organizational scientist, the question for you remains where to put them on your newly devised brain shelves of understanding flat organizations so that you don't get confused and don't waste time storing duplicate approaches for identical problems.

To that end, let's recall that in this book we've paved the way from distinct organizational goals to design solutions. For a subset of goals—namely creativity, speed, and attraction and retention of talent—we examined which workable design solutions would feature decentralization in at least one of the 4+1 dimensions of organizing: task division, task allocation, rewards distribution, information exchange, and exception management.

To connect these goals to design solutions, we developed our own logics of organizing. These are reflected in all the (conditional) arguments we've made over the course of Chaps. 2, 3, 4, 5, 6, 7, 8, and 9. We could, if we wanted to, express these as an explicit set of principles. So, in Chap. 1 we could say that "increase in span of control must lead to more delegation." But even if we don't, these arguments form part of our LoO. Sometimes we actually did explicate the principles that constitute our LoO. In Chap. 3, for example, we explicitly mention that "fostering engagement requires high delegation in task allocation." Importantly, however, our LoO is not born of gut feelings or based on subjective experiences but draws on as much empirical knowledge as I could find for you.

If we now try to understand how the contemporary approaches discussed in this chapter so far map onto the terminology developed in this book, let's make sure we distinguish carefully between goals, LoO, design principles, and design solutions.

Agile

In our notation, the term actually denotes a LoO consisting of the four principles mentioned above. Some of these principles may overlap with our LoO. Notably, "*Responding to change over following a plan*" is an imperative we have not articulated explicitly but a proposition we'd implicitly take for granted when we discuss the advantages of abandoning central planning and allowing for decentral decision-making to become speedier (see Chap. 7). This partial overlap in principles is not surprising if we consider the articulated need of agile: to increase the speed of development, be it software or some other commercial product. To become speedier has been a focus of this book as well.

That said, the agile LoO draws on a set of principles that are otherwise not derived from or supported by empirics. Moreover, just listing a set of principles hardly leads to a robust LoO. For the latter, it takes the articulation of boundary conditions and moderators: the identification of when which principle is relevant or not, and how one parameter interacts with another. Undoubtedly, the simplicity of the agile LoO is one of the reasons why many practitioners struggle in translating the set of principles to actionable solutions themselves.

Given the above difficulty, they instead tend to adopt off-the-shelf implementations like Scrum that are commensurate with the agile principles. The problem is that such templates may be more useful in some instances and less in others, and that they may not necessarily be the best configurations to fulfill agile design principles.

These implementations usually produce solutions of the flavor as depicted in Table 12.1, column 2.

Scrum

Scrum fits this bill perfectly.[32]

"The fundamental unit of Scrum is a small team of people, a Scrum Team. The Scrum Team consists of one Scrum Master, one Product Owner, and Developers. Within a Scrum Team, there are no sub-teams or hierarchies. It is a cohesive unit of professionals focused on one objective at a time, the Product Goal."[33]

At this point you may rightfully wonder: why should these be the only solutions that fit an agile LoO? Having read the book, you may think of many more combinations/permutations that might be consistent with the goal of creating a fast-reacting organization. Our guides in Chap. 9 give a sense of how they may vary. Finally, how to scale these solutions beyond team level remains opaque.

DAOs

DAOs were explicitly designed to foster the decentral collaboration of individuals. The mere devotion to nonhierarchical collaboration requiring voluntary contributions creates an overlap between the DAO-specific LoO and the understanding developed in this book.

Table 12.1 Design solutions emerging from contemporary approaches to nontraditional ways of organizing

Approaches to nontraditional organizations	Scrum	DAO	Holacracy with one circle	Holacracy with multiple circles	RenDanHeYi
Task division	Decentralized	Decentralized	Authoritative	Hierarchical	Largely decentralized
Task allocation	Decentralized	Decentralized	Authoritative	Hierarchical	Decentralized
Rewards distribution	Decentralized	Decentralized	Authoritative	Hierarchical	Decentralized
Information exchange	Decentralized	Decentralized	Decentralized	Decentralized	Decentralized
Exception management	Decentralized	Decentralized	Decentralized	Decentralized	Decentralized

Note: Authoritative = centralized decision rights in a two-layered structure; hierarchical = centralized decision rights in a multilayered structure. © Markus Reitzig 2021

That said, the thinking behind DAOs at best represents a subset of the understanding we've developed here. First, DAOs solely carry out routine operations and are thus unsuited to helping attain the goal of creativity, for example. Second, DAOs require a rather high level of technical skill on the part of the contributor that may restrict their application in a variety of other settings which we also discussed.

Given the relatively narrow range of applications that DAOs can be used for or have been applied to in the past—notably in the financial sector—and given the reminiscence between DAOs and OSSD, it's not surprising that the predominant design solution they offer has a configuration as depicted in Table 12.1, column 3.

Holacracy

Holacracy was created to make companies neither speedier nor more creative per se. It was not, as Brian Robertson admits himself, ever meant to be non-hierarchical: "I think it can be misleading to claim either 'Holacracy is flat' or 'Holacracy is hierarchical'; Holacracy uses a different type of hierarchy than we're used to, for a different purpose."[34]

In light of the above, it isn't surprising that holacracy focuses—apart from perhaps a few exceptions—on very different design principles than we focused on in this book and that, by definition, it suggests design solutions that all have a configuration as depicted in Table 12.1, columns 4 and 5.

Whether to deploy the approach "wholesale"—as my colleague Ethan Bernstein and his co-authors once put it[35]—or not is a question managers must ponder for themselves. In any case, it wasn't designed to help with the creation of flatter structures to become speedier or more creative.

RenDanHeYi

Probably, of the above approaches, this management system shows the most overlap with the writings herein. The goal of being innovative at all times is, at least in some situations, equivalent to our goals of delivering creative solutions and doing so quickly. Principles such as having no distance to the customer are, at least in part, comparable to our contemplations on the locus of decision-making when speed matters (see Chap. 7).

Interestingly, the current RenDanHeYi solution 2.0 has a configuration as depicted in Table 12.1, column 6.

Table 12.2 Categorizing and mapping approaches to nontraditional ways of organizing to the 4+1 framework

Approaches to nontraditional organizations	Agility	Scrum	DAO	Holacracy	RenDanHeYi
Why was it created?	To tackle the perceived problem of too many traditional software projects failing because of the slowness and rigidity of a traditional hierarchy.	See agile.	To prevent computer systems from passing on conflicting information. In organizations, to replace trusted middlemen with computer technology for sensitive information transfer.	To address the perceived problem of contemporary organizational structures preventing employees bringing in their insights and talents.	To provide a better customer experience, release employees' knowledge and innate their entrepreneurial energies.
What does it actually provide for users?	Logic of organizing to make companies faster and more flexible.	Design solution that follows the design principles of agile.	Design solution that blends the decentralized structure of OSS with the use of a supporting blockchain technology. Intended to facilitate virtual decentralized collaboration.	Packaging approach to organizing that has elements of both principles and design solutions. Goal to integrate information across employees and allocate them ideally.	Approach to organizing that has elements of both principles and design solutions. Goal to make companies innovative.
How does it map onto the understanding of organizations underlying and developed in this book?	Addresses a known problem (change is costly and firms need to develop processes to minimize these costs). Evidence on suitability of LoO for designing fast and flexible organizations is unclear.	Addresses a known problem (see agile). Solution seems to provide decent results.	Addresses a known problem (how collectives of individuals can engage in virtual collaboration). No evidence on performance of the solution compared with suitable reference points.	Addresses a known problem (the need to leverage the knowledge of as many employees as possible and allocate them ideally). No evidence on performance of the solution compared with suitable reference points.	Addresses a known problem (the need to delegate provide autonomy in a decentral manner to be responsive to consumers). No evidence on performance of the solution compared with suitable reference points.

Note: © Markus Reitzig 2021

This is the configuration at the teams—or zi zhu jing ying ti—level, and coordination of these teams happened using a very flat, two-layered hierarchy until 2014 and is now facilitated by a platform. So, strictly speaking, today's microenterprise structure no longer has a formal hierarchy, and the design solution at the teams level relies on a highly decentralized structure.

The fact that the solution the RenDanHeYi model offers is the extreme form of what we would have discussed in Chap. 9 suggests that the logics of organizing are also similar. Little detail is known; however, some interview evidence suggests that similar thinking is at work.[36]

The RenDanHeYi model succeeding within a company that was great at hiring suitable employees resonates with our thinking in Chap. 4. "The people that end up working there are entrepreneurial people," as Bill Fischer would assert and continue, "I think they have succeeded to some extent to create this attractive magnet for these kinds of people."

Similarly, Bill finds that Haier's employees are "not all altruistic thinkers, but they're thinking about, 'What can I do that will help me, help advance what I'm doing, and collectively so that the organisation moves forward?'"—in line with our reasoning in Chap. 5.

Finally, the CEO being a humble leader, as Simone Cicero would put in the same interview, also maps onto what we would expect given our contemplations in Chap. 5.

Thus, taken together, the original RenDanHeYi implementation in the form of *zi zhu jing ying ti*s connected via a two-layered hierarchy seems like a special case of a design solution we might also propose under certain conditions. The difference is that we know under which conditions we would suggest it, and under which we would not.

Table 12.2 summarizes all of our contemplations from this chapter so far.

Important Takeaways

For as long as humans have inhabited this planet, they've formed organizations of one sort or another: goal-directed systems in which different actors with different interests and information jointly work toward a common goal. Families, tribes, companies, states—these are all different types of organizations devised for different purposes. The greatest achievements of humans were arguably all achieved through cooperation between different individuals, most of whom were joined by their belonging to a common organization.

In consequence, it isn't surprising that the field of organizational studies is one of the oldest in the field of social sciences. From its origins in the ancient world until today, it has kept some of the finest brains busy thinking about how to divide labor and integrate the different contributions from different individuals.

At the same time, given the ubiquitous nature of organizations in our daily private and professional lives, practice has shaped our understanding of which forms of collaboration work for which purpose and which people.

Fortunately, we continue to learn about how organizations work, and how we can make them work better. That said, this learning must build on the proverbial shoulders of giants from science and practice. Without acknowledging their prior insights, chances are that we reinvent the wheel more often than we stumble upon truly novel insights.

The logics of successful flat organizing that we developed in this book build on the knowledge that others created before us, and they add to this the novel insights that my colleagues and I were able to gain over the past two decades of our own research. There will be a point in time when this book no longer represents the latest thinking—and this will be great for all of us, as it will mean that we've again refined our understanding.

However, given our approach, this point may lie further in the future than just a few years from now. Social science progresses steadily but slowly, and as far as business horizons are concerned, I would thus dare to say that this book qualifies as a timeless book rather than a fad, and that you will be able to rely on its insights for many years to come. Should you prefer taking more fashionable approaches to the design of organizations, that point might come a little earlier.

You have the choice.

Concluding Remarks

Congratulations! You've made it to the end of this book.

We've come a long way in building our joint understanding of what flat structures actually are, when to use them and when not to, and how to design and staff them to be successful if we do use them.

You've had the opportunity to test your own novel understanding by putting yourselves in the shoes of leading executives who experienced the process of delayering or flat growth in their companies.

And we convinced ourselves that our understanding developed in this book would not suffer from our ignoring other contemporaneous approaches that are out there and that are being used.

In doing so, you've acquired a contemporary but also rather timeless understanding of how to think about organizational structures in order to make your companies more creative, speedier, and more attractive to current or future personnel.

I wish you the best of success as you put your new insights to work. And I end on a last piece of insight from many years of advising small and large firms: when you engage in the process, you will need patience and perseverance. Designing and adjusting structures, making sure they're being embraced by management and employees alike, is not a matter of weeks or months. It's a matter of years. And if it's of any comfort to you, it took years to finish this book, too.

Notes

1. Puranam, Alexy, and Reitzig, M., "What's 'New' about New Forms of Organizing?"
2. Greer and Hamon, "Agile Software Development."
3. See https://agilemanifesto.org/ (accessed August 2, 2021).
4. See "A Short History of Scrum."
5. Lamport, Shostak, and Pease, "The Byzantine Generals Problem."
6. See Robertson, "Holacracy," at 3 mins 25 secs.
7. See Gill, "A Conversation with Bill Fischer and Simone Cicero about Haier Group."
8. Interested readers are encouraged to peruse the Agile Alliance website at http://www.agilealliance.org (accessed August 2, 2021).
9. To avoid confusion, note that the founders of the agile manifesto did not call these four principles "principles." In fact, to make matters more confusing, what they refer to as their 12 (!) principles is a derivative elaboration on these four core statements: https://agilemanifesto.org/principles.html, (accessed

August 2, 2021). For the purpose of this book, and in line how organizational experts would speak about the issue, I suggest viewing agility as a set of four core principles from which all other ideas (elaborated principles, design solutions, etc.) are being derived.

10. Alexy, Poetz, Puranam, and Reitzig, "Adaptation or Persistence?"
11. Ibid.
12. Baron, Hannan, and Burton, "Building the Iron Cage."
13. See "What Is Scrum?"
14. See "What Is a Sprint in Scrum?"
15. See "What Is a Sprint Review?"
16. Hsieh, Vergne, Anderson, Lakhani, and Reitzig, "Bitcoin and the Rise of Decentralized Autonomous Organizations,": 2.
17. Hsieh et al., "Bitcoin and the Rise of Decentralized Autonomous Organizations," 4.
18. Robertson, *Holacracy,* 55.
19. See Gill, "A Conversation with Bill Fischer and Simone Cicero about Haier Group."
20. See Liu, "Opportunities Await the Innovators."
21. Muralidhara and Faheem, "Zhang Ruimin: Achieving Excellence," 8.
22. Frynas, Mol, and Mellahi, "Management Innovation Made in China."
23. Ibid. Platform models facilitate coordination between legally independent enterprises using, among other things, the price mechanism, whereas organizational hierarchies are used to facilitate coordination between subunits or agents working for the same enterprise. If you're interested in reading more about recent developments pertaining to platform models, I encourage you to peruse the works of my former colleague Kevin Boudreau and his co-authors.
24. Teece, Pisano, and Shuen, "Dynamic Capabilities and Strategic Management," 521.
25. Ibid.
26. Hippel and Krogh, "Open Source Software and the 'Private-Collective' Innovation Model."
27. Morrison and Milliken, "Organizational Silence."
28. See Tallon and Pinsonneault, "Competing Perspectives on the Link between Strategic Information Technology Alignment and Organizational Agility." See also Hazen, Bradley, Bell, In, and Byrd, "Enterprise Architecture."
29. See Inman, Sale, Green, and Whitten, "Agile Manufacturing."
30. Rising and Janoff, "The Scrum Software Development Process for Small Teams." See also Schatz and Abdelshafi, "Primavera Gets Agile."
31. Hazen et al., "Enterprise Architecture," 575.
32. We focus on Scrum for the purpose of this chapter because the implementation is probably the most prolific among the set of those seeking to meet agile principles. Other implementations, such as Kanban, would produce similar design solution configurations, though.

33. See "What Is Scrum?"
34. Robertson, *Holacracy*, 47.
35. Bernstein, Bunch, Canner, and Lee, "Beyond the Holacracy Hype."
36. See Gill, "A Conversation with Bill Fischer and Simone Cicero about Haier Group."

Bibliography

Alexy, O., K. Poetz, P. Puranam, and M. Reitzig. "Adaptation or Persistence? Emergence and Revision of Organization Designs in New Ventures." *Organization Science* (2021), https://doi.org/10.1287/orsc.2021.1431.

Baron, J. N., M. T. Hannan, and M. D. Burton. "Building the Iron Cage: Determinants of Managerial Intensity in the Early Years of Organizations." *American Sociological Review* 64, no. 4 (1999): 527–47.

Bernstein, Ethan, John Bunch, Niko Canner, and Michael Lee. "Beyond the Holacracy Hype: The Overwrought Claims—and Actual Promise—of the Next Generation of Self-Managed Teams." *Harvard Business Review* 94 (2016): 38–49.

Frynas, J. G., M. J. Mol, and K. Mellahi. "Management Innovation Made in China: Haier's Rendanheyi." *California Management Review* 61, no. 1 (2018): 71–93.

Gill, Lisa. "A Conversation with Bill Fischer and Simone Cicero about Haier Group." *Lisa Gill,* September 27, 2020. https://reimaginaire.medium.com/a-conversation-with-bill-fischer-and-simone-cicero-about-haier-group-aeab970b9bf8 (accessed August 2, 2021).

Greer, D., and Y. Hamon. "Agile Software Development." *Software: Practice and Experience* 41, no. 9 (2011): 943–44.

Hazen, B. T., R. V. Bradley, J. E. Bell, J. In, and T. A. Byrd. "Enterprise Architecture: A Competence-Based Approach to Achieving Agility and Firm Performance." *International Journal of Production Economics* 193 (2017): 566–77.

Hsieh, Y. Y., J. P. Vergne, P. Anderson, K. Lakhani, and M. Reitzig, "Bitcoin and the Rise of Decentralized Autonomous Organizations." *Journal of Organization Design* 7, no. 1 (2018): 1–16.

Inman, R. A., R. S. Sale, K. W. Green Jr., and D. Whitten. "Agile Manufacturing: Relation to JIT, Operational Performance and Firm Performance." *Journal of Operations Management* 29, no. 4 (2011): 343–55.

Lamport, L., R. Shostak, and M. Pease. "The Byzantine Generals Problem." In *ACM Transactions on Programming Languages and Systems* 4, no. 3 (1982): 382–401.

Liu, Cecily. "Opportunities Await the Innovators." *China Daily,* February 19, 2017. https://usa.chinadaily.com.cn/china/2017-02/19/content_28429723.htm (accessed August 3, 2021).

Morrison, E. W., and F. J. Milliken "Organizational Silence: A Barrier to Change and Development in a Pluralistic World." *Academy of Management Review* 25, no. 4 (2000): 706–25.

Muralidhara, G. V., and H. Faheem. "Zhang Ruimin: Achieving Excellence through Reinvention of Business Model and Corporate Culture at Haier." Case no. 315-135-1, IBS Center for Management Research: Telanga, 2015: 8.

Puranam, P., O. Alexy, and M. Reitzig. "What's 'New' about New Forms of Organizing?" *Academy of Management Review* 39, no. 2 (2014): 162–80.

Rising, L., and N. S. Janoff. "The Scrum Software Development Process for Small Teams." *IEEE Software* 17, no. 4 (2000): 26–32.

Robertson, B. J. "Holacracy: A Radical New Approach to Management." *TEDx Talks*, July 2, 2015a, https://www.youtube.com/watch?v=tJxfJGo-vkI.

Robertson, B. J. *Holacracy: The New Management System for a Rapidly Changing World*. New York: Henry Holt and Company, 2015b.

Schatz, B., and I. Abdelshafi. "Primavera Gets Agile: A Successful Transition to Agile Development." IEEE Software 22, no. 3 (May/June 2005): 36–42.

"A Short History of Scrum." *The Scrum Master*, n.d. https://www.thescrummaster.co.uk/scrum/short-history-scrum/ (accessed August 2, 2021).

Tallon, P. P., and A. Pinsonneault. "Competing Perspectives on the Link between Strategic Information Technology Alignment and Organizational Agility: Insights from a Mediation Model." *MIS Quarterly* 35, no. 2 (2011): 463–86.

Teece, D. J., G. Pisano, and A. Shuen. "Dynamic Capabilities and Strategic Management." *Strategic Management Journal* 18, no. 7 (1997): 509–33.

von Hippel, E., and G. von Krogh. "Open Source Software and the 'Private-Collective' Innovation Model: Issues for Organization Science." *Organization Science* 14, no. 2 (2003): 209–23.

"What Is a Sprint in Scrum?" Scrum.org, n.d. https://www.scrum.org/resources/what-is-a-sprint-in-scrum (accessed August 2, 2021).

"What Is a Sprint Review?" Scrum.org, n.d. https://www.scrum.org/resources/what-is-a-sprint-review (accessed August 2, 2021).

"What Is Scrum?" Scrum.org, n.d. https://www.scrum.org/resources/what-is-scrum (accessed August 3, 2021).

Glossary

Ability (cognitive) Refers to "a very general mental capacity that, among other things, involves the ability to reason, plan, solve problems, think abstractly, comprehend complex ideas, learn quickly, and learn from experience."[1]

Agility (organizational) Is "the capacity to be infinitely adaptable without having to change."[2] Organizational agility comprises both flexibility—an organization's anticipated responsiveness to external stimuli—and adaptivity—an organization's responsiveness to unplanned environmental changes.[3]

Authority Denotes a superior's legitimate ability to demand a subordinate's obedient behavior within a specified realm of actions.[4] Having formal authority includes the right to make decisions.[5]

Autonomy Refers to "self-governance, or rule by the self"[6] and is considered a fundamental human need.[7]

Bias (in selection) Occurs when "using nonrandomly selected samples to estimate behavioral relationships. [A] sample selection bias may arise in practice for two reasons. First, there may be self selection by the individuals or data units being investigated. Second, sample selection decisions by analysts or data processors operate in much the same fashion as self selection."[8]

Centralization Refers to a regime in which superiors overrun decisions of their subordinate and hold them accountable to their decisions.[9] Centralization is the opposite of decentralization.

Commitment (organizational) Describes the "relative strength of an individual's identification with and involvement in a particular organization."[10]

Decentralization In its extreme form, refers to a regime within which "the subordinate's decisions are neither subject to reversal by [the superior], nor are they accountable for them."[11] The empirically more frequent scenario of a quasi or de-facto decentralized regime refers to a high-delegation environment in which subordinates do not seek approval for their decisions but in which they can still be overruled in theory and remain accountable for their actions. Decentralization is the opposite of centralization.

Design Principle Refers to a designer's "propositions about which organization design solutions are appropriate to divide labor and integrate effort."[12] Several design principles are "jointly forming the … logics of organizing."[13]

Design Solutions Refer to "what founders actually do to address the universal problems organizations face in terms of division of labor and integration of effort."[14]

Division of Labor Denotes the "decomposition of the overall goal into (clusters of) tasks, and the allocation of these task clusters to distinct agents"[15] and describes a "process that converts interdependence between tasks into interdependence between agents."[16]

Flat Structure Refers to an organizational structure with (comparatively) few hierarchical levels compared to a similarly sized organization operating within the same sector.

Hierarchy (of authority, aka command hierarchy) Denotes a structure in which positions of authority are stacked and create a transitive, asymmetric, and acyclical distribution of (normative) influence. Where different positions with equivalent authority form layers—"equivalence classes whose members have the same rank"[17]—we speak of a containment or nested hierarchy.

Integration of Effort Deals with solving "the problems relating to motivation and knowledge that arise when integrating the efforts of interdependent actors."[18]

Leadership Is "the process (act) of influencing the activities of an organized group in its efforts toward goal setting and goal achievement."[19]

Logics of Organizing Denote "belief systems composed of principles of organization design, which, in turn, describe founders' subjective propositions about which organization design solutions are appropriate to divide labor and integrate effort and are reflected in the first set of design solutions."[20]

Modularity Denotes the idea of independence within and across modules, smaller units in a larger system, that (have to) work together.[21] Units of relevance for this book are task bundles or work-related projects.

Motivation Explains why people initiate, continue, or terminate a certain behavior at a particular time. Thereby, "[i]f a situation contains a specific goal which provides satisfaction independent of the actual activity itself, behavior is said to be extrinsically motivated. On the other hand, if the activity is valued for its own sake and appears to be self-sustained, behavior is said to be intrinsically motivated."[22]

Personality Traits Refer to aspects of a human personality that are relatively stable over time and situations and ultimately influence human behavior.[23]

Reciprocity Means that people "reward kind actions [(positive reciprocity)] and punish unkind ones [(negative reciprocity)]."[24] It manifests itself in a "behavioral response to perceived kindness and unkindness, where kindness comprises both distributional fairness as well as fairness intentions."[25]

Self-determination Theory Seeks to explain how individuals are motivated through the experience of autonomy, competence, and relatedness.[26]

Slack Describes the excess of resources (e.g., human resources, financial resources) above the absolute minimum amount of resources necessary to run operations at a routine level.[27]

TEAL Is a term coined by Frederic Laloux and stands for a stage in human evolution which evolves around the human need of self-actualization. A TEAL organization is built around the core principles of self-management, wholeness, and evolutionary purpose.[28]

Wisdom of the Crowd Describes the phenomenon that aggregating the individual assessments of members within a group on a specific issue can lead to a more accurate assessment on that issue than relying on the information of a single member within the group, even when the latter is an expert.[29]

Notes

1. Gottfredson, "Mainstream Science on Intelligence," 13.
2. Dyer and Shafer, "From Human Resource Strategy to Organizational Effectiveness," 6.
3. Harraf, Wanasika, Tate, and Talbott, "Organizational Agility."
4. Weber, *Wirtschaft und Gesellschaft*; Simon, *Administrative Behavior*.
5. Aghion and Tirole, "Formal and Real Authority in Organizations."
6. Ryan and Deci, "Self-Regulation and the Problem of Human Autonomy," 1562.
7. Ryan and Deci, "Self-Determination Theory and the Facilitation of Intrinsic Motivation, Social Development, and Well-Being."
8. Heckman, "Sample Selection Bias as a Specification Error," 153.
9. Puranam, *The Microstructure of Organizations*.
10. Mowday, Steers, and Porter, "The Measurement of Organizational Commitment," 227.
11. Puranam, *The Microstructure of Organizations*, 94.
12. Alexy, Poetz, Puranam, and Reitzig, "Adaptation or Persistence?," 1.
13. Ibid., 2.
14. Ibid., 1.
15. Puranam, *The Microstructure of Organizations*, 45.
16. Ibid., 66.
17. Ibid., 108.
18. Ibid., s67.
19. Stogdill, "Leadership, Membership and Organization," 4.
20. Alexy et al., "Adaptation or Persistence?," 1.
21. Baldwin and Clark, *Design Rules*, 63.
22. Young, *Motivation and Emotion*, 171.
23. Allport, *Pattern and Growth in Personality*.
24. Falk and Fischbacher, "A Theory of Reciprocity," 293.

25. Ibid., 294.
26. Deci and Ryan, *Intrinsic Motivation and Self-Determination in Human Behavior.*
27. Cyert and March, *A Behavioral Theory of the Firm.*
28. Laloux, *Reinventing Organizations.*
29. Surowiecki, *The Wisdom of Crowds.*

Bibliography

Aghion, Philippe, and Jean Tirole. "Formal and Real Authority in Organizations." *Journal of Political Economy* 105, no. 1 (1997): 1–29.

Alexy, O., K. Poetz, P. Puranam, and M. Reitzig. "Adaptation or Persistence? Emergence and Revision of Organization Designs in New Ventures." *Organization Science* (2021), https://doi.org/10.1287/orsc.2021.1431.

Allport, G. W. *Pattern and Growth in Personality.* New York: Holt, 1961.

Baldwin, C. Y., and K. B. Clark. *Design Rules.* Vol. 1, *The Power of Modularity.* Cambridge, MA: MIT Press, 2000.

Cyert, R., and J. March. *A Behavioral Theory of the Firm.* Englewood Cliffs, NJ: Prentice-Hall, 1963.

Deci, E., and R. Ryan. *Intrinsic Motivation and Self-Determination in Human Behavior* (Perspectives in Social Psychology). New York: Plenum Press, 1985.

Dyer, L., and R. A. Shafer. "From Human Resource Strategy to Organizational Effectiveness: Lessons from Research on Organizational Agility." Working Paper No. 98-12, Cornell University Center for Advanced Human Research Studies, 1998.

Falk, A., and U. Fischbacher. "A Theory of Reciprocity." *Games and Economic Behavior* 54, no. 2 (2006): 293–315.

Gottfredson, L. S. "Mainstream Science on Intelligence: An Editorial with 52 Signatories, History, and Bibliography." "Intelligence and Social Policy," special issue, *Intelligence* 24, no. 1 (1997): 13–23.

Harraf, A., I. Wanasika, K. Tate, and K. Talbott. "Organizational Agility." *Journal of Applied Business Research* 31, no. 2 (2015): 675–86.

Heckman, J. J. "Sample Selection Bias as a Specification Error." *Econometrica* 47, no. 1 (1979): 153–61.

Laloux, F. *Reinventing Organizations: A Guide to Creating Organizations Inspired by the Next Stage in Human Consciousness.* Brussels: Nelson Parker, 2014.

Mowday, R. T., R. M. Steers, and L. W. Porter. "The Measurement of Organizational Commitment." *Journal of Vocational Behavior* 14, no. 2 (1979): 224–47.

Puranam, P. *The Microstructure of Organizations.* Oxford: Oxford University Press, 2018.

Ryan, R. M., and E. L. Deci "Self-Determination Theory and the Facilitation of Intrinsic Motivation, Social Development, and Well-Being." *American Psychologist* 55, no. 1 (2000): 68–78.

Ryan, R. M., and Deci, E. L. "Self-Regulation and the Problem of Human Autonomy: Does Psychology Need Choice, Self-Determination, and Will?" *Journal of Personality* 74, no. 6 (2006): 1557–86.

Simon, H. A. Administrative Behavior: A Study of Decision-Making Processes in Administrative Organization. New York: Macmillan, 1947.

Stogdill, R. M. "Leadership, Membership and Organization." *Psychological Bulletin* 47, no. 1 (1950): 1–14.

Surowiecki, J. *The Wisdom of Crowds*. New York: Anchor Books, 2005.

Weber, M. *Wirtschaft und Gesellschaft*, 1st halfbinding, Tübingen: Mohr Siebeck, 1921 (5th ed. 1980), 122 ff.

Young, P. *Motivation and Emotion: A Survey of the Determinants of Human and Animal Activity*. New York: Wiley, 1961.

Index[1]

A

Ability
　cognitive, 72, 80, 116n19
Accountability, xx, 8, 80, 86, 99, 147
Accountable, 8, 160, 161, 195, 196
Adidas, 5
Administrator, 100
　Wikipedia, 24, 100
Advertisement, 163
Aerospace, 29
Age, 66, 151
　employee, 66, 151
Agile, xx, 4, 15, 141, 142, 173–190, 190n9, 191n32
Agility, xx, 173, 177, 178, 182, 183, 191n9
Agreeableness, 69, 70, 73
　See also Personality trait
AI, 5
Airbus, 5
Alexy, Oliver, xxiii, 19, 20, 174, 177
Algorithm, 74
Allen, John, 31
Altruistic/altruism, 75n11, 88n5, 188
Anarchy, 67

Apparel, 29
Arbitration, 98–101
　See also Conflict resolution
Atlassian, 27, 48, 49, 85, 95, 110, 111
Atos, 27, 28, 31, 35, 48, 50, 87, 132
Attachment, 46, 49–51, 53, 55, 65, 112, 114, 128, 145, 159
　See also Mechanism
Authority
　lateral, 24, 98–101
　managerial, 100
Automobile, 3
Autonomously, 6, 46, 64, 70, 84, 85, 131, 158
Autonomy, 8–10, 27, 30, 31, 43–49, 51–53, 55n1, 55n9, 55n10, 56n12, 57n22, 64–68, 72, 75n3, 75n5, 75n8, 79, 81, 82, 84–87, 89n19, 94, 97, 99–101, 105, 109, 111, 114, 116n12, 116n19, 132, 147, 157–160, 165, 181, 196
　job, 46, 56n12, 65, 75n5, 75n8, 116n12
　at work, 14, 43, 45, 55n10, 64–67, 70, 80

---

[1] Note: Page numbers followed by 'n' refer to notes.

B

Baldwin, Carliss, 89n11, 94, 95
Baron, James, 178
Bell, Andrew, 24
Bernstein, Ethan, 186
Bias, 37n33, 59n52, 195
　selection, 195
Blockchain, 176, 179, 181
Borek, Richard, 15, 150, 155–162, 162n1
Brainstorming, 109
Breton, Thierry, 31
Budget, 4, 111
Bureaucracy, xx, xxi, 4, 9, 28
Burton, Diane, 178
Buurtzorg, 27, 28, 32, 48, 50, 52, 85, 87, 99

C

Cabals, 26
Cannon-Brookes, Mike, 27
Career move, 151
　lateral, 151
Carson, Ryan, 7, 8, 143, 146
Cartel, 89n8
Carter, Dean, 32, 112, 116n15
Casalena, Anthony, 31, 32
Case study, 155, 163
Censoring, 126
Central, 107, 111, 113, 157, 183
Centralized, 5, 10, 15, 51, 105–115, 115n1, 122–123, 127, 132
Change, 4, 6, 8, 10, 13, 22, 37n33, 43, 72, 80, 111, 114, 115, 136, 142, 156, 158–161, 169, 170, 177, 180, 181, 195
Chaos, 35, 67
Chief Executive Officer (CEO), xxi, 7, 9–13, 17n51, 26, 30–32, 36n31, 49, 50, 85, 99, 110, 112, 129, 130, 155, 156, 158–162, 169, 188
Chief Human Resource Officer (CHRO), 112
Chouinard, Yvon, 29, 116n15
Citizenship, 82
　organizational, 70
Clark, Kim, 95
Cloud, 3, 9, 28
Coach, 87, 99
Coalition, 89n8
Co-create, 83
Co-creation, 101, 140, 142
Collaborate, xxii, 28, 31, 181
Collaboration, 14, 19, 20, 24–26, 28, 31, 80–82, 87, 88n6, 158, 168, 177–179, 184, 189
Collectors items, 155
Command
　and control, 142, 157
Commitment, 46, 50, 51, 56n12, 195
　organizational, 46, 51
Communicate, xxiii, 21, 28, 46, 51, 71, 83
Communication, 8, 10, 28, 71, 73, 82, 87, 126, 127, 133n2, 143, 157, 161, 166, 167, 169
Compensation, 4, 8, 22, 29, 30, 45, 49, 55n10, 56n10, 67, 83, 84, 101, 112, 164, 170
Competence, 70, 71, 73, 74, 76n14, 97–100, 196
Complexity, 95
Computer simulations, 131
Condition
　necessary, 53, 83
　sufficient, 55
Conflict, 13, 14, 17n51, 20, 22, 24–27, 67, 71, 83–85, 87, 98–100, 109, 133n2, 158, 164
Conflict resolution, 20, 67, 164
Conformity, 127
Conscientiousness, 65, 73, 75n3
　See also Personality trait
Consensus, 6, 24, 28, 110

Consultant, 168
Contract, 11, 21, 163, 177, 178
    employment, 11
Contributor, 24, 25, 96, 100, 181, 186
Control, 26, 46, 47, 49, 51, 52, 56n12, 65–67, 70, 75n5, 100, 112, 127–129, 132, 138, 150, 157–159, 165, 169, 181, 183
    perceived, 46, 47, 49, 51, 56n12, 65, 112 (*see also* Mechanism)
Convergence, 109, 126
    mental, 109, 126
Coordinate, 6, 12, 21, 68, 96, 132, 161
Coordination, 20, 22, 67, 68, 94–96, 100, 140, 166, 188, 191n23
Corporation, xx, 7, 10, 13, 15, 21, 22, 33–34, 37n33, 43, 46, 49, 52, 54, 68, 74, 84, 99, 107, 110, 112, 132, 137, 155, 167, 170, 175, 176
COVID-19, 5
Creative, xx, 3, 9, 27, 48, 72, 108, 126–128, 136–138, 162, 165–167, 173, 186, 190
Creativity, xx, 4, 5, 10, 31, 106, 108–110, 113, 114, 122, 124, 137, 143, 183, 186
Crowd, 125, 132
    wisdom of (WOC), 125, 130, 133n4
Culture, xxi, 31, 49, 50, 132
Cyber security, 28
Cyert, Richard, 97

D

Darwin, Charles, 88n5
Davis, David, 99
De Blok, Jos, 32, 50, 99
Decentral, 24, 51, 73, 85, 107, 109–112, 122, 124, 137, 138, 143, 147, 176, 183, 184
Decentralization
    de facto, 25, 33–34, 51, 53, 64, 67, 82, 106, 195
    informal, 26, 27, 29, 35, 43, 45, 47, 51–53, 63, 81, 131
    quasi, 35, 47–54, 80–82, 84, 93–101, 111, 112
Decentralized, xxi, 6, 8, 10, 14, 23, 25, 26, 32, 35, 35n4, 37n32, 37n33, 43–54, 64, 65, 67, 68, 70–73, 76n16, 80–82, 85, 87, 93, 95, 101, 106, 111, 112, 114, 116n12, 122, 123, 128, 130, 131, 147, 156, 158, 173, 179, 181, 188
Decentralized autonomous organization (DAO), 173, 176, 179, 181–186
Deci, Edward, 44, 45, 86
Decision
    -making, xx, xxii, 4, 9, 10, 14, 17n52, 24–26, 28, 36n31, 49, 81, 87, 98, 99, 106, 108, 109, 111, 112, 115n10, 116n10, 123, 124, 126, 127, 129–131, 136, 137, 150, 151, 156, 157, 164, 170, 180, 183
    rights, xxii, 14, 25, 35, 44, 48, 72, 88, 109, 113, 128, 130–132, 139, 143, 151, 179
Deflate, 14
Delayer, 80, 135–137, 171
Delegation, 110
    high, xxiii, 25–35, 37n33, 43, 44, 47, 48, 51, 63, 67, 79, 83, 85, 87, 88, 93, 94, 98, 111, 114, 116n10, 121, 122, 136, 142, 147, 160, 183
    scope of, 158
Delta Power, 31

Design
　principle, 174, 177, 178, 180, 183, 184, 186, 196
　solution, 174, 175, 177–180, 183, 185, 186, 188, 191n9, 191n32, 196
Design thinking, 4
Digital, 3, 5
Disney, 7
Division of labor, 20, 111, 167, 169

Ebbsfleet United, 99
Eberle Walker, Kate, 7
E-commerce, 155, 156, 159
Economics, xxi, 75n9, 81, 97
　behavioral, 55n5, 67, 69
Editor, 24, 25
Efficacy, 81, 98, 116n19, 125
Efficiency, 97, 98, 100, 116n19, 125
Effort, 7, 14, 20, 31, 43–47, 53, 63, 65, 68, 71, 72, 81, 83–86, 94, 95, 100, 105, 106, 115, 142, 150, 158, 177
Employee happiness, 112
Employees, xix, xx, xxiii, 3–11, 13, 14, 19–22, 25–32, 35, 43–54, 63–72, 74, 79–87, 89n19, 93–101, 107–109, 112, 114, 116n19, 121–132, 135–143, 146, 147, 150, 151, 151n1, 155, 158–162, 166–168, 170, 171, 173, 176, 180–182, 188, 190
Empowerment, 5, 82, 85–87, 115n10
Encyclopaedia Britannica, 24, 25
Engagement, 46, 49, 51, 65, 66, 71, 73, 75n8, 95, 159, 183
　See also Mechanism
Estée Lauder, 7
Evaluation apprehension, 47, 52, 65, 100
　See also Mechanism

Exception management, 23, 25, 35, 71, 83, 84, 98–101, 107, 109, 111, 113, 133n2, 183
Executive, xxii, xxiii, 5, 6, 19, 87, 114, 143, 150, 151, 156–158, 162, 163, 166, 174, 190
Extrinsic, 21, 44, 45, 48, 51, 151

Fabrics, 29
Fair, xxiii, 37n33, 69, 80, 105, 115n1, 116n12, 116n20, 132, 133n6, 141, 176, 181
Fairness, 71
Farquhar, Scott, 27
Fear, 8, 47, 50–52, 85, 86, 100, 165
Fisher, Bill, 176
Flat, xix–xxiv, 5, 8–10, 14, 15, 19, 47, 51, 67, 79, 86, 105–114, 115n1, 121, 135, 137, 143, 146–150, 163–190
Flat structure, xix–xxiii, 4–10, 14, 15, 26, 27, 32, 59n52, 63–65, 67, 73, 74, 79–88, 93, 94, 100, 101, 105–115, 121–132, 135, 137, 146, 147, 150, 162, 164, 166, 171, 173, 180, 182, 190
Flattening, xx, 3, 11, 14, 27, 53, 156
For-profit, 21, 25
Four + one fundamental problems of organizing, 20–23, 147
Freedom, 4, 46, 49, 66, 68, 97, 130, 171
　at work, 31, 169
Freeriding, 81, 87
Fuzzy set logics, 53

Glassdoor, 48
Goal, xx, xxii, 4, 10, 19–24, 27, 30, 36n4, 45–47, 57n22, 64, 70,

75n10, 80, 82–84, 87, 93–95, 107, 108, 113, 114, 121, 122, 135–139, 143, 147, 151, 156–158, 161, 163, 177, 183, 184, 186, 189
Gore, Bill, 29
Gore, Vieve, 29
Gore, W. L. & Associates, 27, 29, 31, 32, 48–50, 82, 85, 111
Graphic design, 163, 166
Group
  size, 98, 124–127, 133n6
  think, 126, 127
Grow, 9, 45, 80, 126, 132, 136, 146, 159, 166–168, 170
Growth, 5, 6, 74n2, 80, 136, 137, 146, 147, 150, 156, 163–172, 190

Hackathon, 27, 85, 95, 111
Hannan, Michael, 178
Harrington, Mike, 25
HBO, 5
Healthcare services, 28, 117n21
Hidden profile, 124, 125
Hierarchical, xix–xxi, 4, 10, 12, 15, 25, 29, 47, 106, 122, 123, 127–131, 146, 155–162, 169, 171, 179, 186
Hierarchy
  atypical, 132
  command, xx, 7, 10–12, 14, 17n52, 107, 128, 129
  depth of, 12
  traditional, 9, 28, 88, 93, 100, 105, 113, 114, 123, 128–130, 132, 136, 138, 146, 156
Hiring, xxiii, 6, 26, 53, 59n52, 70, 72–74, 79, 80, 101, 142, 188
Holacracy, xx, 99, 173, 176, 179–183, 186
Honest, 76n14, 94, 165

Honesty and humility, 64, 69, 70, 73
  See also Personality trait
Human resources (HR), 6, 32, 65, 84, 96, 97, 101, 115, 116n12, 125, 158
Humble, 86, 89n19, 121, 163, 165, 188

Idea management, 4
Identification, 81, 184
Incentive, 22, 48, 71, 82, 84, 88n6, 112, 159
Indeed, 4, 97, 106
Influence
  bidirectional, 130
  informational, 128
  normative, 128, 130, 131, 151
  unidirectional, 129–131
Information
  access to, 82–85, 94
  analyzing, 106
  costs of, 127
  exchange of, 164, 176
  gathering, 106–108, 111, 113, 123–126, 130, 131
  network, 108
  recombination of, 108
  recombination of, 51 (*see also* Creativity)
  taking action on, 127
Information technology (IT), 3, 4, 25, 28, 182
Infrastructure, 3, 75n9, 80
Innovation, 4, 6, 29
Innovative, xx, 108–110, 137, 186
Integration of effort, 20, 84, 111, 167, 178
Interest, 4, 6, 7, 22, 24, 28, 44, 47, 48, 52, 66, 71, 76n16, 151, 189
  self-interest, 64, 67, 71, 86
Intrinsic, 44, 45, 51, 66, 71, 151

J

Job
  redesign, 45
  satisfaction, 7
Johnson, Alan, 7, 143

K

Kanban, 191n32
Kelly, Terri, 32, 85
Key performance indicators(KPIs), 25, 114, 157, 159, 161
Klapper, Helge, 100, 128
Knowledge
  architectural, 83–85, 94
  expert, 125, 137, 143
Knudstorp, Jorgen Vig, 110
Kopteff, Mikael, 6
Koski, Bob, 31
Krans, Jan, 31

L

Laloux, Frederic, 23
Lamport, Leslie, 176
Larrick, Richard, 125
Lateral authority, 24, 98–101
Law, 22
  labor, 11
Layer, xix–xxii, 4, 5, 10–12, 15, 17n52, 23, 36n5, 47, 72, 105, 128, 132, 138, 143, 147, 155, 157, 166, 170, 171, 196
Leader, xix, 28, 32, 49, 53, 86, 88, 105, 140, 151n1, 155, 157, 158, 168, 169, 175, 188
Leadership, 4, 12–14, 32, 43, 50, 89n19, 114, 140, 160, 196
  style, 86, 88, 158, 161
Learn, 9, 21, 47, 65, 70, 72, 189, 195
Lecuona Torras, Ramon, 97

LEGO, 110
Locus of control, 65, 67, 73, 75n5
  See also Personality trait
Logics, 17n52, 53, 66, 97, 99, 112, 178, 181, 189
  of organizing (LoO), 174, 178–180, 182–184, 188, 196

M

Macario, Rose, 112
Macfarquhar, Colin, 24
Machine learning, 49, 74
Maciejovsky, Boris, 128
Manager
  HR, 6
  middle, 108, 132, 140
  mid-level, xxi, 11, 12, 72, 129, 151, 156, 166, 169
Managerial framework, xxiii
Mannes, Albert, 125
Manufacturing, 3, 182
March, Jim, 97
Marketing, 9, 169
Mechanism, 29, 44–47, 51–53, 65, 81, 98, 100, 112, 124, 171, 191n23
  psychological, 44–47, 51
  social, 81
Microsoft, 25, 27, 125
Mismatch, xx, 22, 113, 114, 121, 146
Mitsuhashi, Hitoshi, 76n16
Modular, 4, 95, 96, 101, 143
Modularization, 94–96
Monitoring, 13, 82
Motivate, 21, 35, 44–53, 66, 80, 94, 109, 130
Motivation
  extrinsic, 44, 45, 117n21, 151
  intrinsic, 44, 45, 66, 71, 117n21, 151
Mr. Green, 30

Need
  for achievement, 65 (*see also* Personality trait)
  psychological, 45
Nelson, Richard, 181
Newell, Gabe, 25, 26, 36n31
New product(s), 108, 110, 139, 141, 182
  development (NPD), 115n10, 116n20
New services, 115
No-boss, 8
Non-hierarchical, 179
Not-for-profit, 23

Openness, 5
Open source software (OSS), 76n16, 83, 179, 181
Operational, 5, 31, 158, 169, 170
Opportunity, 4, 7, 9, 10, 21, 28, 48, 123, 124, 146, 158, 159, 161–162, 176, 190
  costs of time, 123, 124
Organizational behavior, xxiii, 81
Organizational design, xxii, xxiii, 6, 135, 164–165, 171, 174, 176
Organizational transformation, 161
Outcome, 25, 44, 65, 83, 84, 95, 107, 109, 137, 147, 157, 161–162, 182
Outdoor sports, 29

Patagonia, 27, 29, 32, 48, 50, 53, 85, 97, 98, 112, 116n15
Pease, Marshall, 176

Peer(s), xxiii, 8, 21, 25, 27, 30, 36n5, 43, 48, 53, 55n2, 64, 67, 68, 70, 71, 75n9, 76n16, 83–85, 88, 94, 95, 98–100, 112, 124, 126, 128, 142, 150, 163–165, 180
  review, 29, 30, 82
Pentland, Sandy, 126, 127
Performance, xix, xxi, 10, 22, 32, 44–46, 55n9, 56n12, 56n19, 65, 66, 73, 74, 75n3, 75n5, 85, 93, 97, 98, 101, 114, 124–127, 159, 160, 182
Personality
  trait, 64–66, 69, 72, 73, 74n2, 75n3, 76n14, 76n15, 86, 93, 196
  type, 64, 69
Personality trait, 64–67, 69, 72, 73, 74n2, 75n3, 76n14, 76n15, 86, 93, 160–161, 196
Personnel
  turnover, 106, 112, 116n12, 150, 160
Pisano, Gary, 181
Politeness, 69
  See also Personality trait
Power, 5, 17n52, 24, 111, 128–130, 136, 151, 157, 164, 170
  See also Influence
Preferences, 46, 83, 84, 140, 143, 146
Project, 3, 4, 6–9, 24, 26, 27, 29–31, 43, 47, 49, 51, 67, 84, 85, 87, 109, 114, 116n19, 132, 138, 140, 142, 143, 146, 147, 150, 157–160, 162–164, 166, 168, 169, 171, 175, 179, 196
Project architecture, 4, 143, 147
Prosocial behavior, 70
  See also Personality trait
Prototype/ing, 109, 111, 113
Psychology, 65, 70, 182
  personnel and social, 70

Public good, 67, 81, 89n6
Puranam, Phanish, xxiii, 19, 20, 115n1, 128, 174, 177

Quality
  product, 121
  service, 121

R&D, 115, 116n20
Rätker, Georg, 4, 138, 139, 141, 142, 151n2
Reaktor, 5–7, 10, 87, 132, 136, 146, 147, 150, 151, 152n10
Reciprocity
  indirect, 76n16
  non-equivalent, 76n16
Recruiting, 6, 63, 67, 79, 80, 98, 112, 114, 147, 170
Redesign, 7
Reitzig, Markus, 23, 122, 129–131, 136, 138, 144, 148, 178
Remuneration, 4, 20, 21, 27, 112, 140
RenDanHeYi, 173, 176, 180, 181, 183, 186–188
Re-organisation, 114, 137, 142, 143, 155, 156, 159–161
Responsibility, xx, xxii, 4–6, 9, 14, 26, 32, 36n31, 53, 64, 68, 69, 83, 88, 99, 109, 116n11, 139, 140, 146, 147, 150, 158, 160, 168, 169
Restructuring, 168, 169
Retirement, 66, 80, 160
Revenue, xxi, 3, 28–30, 71
Review, 8, 23, 30, 48–51, 56n22, 76n18, 57n22, 82, 88n5, 112, 159, 175, 179
Rewards, 20–22, 32, 81–84, 89n6, 97, 100, 112, 140, 151, 158, 196

distribution, 21–23, 25, 32, 35, 51, 71, 96–98, 107, 111, 112, 183
Robertson, Brian, 176, 181, 186
Ruimin, Zhang, 176, 180
Ryan, LLC, 30
Ryan, Richard, 44, 45

Salary, xxiii, 25, 29, 30, 32, 35, 44, 49, 50, 56n10, 70, 80, 82, 85, 98, 168
Sanctions, 81, 82, 100, 143
Sanger, Larry, 24, 84
Satisfaction, 5, 7, 44–47, 56n19, 196
Savage, Chris, 9, 10, 146
Scaling, xix, 6, 9, 110, 111, 128
Schaumburg Flyers, 125
Schumpeter, Joseph, 181
Schuster, Andreas, 163–171, 172n1
Schwaber, Ken, 175
Schwartz, Brendon, 9, 10, 146
Science
  psychological
  social, 35n4, 56n11, 189
Scientist, 49, 55n10, 76n22, 56n10, 81, 126, 128, 174, 177, 181, 183
Scrum, xx, 173, 175–176, 178–179, 181–184, 191n32
Selection, 37n33, 53, 88n5, 127, 147, 160, 195
Self-actualization, 45–48, 51, 55n8, 56n19, 64, 65, 112, 197
  See also Mechanism
Self-determination, 86, 112, 159
Self-organization, 5, 9, 14, 23–26, 70, 79–88, 94, 150, 158
Self-selection, 35, 64, 85, 140, 150, 164, 171, 195
  See also Task(s), allocation of
Shop-floor, xxii, 11–13
Shostak, Robert, 176
Shuen, Amy, 181

Simon, Herbert, 21, 182
Skill, xxiii, 6, 8, 21, 26, 45, 70–74,
    82–84, 94, 114, 151n1, 171, 186
  job-related, 55n9
Skoll, Jack, 125
Slack, 96–98, 114, 197
  human resource, 96, 97, 197
Smarkets, 27, 30, 32, 48–50, 85
Smellie, William, 24
Smirnova, Inna, 76n16
Smith, Adam, 20, 46
Social norm, 81
Software, 3, 9, 25, 27, 28, 30, 83, 96,
    175, 176, 184
Sopra Steria, 28
Span of control, 11–14, 23, 26, 132,
    138, 150, 157, 169, 183
Specialize/specialization, 20, 168
Speed, 4, 9, 10, 21, 106, 110–111, 113,
    114, 115n10, 116n11, 116n10,
    122, 124, 126, 128, 137–143,
    157, 170, 182–184, 186
Sprint (in Scrum), 181
Squarespace, 27, 30–32, 48, 49
Staff, xx, xxii, xxiii, 4, 9, 14, 26, 32, 35,
    44–48, 50, 53, 56n22, 59n52,
    57n22, 63, 65, 67, 70–72,
    79–82, 86, 87, 96, 97, 105,
    112–114, 121, 190
Startup, xx, xxi, 15, 80, 88n1, 89n9,
    132, 135, 146, 157, 166, 176
Stasser, Garold, 124
Status, 17n52, 21, 128–131, 151, 170
  See also Hierarchy; Influence
Strategic planning, 4
Strategy, 5, 30, 49, 50, 74, 156,
    164, 166
Structure, xix–xxiv, 3–15, 21–25, 27,
    29, 30, 32–34, 35n4, 36n5,
    36n32, 37n32, 44, 47, 48,
    57n22, 63–65, 67, 68, 70, 72–74,
    79–88, 89n11, 93, 94, 96, 100,
    101, 105–115, 121–132,
    135–137, 142, 143, 146, 147,
    150, 151, 155–157, 159–162,
    164, 166–171, 173, 176, 179,
    180, 182, 186, 188, 190, 196
Subordinate, xxii, 4, 13, 17n51, 23, 26,
    43, 47, 50, 52, 53, 63, 72, 79,
    88, 129, 130, 138, 140, 157, 195
Sun Hydraulics, 27, 30, 31, 48, 50, 96
Supervisor, 4, 25, 64
Support
  managerial, 79, 93
  organizational, 53, 86
Sutherland, Jeff, 175

T

Talent
  attracting, 111–113, 143
  retaining, 111–113, 143
Task(s)
  allocation of, 196
  architecture, 71, 83, 84, 95, 96,
    143, 164
  bundle of, 45
  constraints, 94
  division of, 20–23, 25, 32, 35, 51,
    53, 55, 68, 70, 82–85, 94–96,
    107, 109–113, 122, 140, 143,
    147, 157, 158, 171, 183
  interdependence, 94, 196
  nature of, 83, 84
Tax services, 30, 95
TEAL, 23, 197
Teams, xx, xxi, xxiii, 4–6, 8–10, 13, 14,
    24, 27, 28, 30, 36n31, 49, 50,
    71, 72, 74, 80, 85, 87, 94–96,
    99, 105, 108–111, 116n11, 126,
    127, 130–132, 138, 140, 142,
    143, 147, 150, 156–158, 161,
    162, 164, 167–169, 171, 176,
    178, 180, 184, 188

Teams-based, xix, 98, 100, 110, 130, 132, 135, 136, 146, 157, 166, 171, 178
Teece, David, 181
Terävä, Hannu, 6, 87
Testimonials, 49
  employee, 48
Theory, 37n33, 94–96, 130, 174, 175, 196
  self-determination-, 44, 45, 196
Threat, 10
Time (to market), 110
Tipico, 30
Titus, William, 124
Top-down, 132, 147, 179
Traditional organization, 23, 179
Transparency, 5, 6, 8, 26, 30, 31, 50, 122, 140, 143, 159, 160
  of task architecture, 84
Transparent, 4, 8, 30, 87, 147, 158
Treatment, 160
Treehouse, 7, 8, 10, 82, 136, 143, 146, 150, 151n7
Trost, Jason, 32, 49
Trust, 10, 49, 68, 69, 76n14, 76n16, 86, 107, 158
T-Systems, 3–5, 10, 28, 136, 137, 142, 150, 151, 151n2

U

Unfair, 57n22, 68, 69

V

Valve, 25–26, 31, 35, 96, 111, 132
Virgin, 7
von Hippel, Eric, 181
von Krogh, Georg, 181
Voting, 24, 98–101
  See also Conflict resolution

W

Wales, Jimmy, 24, 84
Wikipedia, 24–26, 35, 84, 96, 100
Willingness, 64–66, 86, 108
  to work autonomously, 64
Winter, Sidney, 181
Wirdesign, 15, 150, 163–172
Wisdom of the crowd (WOC), 125, 197
Wistia, 7, 9, 10, 136, 146, 147, 150, 152n8
Word of mouth, 112
Workflow diagram, 21
Workforce, xx, 3, 4, 6–8, 56n10, 105, 123, 137–139, 142, 146, 150, 156, 160, 169
Workplace, 44, 46, 50, 51, 64, 67, 80, 81, 86, 87, 93, 116n12, 143, 147, 165

Z

Zi zhu jing ying ti, 173–190

GPSR Compliance
The European Union's (EU) General Product Safety Regulation (GPSR) is a set of rules that requires consumer products to be safe and our obligations to ensure this.

If you have any concerns about our products, you can contact us on

ProductSafety@springernature.com

In case Publisher is established outside the EU, the EU authorized representative is:

Springer Nature Customer Service Center GmbH
Europaplatz 3
69115 Heidelberg, Germany

www.ingramcontent.com/pod-product-compliance
Ingram Content Group UK Ltd.
Pitfield, Milton Keynes, MK11 3LW, UK
UKHW021252180426
11946UKWH00004B/101